What English Language Need to Know Volume
Designing Curriculum

MW01037511

"This text is a necessity as Ministries of Education are looking at adopting new curricula in their countries."

Dolores E. Parker, Independent Consultant, and Department of State, Regional English Language Officer (ret.), USA

"Very timely for teacher education programs in EFL settings. This text will provide prospective teachers with the theoretical and practical knowledge they need about curriculum development."

Aysegul Daloglu, Middle East Technical University, Turkey

"Authors Christison and Murray are well known throughout the world for their stellar contributions to the field of English language teaching. Their understanding of language curriculum issues is closely tied to their real-world experiences with curriculum design and curriculum renewal projects at their home institutions and in institutions, large and small, around the world. The real-world examples throughout [this text] will be welcomed by both pre-service and in-service teachers."

Fredricka L. Stoller, Northern Arizona University, USA

All English language teachers need to understand the nature of language and language learning, and with that understanding they need to be able to facilitate student learning and design curriculum for effective learning. *What English Teachers Need to Know*, a set of companion texts designed for pre-service teachers and teachers new to the field of ELT, addresses the key question: What do English language teachers need to know and be able to do in order for their students to learn English? These texts work for teachers across different contexts (countries where English is the dominant language, one of the official languages, or taught as a foreign language); different levels (elementary/primary, secondary, college or university, or adult education); and different learning purposes (general English, workplace English, English for academic purposes, or English for specific purposes).

Volume I, on understanding learning, provides the background information that teachers need to know and be able to use in their classroom. Volume II, on facilitating learning, covers the three main facets of teaching: planning, instructing, and assessing. Volume III, on designing curriculum, covers the contexts for, processes in, and types of ELT curricula—linguistic based, content-based, learner-centered, and learning-centered. Throughout the three volumes, the focus is on outcomes, that is, student learning.

MaryAnn Christison is Professor, University of Utah, Department of Linguistics and the Urban Institute for Teacher Education, USA.

Denise E. Murray is Professor Emerita, Macquarie University, Australia and Professor Emerita, San José State University, USA..

ESL & Applied Linguistics Professional Series
Eli Hinkel, Series Editor

Visit **www.routledge.com/education** for additional information on titles in the ESL & Applied Linguistics Professional Series

What English Language Teachers Need to Know Volume III

Designing Curriculum

MaryAnn Christison
and Denise E. Murray

Routledge
Taylor & Francis Group

NEW YORK AND LONDON

First published 2014
by Routledge
711 Third Avenue, New York, NY 10017

and by Routledge
2 Park Square, Milton Park, Abingdon, Oxon OX14 4RN

Routledge is an imprint of the Taylor & Francis Group, an informa business

© 2014 Taylor & Francis

Library of Congress Cataloging in Publication Data
Murray, Denise E.
    What English language teachers need to know / Denise E. Murray and Maryann
    Christison.
        v. cm.
    Includes indexes.
    Contents: v. 1. Understanding learning
    [etc.]
    1. Second language acquisition—Study and teaching.   2. Language and
    languages—Study and teaching.   3. English language--Study and teaching—
    Foreign speakers.   4. Multilingualism in children.   5. Language and culture.   I.
    Christison, MaryAnn. II. Title.
    P118.2M89 2010
    428.0071—dc22
                                                                    2010005148

ISBN: 978-0-415-66254-3 (hbk)
ISBN: 978-0-415-66255-0 (pbk)
ISBN: 978-0-203-07219-6 (ebk)

Typeset in Bembo
by RefineCatch Limited, Bungay, Suffolk

Brief Contents

Contents

17   A Humanistic Curriculum   191

18   A Task-based Curriculum   201

PART VI
Learning Centered Curricula   211

19   Outcome-based Education   213

Preface

English language teaching worldwide has become a multi-billion dollar enterprise, one that the majority of nations in the world are embarking on to lesser or greater extents. For many countries, English is seen as a commodity through which they will become more competitive in the global marketplace. While English may have national and personal advancement potential, it is also pervasive in the global media. Youth culture in particular is influenced by English-dominant media and marketing. As a result, English is being consumed and transformed transnationally.

The settings where English is taught vary from countries where English is the official and dominant language, such as the U.S. or Australia, to those where it is an official language, usually as a result of past colonialism, such as India or the Philippines, to those where it is taught in schools as a subject of study, such as Japan or the Czech Republic. In the first set of countries, when English is taught to immigrants or to international students, the language is often called English-as-a-second-language (ESL), and its teaching TESL. In the second set of countries, where it is taught to citizens and increasingly to international students, it is usually referred to also as ESL. In the third set of countries, the language is often referred to as English-as-a-foreign-language (EFL), and its teaching as TEFL. Because both ESL and EFL carry ideological baggage, there is much discussion in the field about more appropriate terminology and the use of alternate terms. Some prefer to use (T)ESOL—(teaching) English to speakers of other languages—since it acknowledges that the learners may have more than one previous language and can be used to include both ESL and EFL contexts. Others prefer (T)EAL—(teaching) English as an additional language—for the same reason, whereas ESL implies there is only English plus one other. Other terms in use include English as an international language (EIL) and English language teaching (ELT). Whatever the terminology used, distinctions are increasingly becoming blurred as people move around the globe and acquire their English in a variety of different settings, being taught by teachers from a variety of different linguistic backgrounds.

In these volumes, we will use ESL and EFL because they are still the most widely used terms, while recognizing the inherent reification of English in their use. When referring to teaching, we will use ELT to avoid confusion between the field TESOL and the professional association called TESOL.

Similarly, the terminology used to define the users of English has been contested. The most commonly used terms have been native speaker (NS), in contrast to non-native speaker (NNS). Both terms assume ideological positions, especially since the NS is valued as the norm and the model for language learning, not only in those countries where English is the dominant language, but also in many EFL settings. Yet, the majority of English language users and teachers do not have English as their mother tongue or dominant language. In some ESL contexts, such as the U.S., immigrant learners are referred to as English language learners (ELLs), even though all English speakers, no matter their immigration status, are English language learners—we are both still learning English! Leung, Harris, and Rampton (1997) have therefore proposed refining what it means to know and use a language with three terms: language expertise (linguistic and cultural knowledge), language affiliation (identification and attachment), and language inheritance (connectedness and continuity). What is important then about a learner's (or teacher's) language is their linguistic repertoire in relation to each of these criteria, not whether they are a NS. Since there is no general acceptance of such terms, we shall continue to use NS and NNS, while noting that they establish a dichotomy that is neither valid nor descriptive.

Much of the literature also refers to people learning English in formal settings as students and sometimes as learners. We have chosen to use the term learner, except when it leads to infelicitous expressions such as "learners learning." Student implies passivity; learner implies agency. For us, learners are vital collaborators in the educational enterprise.

Who is This Book For?

We are writing this book for pre-service teachers and teachers new to the field of ELT. Whether you are teaching in an English-dominant country, a country where English is one of the official languages, or a country where English is taught as a foreign language, the information in this book is relevant to your context. We have also designed it for whatever level you may be teaching—elementary (primary) school, secondary school, college or university, or adult education. It also includes the information teachers need to teach general English, workplace English, English for academic purposes (EAP), or English for specific purposes (ESP). We realize that this is a big ask, but we have used examples from the diversity of ELT settings. Of course, we cannot include examples from every country or grade level, but we have tried to be inclusive and ensure that whatever your current or future teaching situation, you will find the material relevant to your learners and situation. At the same time, we have been as specific as possible, rather than relying on generic characteristics of the field.

Our own experiences have covered a vast array of different age groups, contexts, and content areas—between us, we have taught in English-dominant countries, EFL contexts in every continent, young people, adults, university students, general English, English for business, English for science and technology, and EAP.

What is This Book About?

In order to teach in these different contexts, teachers need understandings about the nature of language and language learning. With those understandings, they need to be able to facilitate student learning. This book is the third in a set of volumes titled *What English Teachers Need to Know*. Since student learning is the goal, we have oriented these volumes about the notion of learning, asking the question: *What do teachers need to know and be able to do in order for their students to learn English?*

Volume I in this series provides the background information teachers need to know and be able to use in their classrooms. Teachers need to know (or know how to find out about) the characteristics of the context in which they work—the nature of their learners, the features of their institution, the policies and expectations of their nation/state, and the broader world with which their learners will engage. They need to know how English works and how it is learned. To become proficient in English, learners need to be able not only to create correct sentences in the classroom, but also to engage in conversations with other English speakers, and to read and write texts for different purposes. To accomplish this, teachers need to know how learning takes place both within the learner and through social interaction. Finally, teachers need to understand their role in the larger professional sphere of English language education so that they can continue to grow as teachers and expand the profession through their own participation in its various enterprises. They also need to engage in their local communities to be informed of their needs and to inform their communities about the nature of English language learning. While we have provided separate sections on each of these important themes, the challenge of successful teaching is to know how to blend an understanding of learners, language, and language learning with knowledge of their content goals and how to achieve those goals. This is the subject of Volume II.

Volume II is organized around the three main aspects of teaching: planning, instructing, and assessing. However, this is not a linear progression. These three aspects are reiterative. While planning instruction, teachers are assessing what their learners already know and what they need to know to reach their next curriculum goals. While instructing, teachers are constantly assessing whether their learners have acquired the language in focus and planning on the spot by reacting to student learning (or evidence of not learning). While assessing, teachers are constantly reviewing instructional goals to determine whether learners have achieved them and if not, why not, and how to plan for revision or next steps.

With the focus always on student learning, Figure 0.1 illustrates the dynamic, cyclical interaction of these processes.

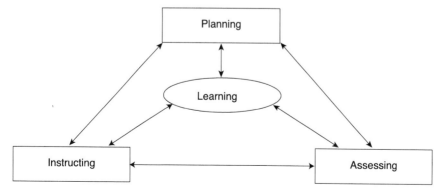

Figure 0.1 Model of the Instructional Process

Overview: Volume III

Volume III helps pre-service teachers, teachers new to the field, administrators, and policy makers understand and work with the theory and practice of developing ELT curricula in a variety of contexts and for a variety of levels. It helps them design curricula that promote student learning. While curricula need to promote student learning they also occur in contexts both historical and political. Curricula are inherently tied to the contexts in which they are designed and to innovation and the management of both learning and educational institutions. Part I provides the contexts for curricula, demonstrating how different stakeholders and different views of education, of language, and of learning impact on the curriculum development process and the content of curriculum. Part II explains and illustrates the process of curriculum design for specific contexts. Parts III–VI provide examples from the different possible orientations to curriculum choice—linguistic, content, learner, and learning. It is situated in current research in the field of ELT and other disciplines that inform it.

In all three volumes we include both theoretical perspectives as well as directions for translating these theoretical perspectives into practice. We illustrate with examples from practice to guide the reader in the translation process. The three books together provide an iterative conversation concerning how to develop language programs that result in optimal student learning. They stem from the view that teaching is a thinking, reasoning, and sociocultural activity in which teachers make decisions based on the context of their classrooms.

The material in these three volumes is based on current research in the field and in other disciplines that can inform ELT. These include psychology, neuroscience, pedagogy, sociology, anthropology, cultural studies, and linguistics. The focus throughout the volumes is on outcomes, that is, student learning.

Each chapter includes activities for the reader—to reflect on the information based on your own experiences, to read further on a topic, or to conduct small-scale investigations into teaching and learning. We hope that you will have as much enjoyment engaging with the materials as we have had writing them.

Reference

Leung, C., Harris, R., & Rampton, B. (1997). The idealised native speaker, reified ethnicities, and classroom realities. *TESOL Quarterly, 31*, 543–560.

Acknowledgments

The English language teaching profession has afforded us so many rich opportunities for teaching, observing English language teachers, educating teachers, participating in discussions, speaking at conferences, conducting workshops, and designing curricula. As we embarked on the third volume in the series *What English Language Teachers Need to Know*, we realized that we were enormously lucky because we were able to draw on such a wide array of educational experiences in so many different contexts and that so many of the ideas and the knowledge base represented in this volume are derived from the work we do and have done over the years. We are grateful to our many students and colleagues over our careers, whose wisdom and experience have contributed to our understanding of the field.

Once again, we are especially grateful to Naomi Silverman, publisher at Routledge/Taylor & Francis, for her enthusiastic support of our ideas as they pertain to expanding the volumes in this series. A big thank you goes to Eli Hinkel as well. She continues to read our work and support us in pursuing ideas for her ESL & Applied Linguistics Professional Series. Last, but certainly not least, we are especially grateful to our wonderful husbands, Adrian Palmer and Bill Murray, who continue to support our work in so many ways, including the incredible amount of patience you have with us when we have little time or energy for discussions about anything but our writing. Your support continues to be the fire that inspires us to be creative and professional.

Part I

Contexts for ELT Curricula

Curricula are sociocultural artifacts that reflect local values and local beliefs about language and language learning. They therefore do not necessarily transfer well to different contexts. However, many curricula have been exported, especially from the BANA (Britain, Australasia, and North America) countries, with variable results. As Edge notes for methodology, which just as easily applies to curricula:

> If what we (and particularly we who live in or draw on such centers of TESOL as the US or Britain) have to offer is essentially methodological, and if those methods are subversive and inappropriate, how exactly do we justify our activities? What sorts of future are we attempting to build with other people?
>
> (Edge, 1996, p. 17)

In Part I we explore the contexts for curricula. We begin with the nature of curricula themselves (Chapter 1), to answer the questions: What is a curriculum? And who is involved in curricular decisions? Chapter 2 provides a social, political, and historical lens through which to view curricula. Chapter 3 explores how English has spread to be the global language for commerce, education, and technology, among other endeavors. This chapter helps to set the stage for many of the curricular examples we use from many different settings in other parts of the book. Chapter 4 explains how current trends in technology are affecting curricula and need to be considered in the curriculum development process.

Reference

Edge, J. (1996). Cross-cultural paradoxes in a profession of values. *TESOL Quarterly*, *30*(1), 9–30.

Chapter 1

The Nature of Curriculum Design

VIGNETTE

I am working with a group of teachers and materials writers on a course for pre- or minimal-literate young refugees to Australia, ones who have some proficiency in spoken English, but disrupted or limited experiences of formal schooling. The government has provided additional hours of English instruction to help them prepare for the regular adult program. We have already had several meetings and, based on research our center conducted, have decided to develop several modules on topics of interest to this clientele, but also ones vital to their successful settlement in Australia: Your Future (work and study); Your Time Out (recreation); Your Money; Your Communication (including technology); Your Health and Well-being; and You and Me (interpersonal relations, cross cultural communication). The overall approach is content-based, with language determined by the content. At this particular meeting, we are working on the module on money. We begin by determining the outcomes we expect learners to be able to achieve at the end of the module, such as "Demonstrate an awareness of different forms of money (cash/virtual) and their use in various transactions (e.g., EFTPOS,[1] online banking, phone, post office, hire purchase)" and "Demonstrate an awareness of implications of signing any contracts." We agree that the content needs to motivate and inform learners. So, we decide to include topics around paying rent, banking, food shopping, budgeting, and cell phones. This leads to four units for the module. To achieve the language and subject matter outcomes, we discuss the language learners will need—structures, lexis, functions, and text types. We discuss the skills they will need—numeracy, critical literacy, and writing a note. A lot of discussion is focused on Australia being a highly literate country and that this group of learners needs to navigate literacy. The question is how to achieve this with pre- and minimal-literate learners. We discuss how to assist learners in seeing the connections between spoken and written language, how to use visuals, how to work with peers, and learning to learn. Content, outcomes, and language were mapped across each module to ensure sequencing of units within the module and across modules. Once the draft materials were developed, they were trialed with teachers in youth refugee classrooms and revised based on teacher feedback. [Murray, research notes]

Task: Reflect

1. What do you think was the advantage of starting the curriculum design process with content, rather than language?
2. Do you think it is appropriate to include non-language content in an English course? Why? Why not?
3. How can you assist learners to see the connection between spoken and written language, given that English does not have one letter/one sound correspondence?

Introduction

"It [the curriculum] informs teachers, students, parents, teacher educators, assessment developers, textbook publishers, technology providers, and others about the goals of instruction. It provides direction, clarity, and focus around worthy ends, without interfering with teachers' decisions about how to teach" (Ravitch, 2010, p. 231).

A curriculum is not a static set of documents, nor is it a list of things to be taught; it's a reiterative, dynamic process, one that is constantly being planned, implemented, and evaluated. Curricula are context-dependent, reflecting the needs of learners, institutional values and policies, and teachers' beliefs. In addition, stakeholders can perceive the same curriculum in different ways. In this chapter, we will focus on what is meant by curriculum, on its essential scope, differing views of curriculum, and curriculum change. For example, there is the recommended curriculum, the written curriculum, the taught curriculum, and the learned curriculum, and they are each different. In all contexts, there is also a hidden curriculum. (See Chapter 2 for further explanation and discussion of each of these types of curriculum.)

Task: Reflect

Directions: Think about your own language learning. How was the curriculum organized? Respond with "yes" or "no" to each statement. Share your reflections with a colleague.

___1.   The curriculum was organized around grammatical structures
___2.   The curriculum was organized around texts
___3.   The curriculum was organized around themes
___4.   The curriculum was organized around the content I needed to study
___5.   The curriculum was organized around competencies I was expected to master
___6.   The curriculum was organized around tasks I was expected to carry out
___7.   The curriculum was organized around projects I was expected to conduct
___8.   The curriculum was organized by the class in negotiation with the teachers
___9.   The curriculum was organized around a textbook.

Defining Curriculum

Educators often define curriculum differently. The literature often does not clearly differentiate among curriculum, syllabus, program, and course. In many British and Australian publications, syllabus seems to be the preferred term, while curriculum is used more in the U.S. *Curriculum* for us is the name for the broadest organization of instruction, involving planning, teaching, and evaluating any plan for the teaching and learning of English. *Syllabus* refers to an instantiation of a curriculum, that is, "that part of curriculum activity concerned with the specification and ordering of course content or input" (Nunan, 1988, p. 14). *Program* encompasses all of the *courses* in a particular institution.

Let's take as an example an institution in an English-dominant country such as the U.S., which prepares international students for their future university study in the U.S. The institution has seven different courses of study: a TOEFL preparation course, an IELTS (academic) preparation course, three levels of general academic English preparation courses, one course for preparing students going into accountancy, and one course for preparing students going into nursing degrees. These seven courses constitute a program. The TOEFL, IELTS, accounting, and nursing-focused courses each have their own curriculum. The three levels of general academic English, however, have one overarching curriculum so that students can move from one course to the next. When a particular teacher teaches the TOEFL preparation course, she follows the curriculum, but uses her own instructional strategies. Her plan for the entire course is a syllabus.

Curriculum Approach

The overall approach to the curriculum may be determined at national or local levels and depends on policies and beliefs about language and language learning. There are four general approaches, each of which has different specific ways of organizing the curriculum:

- Linguistic-based
    - Structural
    - Notional/functional
    - Academic functions
    - Genre/text
    - Vocabulary
    - Skills

- Content-based
    - The integration of language and content
    - Topic and situational

- Learner centered
    - Negotiated
    - Humanistic
    - Task-based

- Learning centered
  - o   Outcome-based
  - o   Competency-based
  - o   Standards-based

Each of these approaches is dealt with in separate chapters, but here, we need to introduce the possible choices because the approach taken influences the content of the curriculum.

Curriculum Content

No matter what approach is taken, in language instruction all aspects of language in use need to be included in instruction and assessment. We say "language in use" because language varies with context, with what is being talked about, with whom it is being used, and who the speaker is. As Fishman eloquently (1965) noted, "who speaks what language to whom and when?" English language in use consists of the following components:

- English sound system.
- English word system.
- English sentence structure.
- Speech acts.
- English discourse structure, both written and spoken.
- Varieties of English—by place and person.
- Cultural contexts (see Murray & Christison, 2011 for details).

Therefore, whatever approach is taken, the curriculum must consider where and how to include all these aspects of the language.

Scope and Sequence

A curriculum needs to include both *scope* and *sequence* of content to be taught. Scope refers to the type and amount of content to be taught, while sequence refers to the order in which the content will be taught. Thus, for example, the scope for the IELTS preparation course would be the language needed for the test, along with sample tests and test-taking strategies. The course would need to teach:

- Listening
  - o   Conversation between two people in an everyday context.
  - o   Monologue in an everyday context.
  - o   Conversation between up to four people set in an educational or training context.
  - o   Monologue on an academic subject.
- Academic reading
  - o   Authentic, academic texts written for non-specialists.

- Academic writing

  o Description, summary, or explanation of graphs, tables, charts or diagrams.
  o Description of an event or of an object.
  o Description and explanation of data.
  o Description of stages in a process.
  o Written response to a point of view, argument, or problem.

- Speaking

  o Introducing oneself.
  o Talking about a given topic.
  o Two-way discussion.

- How performance is measured in each section of the test.
- Test-taking strategies

  o Types of multiple choice questions, e.g., true/false, matching.
  o Specific IELTS instruction, e.g., number of words in writing tasks.
  o Taking notes during listening test.
  o Completing the answer booklets.
  o Preparing for the actual test day, e.g., resting the night before.

- English structure: word, sentence, and discourse level.

Note that in this example, the scope includes the English sound, word, sentences, and discourse systems. It also includes specific cultural contexts, both academic and everyday. Because IELTS includes speakers with different varieties of English in the listening task, language variation also needs to be included in the scope of the curriculum.

The sequence for the course would be the order in which these items were presented, practiced, and reviewed. So, for example, the teacher would probably choose to teach the language of description (both syntactic structures, such as *be* and *have* verbs, and discourse structure) before having learners attempt to describe a graph or diagram.

However, in language teaching, sequencing is quite tricky. It's difficult because, unlike some other subject areas such as arithmetic, there is no pre-defined linear progression and much depends on what learners achieve along the way. Also, the sequencing depends largely on which approach to curriculum design is taken. For example, if an institution chooses a structure-based approach, then the curriculum will begin with what is generally considered the easiest structures to acquire. If a competency-based approach is used, then the sequencing will start with competencies on which others build. For example, teaching *greetings* before teaching *conducting a short telephone conversation*. If a content-based approach is chosen, then what language is taught in what sequence depends on what learners need to know to be able to work with the particular content.

> **Task: Explore**
>
> Find a curriculum document in current use in your context. Which approach is used? Are scope and sequence described so that teachers know what is expected? How is the curriculum evaluated?

The Role of Textbooks and Materials

Because curriculum in our view includes planning, teaching, and evaluation, it necessarily involves consideration of materials that facilitate instruction (see Chapter 6 for a fuller discussion of the interaction among program, courses, lessons, and curriculum). In many contexts, a textbook is the default curriculum. As Ravitch (2010) notes for K–12 education in the U.S., "To have no curriculum is to leave decisions about what matters to the ubiquitous textbooks, which function as our de facto national curriculum. To have no curriculum on which assessment may be based is to tighten the grip of test-based accountability, testing only generic skills, not knowledge or comprehension" (p. 237). In US K–12 education, textbook publishers design textbooks that meet the goals of the largest states, because this brings in the largest profit. However, they also don't want to align the textbooks too closely so they can be used in other states. In general, "The textbooks avoid controversy—which would hurt sales—and maintain a studied air of neutrality, thus ensuring the triumph of dullness" (p. 234). In some institutions, new teachers are handed a textbook and left to their own devices. For inexperienced teachers or ones new to the particular context, the textbook becomes a crutch.

In the context of the vignette, the curriculum and the textbook and materials were closely aligned because we were commissioned to develop both. Because one of the goals was to motivate learners, each unit begins with a DVD of a scenario related to the topic. Prior to watching the DVD, learners look at one shot from the DVD and have to predict what they think the DVD will be about. The actors in the scenarios are young and of different ethnicities. In the first unit of the module on money, two young men are sharing an apartment and having difficulty meeting the rent payments. They meet on the street and one discovers that his roommate has just bought very expensive running shoes because they were on sale. He offers his ATM card and PIN number to his roommate when he's reminded that the rent is due. However, there isn't enough money in the account because he paid for the shoes. They meet another friend who is not happy living with his brother, and so they invite him to share their apartment (and help defray rental costs). He agrees. The textbook provides follow up comprehension tasks, such as sequencing pictures of events, answering comprehension questions, advice on not giving ATM cards and PINs to friends, and so on. The mapping of the language outcomes for this unit is provided in Table 1.1.

Curriculum in Practice

How the curriculum is resourced, implemented, and learned can be quite different from the intention of the curriculum developers. These differences result from

Table 1.1 Mapping Language Outcomes for a Teaching Unit on Money

Text Types	Functions	Structures	Lexis
Calendar ATM screen, ATM printout, EFTPOS receipt Bank statement Surveys Tips on security— from a bank website	Talking about frequency of activities Expressing necessity, obligation, lack of obligation	Frequency—every month/two weeks/ week Monthly, weekly, fortnightly Regular and irregular verbs— past tense Past tense time markers used for sequencing: one day, then, after that Present simple: I pay, we pay Modals: I have to … pay the rent, clean my room I don't have to … How old do you have to be to … drive, vote, drink in a hotel, go to college, etc.	Banking language: debit, credit, balance, transaction, cash withdrawal, account number, fee, EFTPOS machine, ATM, receipt, other bank ATM, statement Chores and responsibilities for sharing a house: pay bills, clean my room, cook, buy food, do my washing, pay rent

decisions made by different stakeholders, such as teaching institutions, teachers, and learners. Consequently, different curriculum scholars have posited various ways of thinking about the curriculum enterprise. To illustrate, we discuss a traditional model and one resulting from research in Hong Kong. We also address the issue of the way curricula transmit culture in covert ways, referred to as the hidden curriculum.

Models of Curriculum Development

Tyler (1949), considered the father of curriculum development in the 20th Century, stated that four fundamental questions should guide all curriculum development, whatever the subject matter:

1. What educational purposes should the school seek to attain? (Defining appropriate learning objectives.)
2. What educational experiences can be provided that are likely to attain these purposes? (Introducing useful learning experiences.)
3. How can these educational experiences be effectively organized? (Organizing experiences to maximize their effect.)
4. How can we determine whether these purposes have been attained? (Evaluating the process and revising the areas that were not effective.)

These four questions, referred to in the literature as the Tyler Rationale, comprised the titles of four of the five chapters in his book. While Tyler's model has been a dominant force for curriculum design, it has been roundly criticized for implying discrete stages. He did, however, note that any of these four questions can be the entry point for the design process. He also recognized that learners do not necessarily learn what teachers teach. "It is what he (sic) does that he learns, not what the teacher does" (Tyler, 1949, p. 63) that results in learning. A further criticism was that his claim that the process was value-free (Kliebard, 1971) was invalid. Indeed, his model overlooked how curriculum is interpreted and influenced by different stakeholders.

A model that seeks to recognize the social, historical, political, and personal forces that affect curriculum is that of Glatthorn, Boschee, and Whitehead (2006). They suggest six types of curriculum: *the recommended curriculum, the written curriculum, the supported curriculum, the taught curriculum, the tested curriculum,* and *the learned curriculum* (see Chapter 4 for a full discussion of this model).

In English language teaching, Adamson, Kwan, and Chan (2000) developed a model based on their research into curriculum change in Hong Kong. This model (Figure 1.1) articulates four types of curriculum, who was involved, and what the process and product were for each.

These decision-making steps are presented in a linear fashion, as are most of the models of the curriculum design process (see Chapter 5 for a discussion of the cycle of curriculum design). In practice, these different curricula interact. As teachers put the curriculum into practice, they may add resources and suggest changes to the policy documents. As policy makers and others see what learning takes place (or does not), they may revise or add to learning resources or provide professional development for teachers so that they better understand the intent of the curriculum. However, what their model does provide is four interpretations of the curriculum. The learning resources may not completely match the intended curriculum; the teaching acts may not implement the intended curriculum; teachers may not use the resources provided; and learners may not learn what teachers teach (as indicated by Tyler in his quote earlier). Although different terms are used by different scholars, all are in agreement that multiple meanings can underpin definitions of curriculum.

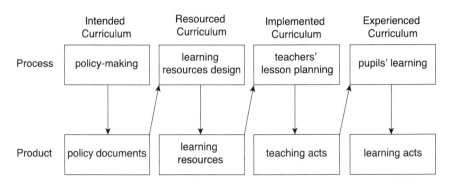

Figure 1.1 Steps in Curriculum Decision-Making

Reprinted with permission from Adamson et al. (2000). *Changing the curriculum: The impact of reform on primary schooling in Hong Kong.* Hong Kong: Hong Kong University Press.

Hidden Curriculum

Another aspect of curriculum seldom discussed in models is the hidden curriculum (see also Chapter 4 for additional information on the hidden curriculum). Curricula are embedded in the sociocultural setting in which they are used. Consequently, they reflect the sociocultural and political beliefs of that setting. For example, Benesch (2001) has criticized English for specific purposes (ESP) for being pragmatic, for focusing on the needs of content courses because of the "efforts of governments and private companies to promote English worldwide for political and commercial purposes" (p. 24). These purposes are hidden from the learners, whose own purposes and sociocultural backgrounds are not considered relevant to instruction. She calls for a critical perspective in ESP, where pedagogy is based on consultation with learners and issues of race, gender, culture, and power are discussed in relation to the learners' own lives. Similarly, Auerbach and Burgess (1985) have pointed out that the life skills content for adult immigrants contains a hidden curriculum that trains refugees/immigrants to be obedient workers, accepting of their low social status.

Topics chosen for study indicate to learners what society considers important and not important. These may not be as overt as in courses in citizenship or culture. For example, an ESL/EFL textbook that includes topics about London, but shows only white, upper- or middle-class activities and places to visit conveys to students that oppression of Britain's multicultural inhabitants, working class, and alternative young people is acceptable. How learners are expected to behave in schools reflects social norms—how they address teachers, how they ask (or don't ask) questions, how they are permitted to dress, or whether they have a pledge of allegiance. In general education in the U.S., there has been much research showing how teachers, despite their stated intentions to treat all children equally, call on boys more than girls, call on students like them more than those from different ethnic or social backgrounds (see, for example, Spindler, 1982). Such teacher behaviors convey social status norms to the children. Therefore, it is incumbent upon curriculum developers to consider what sociocultural values are implied in the curriculum.

Curriculum Change

Curricula are, as we have already said, dynamic. Built into the curriculum process model we describe in Chapter 5 is constant renewal, based on feedback from curriculum assessment. As well as this renewal process and the various interpretations of the intended curriculum, over time any of the stakeholders may choose or be required to change the curriculum. Often change is implemented from above because political leaders change, trends in pedagogy change, and national priorities change. However, if the change is top-down, without buy-in from all stakeholders, change rarely is diffused throughout the educational enterprise (Adamson & Davison, 2008; Goh & Yin, 2008). If all aspects of English language instruction are not aligned with the reform, then it is rarely adopted. For example, Japan became concerned that, despite six years or more of English language instruction in secondary school, students were unable to interact in English with other English users. Japan's curriculum focus was on grammar, rather than on the ability to speak the language, and teachers often taught English through the medium of Japanese.

They therefore instituted curriculum reform that required teachers to focus on communication (Mondejar, Valdivia, Laurier, & Mboutsiadis, 2011). However, the high stakes tests were not changed. They still focused on grammar and the written word; there was no speaking component. Consequently, teachers either did not implement the changes (Underwood, 2012) or, if they did, parents enrolled their children in private after-school tutoring so that their children would pass the tests, tests that determined whether students would be able to enter university. Of course, Japan is not alone in trying to implement curriculum change top-down and finding it unsuccessful. In Hong Kong, Adamson and Davison (2008), and in Singapore, Goh and Yin (2008) found unexpected outcomes in implementation of top-down K–12 reforms. In both contexts, reforms were reformulated by teachers and others.

Conclusion

Because curricula reflect the beliefs and values of language and language learning in the local community, they are usually best developed as close to the local community as possible. Unfortunately, in the field of ESL/EFL, very often curricula and/or textbooks are adopted from elsewhere, usually from an English-dominant country. It is no wonder, therefore, that they find minimal acceptance from teachers or learners. Curriculum development is a complex enterprise, which, to be successfully adopted, needs to involve all stakeholders in the process, a point we expand on in Chapter 5.

Task: Expand

Re-read the example above about teaching money skills to refugees. Adapt this example to your own context. Using Table 1.1, choose what text types would be relevant for your learners. Then, map the language outcomes that result from teaching and learning these particular text types. Share your findings with a colleague.

Questions for Discussion

1. Explain how you would best use textbooks in your context.
2. What non-language beliefs are reflected in the curricula with which you are most familiar? Is it appropriate that these values be imparted to learners? Why? Why not? To what extent are the views of Benesch and Auerbach and Burgess applicable to your teaching context? Why?
3. If you were to teach in an unfamiliar context, how might you uncover the hidden curriculum in the school where you teach?
4. What approaches could the Japanese Ministry of Education have adopted in order to ensure that teachers would be willing and able to implement a communicative curriculum?
5. Go to the IELTS website and check whether the scope and sequence presented here maps onto the specifications of the IELTS test (academic). In what ways could the scope and sequence be different?

Note

1. EFTPOS: Electronic funds transfer at point of sale.

References

Adamson, B., & Davison, C. (2008). English language teaching in Hong Kong primary schools: Innovation and resistance. In D. E. Murray (Ed.), *Planning change, changing plans: Innovations in second language teaching* (pp. 11–25). Ann Arbor, MI: University of Michigan Press.

Adamson, B., Kwan, T., & Chan, K. K. (Eds.). (2000). *Changing the curriculum: The impact of reform on primary schooling in Hong Kong.* Hong Kong: Hong Kong University Press.

Auerbach, E. R., & Burgess, D. (1985). The hidden curriculum of survival ESL. *TESOL Quarterly, 19*(3), 475–495.

Benesch, S. (Ed.) (2001). *Critical English for academic purposes: Theory, politics and practice.* Mahwah, N.J.: Lawrence Erlbaum Associates.

Fishman, J. A. (1965). Who speaks what language to whom and when? *Linguistique, 2,* 67–88.

Glatthorn, A. A., Boschee, F., & Whitehead, B. M. (2006). *Curriculum leadership: Development and implementation.* Thousand Oaks, CA: Sage Publications.

Goh, C. C. M., & Yin, T. M. (2008). Implementing the English Language Syllabus 2001 in Singapore schools: Interpretations and re-interpretations. In D. E. Murray (Ed.), *Planning change, changing plans: Innovations in second language teaching* (pp. 85–107). Ann Arbor, MI: University of Michigan Press.

Kliebard, H. (1971). Reappraisal: The Tyler rationale. *School Review, 78*(2), 259–272.

Mondejar, M., Valdivia, L., Laurier, J., & Mboutsiadis, B. (2011). Effective implementation of foreign language education reform in Japan: What more can be done? [Electronic Version]. *JALT2011 Conference Proceedings*, 179–191. Retrieved from http://www.academia.edu/1907048/Effective_Implementation_of_Foreign_Language_Education_Reform_in_Japan_What_More_Can_Be_Done

Murray, D. E., & Christison, M. A. (2011). *What English language teachers need to know: Volume I Understanding learning.* New York: Routledge.

Nunan, D. (1988). *The learner-centred curriculum: A study in second-language teaching.* Cambridge: Cambridge University Press.

Ravitch, D. (2010). *The death and life of the great American school system: How testing and choice are undermining education.* New York: Basic Books.

Spindler, G. (1982). *Doing the ethnography of schooling: Educational anthropology in action.* New York: Holt, Rinehart and Winston.

Tyler, R. (1949). *Basic principles of curriculum and instruction.* Chicago: University of Chicago Press.

Underwood, P. (2012). Teacher beliefs and intentions regarding the instruction of English grammar under National Curriculum Reforms: A Theory of Planned Behavior perspective. *Teaching and Teacher Education, 12*(6), 911–925.

Chapter 2

Social, Political, and Historical Contexts

VIGNETTE

I have been working with a group of in-service teachers on a US federal grant for two years. Each week I am in the schools observing classes and helping teachers implement a model of instruction that integrates content and language. I have been "invited" by one of the teachers on the grant to visit her eighth grade language arts class. I say that I am "invited" (and not simply invited in the usual sense) because one of the requirements of participation for the Middle School teachers (grades 6–9) who are involved in the grant is to collaborate with the university professors on the grant and to "invite" them to their classrooms for observations on a regular basis. The observations are followed by discussions that are related to the implementation of the model. The collaboration is meant to help all stakeholders learn more about how to help English language learners achieve academic success.

For this observation, the focus was on the part of the model related to Purpose. In the class observation, I looked for teacher indicators that the content concepts and content and language objectives were identified and clearly communicated to learners. I was also concerned with how the content being taught related to the State Core Curriculum for Language Arts.[1]

There were many good things about the lesson I observed, such as the fact that the content concepts were clearly identified for the learners and the objectives were posted. So, all in all, I was pleased with what I observed in terms of how this teacher was using the model for content and language integration. However, when I asked the teacher to talk to me about how the lesson related to the mandated curriculum for the state in terms of the specific standard and objectives it was addressing, she had to admit that it didn't really fit the required curriculum directly. However, she said that she really liked the lesson, had taught the lesson previously, and believed that the students liked it. She said that she would look at the core again and try to determine where her lesson fit. [Christison, research notes]

Task: Reflect

1. How does the teacher in the vignette view the state required curriculum in relationship to her own planning? How might her views be different from the administrators in the district[2] in which she works?
2. Do you think her views about required curricula are typical or atypical of teachers? Do you think teacher views differ according to context?
3. In what other contexts are teachers asked to plan for and deliver instruction based on a required curriculum?

Introduction

Developing an awareness of the extent to which curricular changes are influenced by and are manifestations of social forces is an important understanding for curriculum developers. As was introduced in the vignette, K–12 public school teachers in the U.S. are expected to follow a required curriculum for content and grade level. A required curriculum does not specifically dictate to teachers how they are to deliver the required curriculum. The assumption that most public school administrators make is that it is clear to all K–12 teachers that there is an expectation that they must teach to the core. In the vignette above, we see that even though there is a required curriculum for language arts and the teacher knew that she was expected to follow it, she did not. It was not the primary force that drove her teaching or her decision-making process. There are always social forces and educational trends at work that influence how teachers will implement existing curricula. Both language teaching and curriculum development can best be understood if viewed in relationship to societal and contextual factors that influence decision-making. Curriculum must also be viewed against a historical backdrop of societal change both in terms of the field of English language teaching and specific contexts, such as within public schools, private language schools, government sponsored programs, intensive English programs (IEPs), or higher education within the field.

Curriculum is created to meet specific expectations; nevertheless, what ends up being taught in a classroom is the result of many different social and political forces, such as government initiatives and the influence of professional associations, publishers, researchers, parents, communication groups, and administrators. In this chapter, we focus on social, historical, and political factors that can influence the implementation and creation of curriculum. We want you to see that curriculum is not a static concept; it changes in response to social, historical, and political forces.

Social, Political, and Historical Influences

Goodlad (1979) was perhaps the first to write about the social, historical, and political forces at work in curriculum development. He suggested that there were different types of curricula that result from social, political, and historical influences and offered some key distinctions among them. For example, he stated that in most educational units there is an *ideological curriculum*—a curriculum created by scholars and/or teachers. The ideological curriculum is intended to reflect the ideal blending of theory and practice as supported by training studies. The ideological curriculum is quite different from a *sanctioned curriculum*, a curriculum that has been officially approved by local leaders or administrators and may be subject to the political and social views expressed by these stakeholders.

Glatthorn, Boschee, and Whitehead (2006) agree with Goodlad (1979) concerning the usefulness of thinking about different types of curricula that arise in response to social, political, and historical factors; however, they suggest a different taxonomy that they believe to be more useful for curriculum workers, as the terms they use are directly related to issues that curriculum developers face (see also Adamson, Kwan, & Chan, 2000). Although curricula may be derived from a set of fundamental concepts, skills, and beliefs, they are manifested in reality in quite different ways. The types of curricula that we will discuss from Glatthorn et al. (2006) that are socially, politically, and historically motivated are *the recommended curriculum, the written curriculum, the supported curriculum, the taught curriculum, the tested curriculum,* and *the learned curriculum.*

The Recommended Curriculum

A recommended curriculum stresses content and skills that should be emphasized, and as such, is representative of what an ideal curriculum might be if the curriculum is focused on educational factors related to teaching and learning. Therefore, it is often recommended by schools, local and national educational agencies, and by highly regarded professionals. It is general in nature and is often presented as a list of goals, requirements, or policy recommendations. It often outlines the content and sequence for fields of study, such as biology, math, or language arts. In the vignette that introduces this chapter, the state's core curriculum for language arts is an example of a recommended curriculum.

Recommended curricula are shaped by several key factors. Societal trends have a strong influence on policy makers who, in turn, have the capacity to influence policies that affect curricula. Advancements in technology can also play a role as schools strive to help learners in attaining technological literacy (Dugger and Nichols, 2003). In the U.S. professional associations, such as Teachers of English to Speakers of Other Languages (TESOL), the National Council for the Accreditation of Teacher Education (NCATE), the National Council of Teachers of Mathematics (NCTM), the American Association of Intensive English Programs (AAIEP), the Consortium of English Accreditation (CEA) and Comprehensive Adult Student Assessment Systems (CASAS), play a role in shaping and influencing recommended curricula. Other countries also have a variety of professional movements that influence the content of recommended curricula, for example, the European Common Framework of Reference for Languages. Professionals who translate research into recommendations in their writing and published works also play a significant part in recommended curricula.

A recommended curriculum serves a useful function. It can establish boundaries and endpoints for curriculum planning and promote equity and excellence in learning, including equal access to resources for all learners (Glatthorn et al.,

2006) and can help both teachers and programs in the development of effective instructional programs. In these ways, it is similar to the intended curriculum (Adamson et al., 2000) presented in Chapter 1.

The Written Curriculum

A written curriculum is more specific than a recommended curriculum. It is similar to the resourced curriculum (Adamson et al., 2000) presented in Chapter 1. The purpose of a written curriculum is to "ensure that educational goals of a system are being accomplished" (p. 8). In order to do this a written curriculum must provide more detail than a recommended curriculum. In some contexts a written curriculum is referred to as a curriculum guide because curriculum developers include not only the general goals and objectives of the recommended curriculum but the specific learning activities that should be used to guide learners in the achievement of the objectives. Curriculum guides also include a list of the materials to be used with the specific learning activities.

Although written curricula are intended to help teachers implement the recommended curriculum, they are often subject to criticism. In order to understand the nature of the criticism, it is useful to look at the three functions of a written curriculum: mediating, controlling, and standardizing. By looking carefully at these three functions we are able to gain insight into teachers' views and preferences. Written curricula are often used to "mediate between the ideals of the recommended curriculum and the realities of the classroom" (p. 9). What the educational experts, administrators, and local stakeholders think should be taught might be quite different from what the teachers think should be taught. Written curricula are meant to mediate "between the expectations of administrators and the preferences of teachers," thereby helping these two very disparate groups reach general consensus.

Another function of a written curriculum is controlling. Written curriculum may come about because administrators wish to control what and how the curriculum is being taught. However, teachers and administrators may respond very differently to the controlling function of written curricula. Administrators use a written curriculum to ensure the curriculum is being taught and see a written curriculum as important in management responsibility and student achievement (Marzano, Waters, & McNulty, 2005). On the other hand, if the learning activities specified in the curriculum guidelines do not reflect current knowledge about teaching and learning and best practices, they may not be well received by the teachers. In addition, the learning activities may not reflect what has been traditionally done, and so the guidelines are rejected.

A third function of a written curriculum is standardizing. Although it is an important function of a written curriculum, it is a function that is difficult to implement for two reasons. As humans we are all unique, and as such, we each see the world from our own individual perspective; consequently, even in local contexts, there will be an uneven quality to the delivery of written curricula because of the individual approaches of the teachers. In addition, not all curriculum guides or written curricula are equal. The guides that are best received and implemented by teachers are those in which clear relationships have been established among stated goals, instructional objectives, and learning activities and are aligned with teachers' beliefs about language and language learning (see Chapter 6 in this volume).

The Supported Curriculum

The supported curriculum is the curriculum as reflected in and shaped by the resources that are allocated to support delivery of the curriculum. It is also similar to the idea of the resourced curriculum (Adamson et al., 2000) discussed in Chapter 1. In a supported curriculum resources are hierarchically situated as presented in Figure 2.1. Curricula are influenced by the time allocated at the level of the school and the classroom. In addition, curricula are influenced by personnel decisions, which determine how many students are in a class and how much time teachers have to work with students. For example, Zahorik, Molner, Ehrie, and Halbech (2002), found that fourth graders were more engaged in learning in smaller classes. In addition, a curriculum is influenced by the access that teachers and learners have to textbooks and other learning materials.

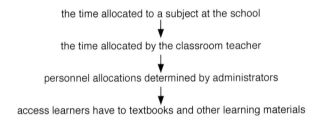

the time allocated to a subject at the school

the time allocated by the classroom teacher

personnel allocations determined by administrators

access learners have to textbooks and other learning materials

Figure 2.1 Patterns of Curricular Influence

The Taught Curriculum

We have seen that there is a difference in the recommended curriculum and the written curriculum. Now we will focus on the differences between the taught curriculum and the recommended and written curricula. The taught curriculum is similar to the implemented curriculum (Adamson et al., 2000) presented in Chapter 1. The difference between a taught curriculum and the written and recommended curricula was highlighted in the vignette when the teacher readily admitted that factors other than the concepts (i.e., the standards and their accompanying learner objectives) that were delineated in the recommended curriculum led her to select the content for her own lesson. While some differences among teachers are to be expected, the extreme situation where each teacher develops his or her own curriculum is to be avoided. Without systematic monitoring, the taught curriculum, in effect, becomes the written curriculum. The taught curriculum represents the curriculum that outsiders would see if they observed teachers in the classrooms. Outsiders assume that the actions they see in the classroom and the content that is covered represent the recommended and written curricula.

The question that both teachers and administrators in any context must ask is if there is a relationship between the written and taught curricula. Glatthorn et al.

(2006) ask, "How does the taught curriculum, regardless of its fit with the written curriculum, become established?" (p. 14). Answering this question is a complex process. What both administrators and teachers in any language program must consider is how to monitor the taught curriculum and determine its relationship to the written curriculum over time and across individual teachers.

The Tested Curriculum

The portion of the curriculum that is assessed by teachers in the classrooms or at the program or district level represents yet another view of curriculum. There are a number of factors to consider in thinking about the content of a tested curriculum. For example, teacher-made tests may not correspond to what has actually been taught in the classroom. The reason for this is that teachers are most often not skilled test developers. Curriculum-referenced tests often seem to drive instruction; consequently, the overall effectiveness of the tests is determined by how the tests are constructed. In other words, if a curriculum-referenced test has been created to measure an understanding of the main concepts covered in the written curriculum and those main concepts have been the focus of instruction, the test is likely to have a positive effect on both teaching and learning. If the curriculum-referenced test covers primarily incidental concepts that are not covered in the written curriculum, the effect on teaching and learning will not be positive. In addition, research on standardized tests suggests that there is not a good fit between the content of the standardized test and the content that teachers cover in the classroom (Berliner, 1984).

The Learned Curriculum

The learned curriculum is the curriculum that represents what students actually know based on what behaviors they exhibit in relationship to the written curriculum. The learned curriculum is similar to the experienced curriculum (Adamson et al., 2000) presented in Chapter 1. As most teachers are aware, students do not learn everything that they are taught even in the most effective instructional environments. Even though teachers establish objectives for learning that are inclusive of major content and language concepts, students will often focus on what is going to be assessed or tested and often only take seriously the information for which they will be held accountable.

The Hidden Curriculum

As we discussed in Chapter 1, a hidden curriculum refers to the pieces of a curriculum that are outside the boundaries of intentional efforts or plans (Glatthorn et al., 2006). All students learn content and behaviors in formal learning contexts that are not part of the intended or recommended curriculum. It is reasonable to assume that the hidden curriculum would include social, political, and historical influences. The ideologies of society permeate most formal classrooms; consequently, students unconsciously learn the skills and traits of the larger society whether those are consciously taught or not.

Task: Explore

1.   Educators define curriculum as *what is taught* and instruction as *how something is taught*. Now that you have been introduced to different types of curricula in this chapter, do you think these general definitions can still be useful? Why or why not?
2.   Do you think you can influence the hidden curriculum? If so, how? If not, why?

Perspectives on the Past

Understanding how historical factors may influence curriculum development in any context is useful for teachers, curriculum designers, and administrators. Yet, history itself is an artifact of the way in which humans have agreed to analyze certain events. In reality, historical events can be viewed from different perspectives and specific historical events are packaged and presented in different ways based on cultural, social, and educational influences. In presenting the information in this section, we recognize that there may certainly be other ways of viewing the events that we present.

One context that we know quite well is the US curriculum perspective in terms of the major historical trends and developments that have influenced education in both public schools and institutions of higher education. In the last century there have been at least eight different "periods" with each period resulting in predominant trends, exemplary leaders, and important and influential research. Because English language teachers work in many different contexts throughout the world, detailing all of the specific periods associated with one country would not be a useful exercise. However, to illustrate the importance of historical perspectives in understanding curriculum design and in understanding the contextual nature of curriculum development, we will provide two US-based examples.

Progressive Functionalism

The period in the U.S. between 1917 and 1940 can be characterized by the confluence of two very different perspectives. One perspective can be characterized as progressive while the other represents basic functionalism. These different perspectives are evident in curricular movements in public school and higher education during this time.

The years from 1917 through the 1920s were filled with optimism and economic growth. Then, the Great Depression hit with the Wall Street crash on October 29, 1929. Throughout the early 1930s, schools began to shut down and eventual recovery was slow and difficult. The 1930s also marked the rise of dictators in European countries—Germany, Italy, and Russia—and also in Japan. As a result of these events, the influence of Western democratic ideals on society in the U.S. was weakened. If we consider the predominant trends in education during this time, we can see how they were influenced by these societal events.

Progressivism as an educational trend can be characterized as a learner centered movement with a focus on paying attention to learners' interests and needs by making relevant and interesting content a starting point for curriculum development. Both learner tasks and curricular content were influenced as the arts received more attention and developing learner creativity became more important. Progressivism is associated with the optimism and economic growth of the 1920s and is represented in the early works of John Dewey (1902), who saw the developing child as central to the development of curriculum.

The essence of functionalism as a predominant educational trend is the belief that a curriculum should represent the functions and activities of adult life as represented in a given society. These functions can best be understood by analyzing learning tasks and the operations needed to carry them out efficiently. The move to functionalism as an educational trend is associated with the difficulties that Americans faced during the Great Depression years. As a society, Americans were focused on how to improve their lives. To this end, they focused on how to improve efficiency in the workplace and eliminate waste. Functionalism is quite strongly associated with the works of Franklin Bobbit (1913) who focused on the study of model adult behaviors.

Romantic Radicalism

The period associated with Romantic Radicalism extends from the mid-1960s to the mid-1970s. In the U.S. it was a time of upheaval, and the fabric of society was, in many ways, stretched to the limit. The country's youth were vocal about their support of a counterculture that espoused drugs, rock and roll, and openness in relationships while lashing out against the traditional values of hard work and the traditional family values.

During this period the very concept of an educational curriculum came under fire as some educational reformists argued for doing away with a scope and sequence, clearly articulated objectives, and explicit learning tasks (Holt, 1964). Instead, some argued that schools should focus on attracting highly exciting and imaginative teachers who could involve students in learning in unique and exciting ways.

Alternative schools were established in public education. Some alternative schools were completely unstructured (also called "free schools") while others shared many characteristics of traditional schools. The defining feature of an alternative school is that it is both strongly teacher centered and child centered. Teachers shaped the curriculum and assumed many of the roles covered by administrators and specialists in traditional schools. Conventional methods of accountability and evaluation were replaced by learner self-assessments and teachers' anecdotal reports.

Many elementary schools (i.e., kindergarten through Grade 6) moved to open classrooms in an attempt to respond to societal moods and pressures (Ravitch, 1983). At the heart of the open classroom movement was a desire to provide rich learning environments with centers of interest that would appeal to children and allow them freedom to choose what was of interest to them. Children were free to move from center to center at will, so there was little concern for order or discipline. The secondary equivalent to open classrooms was elective programs in which students were given the option of taking a series of short-term courses to replace required courses.

Task: Explore

The above section of this chapter has focused on how social forces influence educational curricula by providing examples from US historical perspectives. What societal forces do you think are influencing curricular changes today in the country in which you work? Use the Internet to locate several sources or websites to support your perceptions. Discuss your answers with a peer or a colleague, if you can.

The Politics of Curriculum

Most teachers think of curriculum development in terms of preparation for their classroom teaching and, therefore, associate the concept of curriculum development with the process that is centered around defining content, establishing goals and objectives, and delineating learning tasks. While these curricular concerns are true for most teachers, there is also another level in the curriculum development process that affects teaching and learning. It is particularly evident in sanctioned, recommended, and written curricula, and we call it the politics of curriculum.

The politics of curriculum refers to the individuals and groups in any context that have the potential to influence and change curricula. Within this curriculum-making process there are struggles for power as groups with differing points of view and different agendas advocate for their positions. It is a process that is evident in all contexts and ultimately determines which belief systems and practices will gain the widest audience and receive approval from the most powerful people. Although major sources of influence vary greatly among different contexts, the process seems to be similar as issues of power and control are resolved in curriculum decision-making. An important question for English language curriculum developers to ask is the following: Who has the potential to influence the curriculum that I develop?

Because English language programs and curriculum developers reside in many different contexts, it may be useful to take a closer look at the potential stakeholders who can and do influence the process both directly and indirectly. The list in Figure 2.2 was created to help you explore the relative influence of different individuals and groups. As you review the list, make note of the level of influence from none to considerable. Not all groups will apply in your context, so also mark the ones that are not applicable. For some groups, you may not know the answer. In these cases, indicate that you do not know.

1. National or federal governments, such as ministries of education in most countries or the Department of Education in the U.S.
2. State or provincial governments (such as state legislatures in the U.S.).
3. State Boards of Education in the U.S. or Boards of Directors in English language teaching programs.
4. Chief educational officers at the national, state, or provincial level.
5. Local Boards of Education in the U.S.
6. Local educational leaders, such as program directors or school principals.
7. Local teachers.

8. Local community members.
9. Parents.
10. State and local non-teaching organizations.
11. National and international teacher associations such as TESOL and IATEFL.
12. State and local professional teaching associations.
13. Publishers.
14. Teacher unions.
15. Employers.
16. Other.

Task: Expand

Work with a partner or in a small group if you can. Use the list above. Prepare a chart in which you list all of the stakeholders that could influence the curriculum decision-making process in your context. Rate the influence of each one. Share your perceptions with another group or another colleague in the context in which you work.

Questions for Discussion

1. In the U.S., charter schools, home schooling, and school vouchers are becoming commonplace. If you know about these practices, do you agree or disagree with them? Why or why not? If you do not know about these practices, ask a colleague or do some research to discover what these practices entail. Then, determine if you agree or disagree with them and explain why or why not.
2. If you are working in a non-US-based context, identify the most current educational trends. What might be the basis for them as they relate to societal forces at work?
3. What role do you think that politics plays in the development of curriculum in the context in which you work?

Notes

1. A mandated curriculum specified by a state for content and grade level. It is a curriculum that all K–12 teachers must follow.
2. Public schools in the U.S. are run by school districts, which are under the control of state and local governments. The governing body is called a school board and the chief administrator is called a superintendent. There are over 13,500 school district governments in the U.S.

References

Adamson, B., Kwan, T., & Chan, K. K. (Eds.). (2000). *Changing the curriculum: The impact of reform on primary schooling in Hong Kong*. Hong Kong: Hong Kong University Press.
Berliner, D. C. (1984). The half-full glass: A review of research on teaching. In P. L. Hosford (Ed.), *Using what we know about teaching*. Alexandria, VA: Association for Supervision and Curriculum Development.

Bobbit, F. (1913). *The supervision of city schools*. (Twelfth Yearbook of the National Society for the Study of Education, Part I). Chicago: University of Chicago Press.

Dewey, J. (1902). *The child and the curriculum*. Chicago: University of Chicago Press.

Dugger, W. E., Jr., & Nichols, C. (2003, December). Advancing excellence in technological literacy. *Phi Delta Kappan, 85*, 316–17.

Glatthorn, A. A., Boschee, F., & Whitehead, B. M. (2006). *Curriculum leadership: Development and implementation*. Thousand Oaks, CA: Sage Publications.

Goodlad, J. I., & Associates. (1979). *Curriculum inquiry: The study of curriculum practice*. New York: McGraw-Hill.

Holt, J. (1964). *How children learn*. New York: Pitman.

Marzano, R. J., Waters, T., & McNulty, B. A. (2005). *School leadership that works: From research to results*. Alexandria, VA: Association for Supervision and Curriculum Development.

Ravitch, D. (1983). *The troubled crusade: American education 1945–1980*. New York: Basic Books.

Zahorik, J., Molnar, A., Ehris, K., & Halbech, A. (2002). Teaching reduced-size classes: Lessons from the classroom. In J. D. Finn and M. C. Wang (Eds.) *Taking small classes one step further* (pp. 1–18). Charlotte, NC: Information Age.

Chapter 3

The World of English Language Teaching

VIGNETTE

*I am teaching a workshop for graduate students in an MA TESOL program. The course is designed to help them "further develop their academic reading and writing" so that they can successfully undertake the other courses in the MA program. The class is multinational, with students from Japan, Thailand, Taiwan, and the U.S. Some of the students from the U.S. are immigrants; some are native speakers of English. What all have in common is the need to improve their **academic** reading and writing. Michiko studied English for eight years in Japan, where the school used a grammar-translation methodology and all the teachers were Japanese. She completed her BA in English at a Japanese university and began teaching English in Japanese government schools. She decided to complete an MA TESOL so that she could return and work in a private school. In order to gain entrance to the program, she took several general English courses to prepare her for the TOEFL examination. Like Michiko, Noy studied English in school in Thailand. However, she attended an international school, where most of the instruction was in English and the instructors were British. She completed her BA in accounting in the U.S. and decided to become an EFL teacher on her return to Thailand. So, she enrolled in the MA TESOL program. Joyce, from Taiwan, also studied English at school, completing her BA in English in Taiwan before coming to the U.S. for the MA TESOL. In high school, her parents sent her to an after-hours school to practice her English with an American teacher. She plans to open a private English language school on her return to Taiwan. Patricia's family emigrated to the U.S. from Mexico when she was 12. She had studied no English during her schooling in Mexico. Her parents still speak limited English. She graduated from a California high school and received her BA in linguistics from a university in California. On receiving her MA degree, she plans to teach in a community college or adult education center in California. Adileh came to the U.S. with her parents as refugees from Iran when she was a baby. She completed all her education in the U.S. She plans to seek admission to a doctoral program in language education once she's completed her MA TESOL. Rosario is an older student, having gained admission to the MA through a special seniors program. She emigrated from the Philippines with her husband and two children. Now that he has died, she is taking classes for interest only.* [Murray, research notes]

Task: Reflect

1. Noy was exposed to British English; Joyce to American English; Rosario to Philippine English. How do you think that affected their reading and writing for academic English at a US university?
2. If you learned English in a school setting, for how many years did you study English? What variety of English was used?
3. If you are a native speaker of English, what variety do you speak?
4. How important is it for language learners to understand speakers from different countries?
5. In what ways is this class a microcosm of how English speakers interact in the work world worldwide?

Introduction

English has become the global language for communication in industry, business, scholarship, entertainment, advertising, and diplomacy and, more recently, the Internet. As a result, it is taught and learned around the world and is estimated to be a multi-billion industry (the most recent available estimates were US$9.2 billion in 2005 just for the international student sector [Blundell, 2006]). It is taught in different settings with learners of different sociocultural backgrounds, different aspirations, and of different ages. Many of the teachers who teach in these settings are highly mobile, moving from country to country or from school to university settings. Consequently, any volume on curriculum needs to account for the possible different settings in which English is taught and in which English teachers may find themselves at some point in their lives. In this globalized use of English, we find that English is no longer the sole province of those speakers from English-dominant countries such as the U.S. and U.K. How has this expansion of users affected the language? To answer this question, this chapter will discuss world Englishes and a model which sought to theorize these Englishes (Kachru, 1986). We will conclude with a discussion of what is the appropriate target English for the field of ELT.

World Englishes

English is used differently depending on both the characteristics of the person using it and the purpose for which it is being used. In this chapter, we will focus on user characteristics. Differences because of use will be discussed in Chapter 11.

Language (including English) varies depending on user characteristics, such as age, geographical area, social class, gender, and ethnicity. When language varies in these ways, the result is often referred to as a *dialect*. How do linguists determine what is a dialect and what is a language? There are actually no "rules" to make this determination. Different criteria have been used. Mutual intelligibility is the most common criterion. However, there are many different mutually intelligible varieties that are considered to be different languages. For example, Swedish and Danish are mutually intelligible, but they are considered separate (but related) languages. In contrast, speakers of different dialects of Chinese are not intelligible to one another; yet, they all consider themselves to be speakers of Chinese. Why? National boundaries may be a determining factor in considering a variety to be a language, as in the case of Swedish and Danish. Another criterion is a shared literature, as in the case of Chinese. We can see from these two examples that determining whether a variety of a language is perceived as a language or dialect is a sociopolitical construct, not based solely on linguistic features. To avoid this dilemma, Kachru (1986) developed the concept of World Englishes, identifying three concentric circles of Englishes.

Kachru's Concentric Circle Model

According to Kachru's model (Kachru, 1986; Kachru & Nelson, 1996) the three different circles of countries are the *Inner Circle* representing the traditionally dominant English-speaking countries (e.g., Australia, Canada, the U.K., and the U.S.), the *Outer Circle* of former British colonies where English is an official language and/or used in public domains (e.g., India, Singapore, and Uganda), and the *Expanding Circle* which, as the name suggests, is an ever growing circle of countries where English is gaining significant status in some domains (e.g., Brazil, Czech Republic, Japan, Thailand, and Turkey). In the Outer Circle, English is used in *intra*national domains; in the Expanding Circle, it is used in *inter*national domains (Lowenberg, 2002).

Kachru's model and even Lowenberg's differentiation are contested (see, for example, Crystal, 1997; Modiano, 2003; Seidlhofer, Breitender, & Pitzl, 2004), especially because of the current blurring across the boundaries of the circles. Many Outer Circle users of English are native speakers (NS), a term previously used as a delineator of the Inner Circle. For example, in Singapore, where many families use English in the home, as well as in education or government, many Singaporeans acquire English as their first language in the home. The division between Outer and Expanding Circles is similarly blurred. Many countries in the Expanding Circle teach bilingually or even use English as the *medium of instruction* (MOI) for some subjects, for example, Germany (Klippel, 2008). The model also does not account for the complexities of language use in immigrant countries such as Canada, nor in multilingual countries such as India with its code-switching,[1] pidgins,[2] and creoles.[3] The Expanding Circle countries are also using English in *intra*national domains such as television, popular music, and advertising.

Despite these criticisms the Kachru model is useful for highlighting the differences in context between learners of English in the three circles. We will, therefore, use it as a framework for discussing ELT as a worldwide phenomenon, while acknowledging that within each circle are many different contexts and that the circles themselves are porous and ever changing.

Task: Reflect

In which circle do you work or live? Think about the other two circles. How similar is your particular context to the other two? How different (or similar) do you think it would be to teach in those other circles? What questions would you want to have answered before you taught there?

English in the Three Circles

The use and teaching of English in each circle, as we have previously indicated, is complex and in flux. However, we can make some generalizations about different contexts within each circle.

Inner Circle

The Englishes of the Inner Circle countries are not all the same. Within countries, especially Britain, Canada, and the U.S., there is also variation. Some varieties are perceived by some to be more prestigious than others. For example, great stigma has been attached to the variety called African-American Vernacular English (AAVE) and controversies have waged over whether this variety has a place in schools. Similar battles have occurred over the years with, for example, Australian English not being deemed sufficiently prestigious for use in schools in Europe (Murray, 2010).

The Inner Circle countries have large immigrant populations, as well as international students coming there to study. ELT in these countries, therefore, has largely focused on these two communities. This form of ELT is often referred to as English-as-a-second-language (ESL) because it is the learners' second or third language after their mother tongue. This distinguishes it from Expanding Circle countries where English had traditionally been taught as a foreign language (EFL). Just as the boundaries between Kachru's circles are permeable, so, too, is the boundary between EFL and ESL flexible. Because it is a convenient and traditional way of referring to the two situations, we will use it here.

The immigrant populations that are not proficient in English are served in K–12 schools, adult schools, workplace programs, and colleges/universities. In K–12 schools, ESL instruction may occur as stand-alone courses, as part of a bilingual program, or in special delivery of school subject areas. In adult schools, programs vary considerably across the different BANA (Britain, Australasia, North America) countries (see Murray, 2005 for a full exploration of these programs). Vocational programs may take place on site in workplaces or as pre-vocation programs offered by adult schools or colleges. Again, the organization of these programs differs across the BANA countries (see Murray, 2011 for a full exploration of these programs). At college/university level, programs to help immigrant students are often stand-alone ESL courses or adjunct courses, attached to discipline subjects (see Chapter 14 in this volume). The ESL courses can be general English, preparation for specific university subject matter (e.g., accountancy), or preparation for academic study, called English for academic purposes (EAP).

ESL curricula for international students may be in K–12 schools, preparation for university content study, EAP, or adjunct programs.

Outer Circle

The varieties of English used in the Outer Circle are *nativized* (Kachru, 1986), that is, the process through which English, in contact with other languages in multilingual settings, develops new, systematic linguistic features. Nativization is "The linguistic readjustment a language undergoes when it is used by members of another speech community in distinctive sociocultural contexts and language contact situations" (Kachru, 1992, p. 235). These are systematic forms that are features of a variety used widely in a community that accepts them as norms. They can occur at all levels of language—sound, word, sentence, and discourse. They differ from the interlanguage forms used by those learning English (see, for example, Lowenberg, 1992). When this nativized variety is accepted as a legitimate variety with its own independent model of usage across a variety of sociolinguistic contexts, it is institutionalized (Kachru, 1992). However, often this local variety is not institutionalized.

For example, Singapore has conducted campaigns to teach people "grammatically correct English." One such campaign launched in 1999, "The Speak Good English Campaign," includes lessons in newspapers, on television, and on the web. These lessons identified Singapore English (Singlish) features and then provided Good English alternatives. *Lah*, *lor*, and *leh*, which are particles from Malay, are used in Singlish for emphasis at the end of words or phrases. However, authorities within Singapore consider it (and other nativized forms) unacceptable because it is from Malay and does not occur in the Englishes of the Inner Circle, especially that of Standard British English.

Different countries in the former British colonies have chosen different orientations towards English, such as the example of Singapore above. We will discuss how two different perspectives affect the role of English(es) in education.

India is a multilingual country with 1,576 languages/dialects classified as mother tongues, according to the 1991 census. The official language of the Central Government of the Republic of India is Hindi, with English as a secondary official language. "Throughout India, there is an extraordinary belief, among almost all castes and classes, in both rural and urban areas, in the transformative power of English. English is seen not just as a useful skill, but as a symbol of a better life, a pathway out of poverty and oppression" (Graddol, 2010, p. 120).

In education, there is a three-language policy:

1. The mother tongue or the regional language.
2. The official language of the Union or the associate official language of the Union as long as it exists.
3. A modern Indian or foreign language not covered in (1) or (2) and other than that used as the medium of instruction (Ministry of Education, 1966, p. 192).

In 1988 the Central Board of Secondary Education (CBSE) engaged in curriculum renewal for the courses taken by students in English-medium contexts, with the goal of improving communicative language learning. Teachers and learners did engage in more communicative activities and the final exam was changed in 1995. However, it remained a paper-and-pencil test, with the focus on reading, writing, grammar, and literature, and its revision in 2005 was even more based on memorization (Matthew, 2012). Consequently, the exam became the de facto curriculum.

Malaysia has followed a rather different path from that of India.

Among Malaysians, English is viewed rather equivocally. On the one hand, it is regarded as an important second language for instrumental purposes, a neutral language for social integration and a pragmatic one for professional growth and career advancement. On the other hand, it is perceived in certain quarters as a language that threatens the status of the national language and erodes local cultures.

(Lee, Lee, Ya'acob, & Wong, 2010)

As a result of British colonialism, English was the medium of instruction (MOI) in Malaysian schools. However, in 1970, this was changed to Bahasa Melayu, the official language of the country. In addition, there are primary schools where Chinese or Tamil are the MOI to meet the needs of the large Chinese and Tamil populations. As a result of these changes, over time there was concern that Malaysians were no longer competitive globally because they were no longer fluent in English. Consequently, in 2003 the government implemented a policy of teaching mathematics and science through English. Both primary and secondary teachers were given in-service training in the new curriculum, as well as in English language. The policy was abandoned in 2009 because of a perceived lack of improvement in English. There are actually a number of reasons why the policy was not successful (see Patel, 2012 for further details), including issues of stakeholder involvement discussed in Chapter 1 in this volume.

What these two examples from the Outer Circle demonstrate is the tension between English and indigenous languages, as well as the importance of planning curriculum change with care and sensitivity.

Expanding Circle

Some writers have posited that nativization has occurred in Expanding Circle varieties such as Europe (Kelch & Santana-Williamson, 2002) and China (Modiano, 2003), in addition to in Outer Circle countries. But there is no general agreement that they are sufficiently established to have become norms of use.

More typical of the Expanding Circle is the teaching of English in the school system as a subject, with teachers sharing the mother tongue of their students. In many countries, universities use English as the MOI or textbooks and research the students are expected to read are in English. Because of the perception that even after years of English, students are not prepared to use English as a MOI or to communicate with other speakers of English, countries have adopted different strategies. The European Union (EU) has adopted Content and Language Integrated Learning (CLIL), in which subject matter is taught using English as the MOI so that students learn both language and content at the same time (see Chapter 14 in this volume for a discussion of CLIL). A different strategy has been to begin language instruction at earlier and earlier ages, leading to the growing field of Teaching English to Young Learners (TEYL).

In Japan, EFL became compulsory in primary schools as of April 2011, following a trial stage from 2002 to 2010. Prior to this, English was taught for six years in secondary schools and two further years in tertiary education, where the methodology was audiolingualism and grammar-translation, in an exam-oriented curriculum. The goal of introducing English in primary school was to foster positive attitudes and experiences with foreign languages, rather than to develop language proficiency. For teachers with negative experiences of learning English themselves and with limited models of instruction, and limited spoken English proficiency themselves, and with large class sizes, the challenges were enormous (Araki-Metcalfe, 2012). Japan is not alone in facing this dilemma. Many other countries have introduced English in primary school, with similar difficulties and limited success, for example, Hong Kong (Adamson & Davison, 2008), China (Wedell, 2011), and Indonesia (Damayanti, 2008).

Standard Varieties

All speakers have a range of varieties in their repertoire. However, within a speech community, often a "standard" evolves, usually based on the variety of those with power in the society. Thus, in both Britain and the U.S. standards have developed such that regional or ethnic varieties within these countries have not been considered appropriate or "good English," especially for formal or public use. These attitudes were exported along with the spread of English, as we saw with the case of Singapore, and the preference for a particular variety expressed in some Expanding Circle countries (see below). Standard varieties are no more linguistically pure or special than any other variety. They have achieved their status because of the political and economic power of those who speak that variety.

Traditionally, as previously mentioned, the Inner Circle was considered to be the one with NS of English. So, what do we mean by NS?

Who Is a Native Speaker?

The term NS is also highly contested. The traditional approach was to define NSs as "people who acquired the language naturally and effortlessly in childhood . . . in the community which uses the language" (Cook, 2003, p. 28). It is the latter part of the definition that denies the reality of language use. Children of expatriates or in bilingual homes in all three circles may "acquire English naturally and effortlessly from childhood," but are not living in the community that uses the language. As Paikeday (1985, p. 2) so eloquently states, "One would like to be able to assign each and every individual to one class or other (here native and non-native speaker), but the situation does not allow it." Yet, the myth of the native speaker continues and its consequences are dire for both language learners and teachers. While there may be no sociolinguistic basis for defining native speaker, and evidence that the native speaker concept is a myth, some would still claim that "we need it as a model, a goal, almost an inspiration" (Davies, 1996, p. 157). However, this issue of "model" and "goal" becomes problematic once one attempts to invoke the NS as the target for English language teaching. Which NS variety should be the goal, model or inspiration?

Appropriate Variety of English for Instruction

Traditionally, many countries have shown a preference for one Inner Circle standard, either British or American, as the model language for both instruction and educators. So, for example, Japan has traditionally chosen American English as the standard as a result of the intense contact post–World War II. In contrast, Italy, being part of Europe, has chosen British English. These countries often will not hire speakers of other varieties such as Australian, Singaporean, or Indian English. As a result of this preference, often one expressed by non-native speakers, NS teachers are hired as adjuncts, especially to provide NS models to learners. In many countries, such as Taiwan, these programs pay NS teachers more than local teachers.

While it is not too difficult to envisage accepting nativized varieties in classrooms and interactions, implementing such an approach in assessment is far more complex; for it is in tests, especially internationally standardized tests with their one correct answer, that variation becomes unacceptable. Lowenberg (for example, 2007) has written extensively on the ethics of using Standard American or British as the norm in test development.

About 80% of the English speakers in the world are non-native speakers (NNS). They are having a great impact on the English language such that the Inner Circle countries will no longer be the only models of English.

One movement that has gained currency has been the establishment of a new variety of English as a lingua franca. This program is designed to describe mutually comprehensible and intelligible features of English and remove English features that are difficult to learn but not necessary for comprehension. In other words, the aim is to replace a standard based on Inner Circle Standard English(es) with a simplified standard (Jenkins, 2006; Kirkpatrick, 2007; Seidlhofer et al., 2004). While superficially there appears to be some merit in reducing English to a comprehensible, intelligible core to use as a lingua franca, this direction competes with "the diverging force to establish institutionalized varieties for intranational use" (Yano, 2009, p. 249). Yano (2001), therefore, predicted that instead of an international lingua franca emerging, English would converge naturally into six regional standards because of the frequency of intraregional use, as opposed to inter-regional use. Further, there are those advocating for such a lingua franca position themselves, more as prescriptivists than descriptivists, because their work describes what should be, rather than what is. As Mollin (2006, p. 1) claims, the lingua franca English is a mere "Yeti of English varieties: everyone has heard of it, but no one has ever seen it."

> There needs to be recognition that people learn the language in their own terms and to their own ends and these do not necessarily relate to the UK or any other country of which English is the mother tongue ... Policies must be sensitive to a global population of English speakers. English is more a family of languages than a single language with set rules and orthodoxies.
>
> (Jones & Bradwell, 2007, pp. 89–90)

Furthermore, English learners may not relate to the standard taught in schools. In the U.S., Goldstein (1987) found that some Hispanic learners adopted AAVE through their contact with African-American peers. Similarly, in Canada Ibrahim (1999) showed that African immigrants chose to identify with AAVE speakers and acquired that variety. Immigrants to regional areas in Britain may choose to acquire the local variety, identifying with their peers. The issue for curriculum developers and teachers is which variety to choose as the model for instruction (and assessment). Such decisions need to be part of the curriculum development process and be responsive to local contexts.

Task: Explore

Conduct a short questionnaire with some of your colleagues or peers. If you are in a pre-service course or in-service workshop, give the questionnaire to ten of your peers. If you are teaching, give the questionnaire to five of your colleagues. Collate your results and share with a colleague or peer.

Questionnaire

Below are several statements about English. Rate your agreement with them on a five point scale.

1 = Strongly disagree; 2 = Disagree; 3 = Neutral ; 4 = Agree; 5 = Strongly agree

1. Only standard American or British English should be taught in EFL programs.	1 2 3 4 5
2. Indian English should be taught in schools in India.	1 2 3 4 5
3. Immigrants in Australia should learn to speak Australian English.	1 2 3 4 5
4. Students will learn English better if it is used as a medium of instruction for subjects like mathematics or science.	1 2 3 4 5
5. Students should learn to understand speakers of different varieties of English.	1 2 3 4 5

Conclusion

Although English has become the global language for use in many contexts, how it is used, how it is taught, and attitudes towards it vary across different countries. As it has spread, different Englishes have developed so that Standard British English or Standard American English can no longer be the only appropriate models used in education. Curriculum developers need to determine the most appropriate models for their particular contexts.

Task: Expand

Kachru, B. B., Kachru, Y., & Nelson, C. (Eds.). 2009. *Handbook of World Englishes*. London: Wiley-Blackwell.

This collection focuses on critical aspects and case studies of the theoretical, ideological, applied, and pedagogical issues related to English use around the world.

> TESOL positions papers are available at: http://www.tesol.org/about-tesol/press-room/position-statements/social-issues-and-diversity-position-statements
>
> TESOL, the international professional association, has a variety of position papers about ELT. This URL takes you to the section of papers on social issues and diversity including English as a global language, multilingualism, and language varieties.

Questions for Discussion

1. What has been the effect of colonialism on the teaching and learning of English in the Outer Circle?
2. Why is Kachru's model arbitrary for describing the different Englishes in the world?
3. How would you best define native speaker?
4. How can curriculum developers decide which variety of English to use in instruction and assessment?
5. How important is it for learners to understand speakers of many different varieties of English? Why?

Notes

1. Code-switching refers to the systematic way in which bilinguals shift from one language to the other.
2. A pidgin is a contact language that develops when a dominant group does not learn the local variety. To communicate, the subordinate group adopts aspects of the dominant language. However, they simplify it and include features from their own language. Pidgins have no native speakers and are used for a restricted range of uses.
3. A creole is a pidgin that has acquired native speakers as children grow up using the pidgin. As more demands are put on the language, it becomes more complex, often as complex as any other language.

References

Adamson, B., & Davison, C. (2008). English language teaching in Hong Kong primary schools: Innovation and resistance. In D. E. Murray (Ed.), *Planning change, changing plans: Innovations in second language teaching* (pp. 11–25). Ann Arbor, MI: University of Michigan Press.

Araki-Metcalfe, N. (2012). Top-down education reform in English language curriculum in Japanese primary schools: Its implementation and evaluation. *Journal of Asian Critical Education, 1*(1), 70–90.

Blundell, S. (2006). *Leading trend indicators—an ELICOS sector perspective.* Paper presented at the Australian International Education Conference, Perth, Australia, October 10–13, 2006.

Cook, G. (2003). *Applied linguistics.* Oxford: Oxford University Press.

Crystal, D. (1997). *English as a global language.* Cambridge: Cambridge University Press.

Damayanti, I. L. (2008). Is the younger the better? Teaching English to young learners in the Indonesian context. *Educare: International Journal for Educational Studies, 1*(1), 31–38.

Davies, A. (1996). Proficiency or the native speaker: What are we trying to achieve in ELT? In G. Cook & B. Seidlhofer (Eds.), *Principle and practice in applied linguistics* (pp. 145–157). Oxford: Oxford University Press.

Goldstein, L. M. (1987). Standard English: The only target for nonnative speakers of English. *TESOL Quarterly, 21*(3), 417–438.

Graddol, D. (2010). *English next India.* New Delhi: British Council.

Ibrahim, A. E. K. (1999). Becoming Black: Rap and Hip-Hop, race, gender, and identity and the politics of ESL learning. *TESOL Quarterly, 33*(3), 349–369.

Jenkins, J. (2006). Current perspectives on teaching world Englishes and English as a lingua franca. *TESOL Quarterly, 40*(1), 157–181.

Jones, S., & Bradwell, P. (2007). *As you like it. Catching up in an age of global English.* London: Demos.

Kachru, B. B. (1986). *The alchemy of English: The spread, functions and models of non-native Englishes.* Oxford: Pergamon Press.

Kachru, B. B. (1992). The second diaspora of English. In T. Machan & C. Scott (Eds.), *English in its social context and second language acquisition: Essays in historical linguistics* (pp. 230–252). New York: Oxford University Press.

Kachru, B. B., & Nelson, C. L. (1996). World Englishes. In S. L. McKay (Ed.), *Sociolinguistics and language teaching* (pp. 71–102). Cambridge: Cambridge University Press.

Kelch, K., & Santana-Williamson, E. (2002). ESL students' attitudes toward native- and nonnative-speaking instructors' accents. *The CATESOL Journal, 14*(1), 57–72.

Kirkpatrick, A. (2007). Asian Englishes: Implications for English language teaching. *Asian Englishes, 9*(2), 4–19.

Klippel, F. (2008). New prospects or imminent danger? The impact of English medium of instruction on education in Germany. In D. E. Murray (Ed.), *Planning change, changing plans: Innovations in second language teaching* (pp. 26–42). Ann Arbor, MI: University of Michigan Press.

Lee, S. K., Lee, K. S., Ya'acob, A., & Wong, F. F. (2010). English language and its impact on identities of multilingual Malaysian undergraduates [Electronic Version]. *GEMA Online™ Journal of Language Studies, 10,* 87–101, Retrieved from http://pkukmweb.ukm.my/~ppbl/Gema/GEMA%202010/pp%2087_101.pdf

Lowenberg, P. H. (1992). Testing English as a world language: Issues in assessing non-native proficiency. In B. B. Kachru (Ed.), *The other tongue: English across cultures* (pp. 108–122). Champaign, IL: University of Illinois Press.

Lowenberg, P. H. (2002). Assessing English proficiency in the Expanding Circle. *World Englishes, 21*(3), 431–435.

Lowenberg, P. H. (2007). Issues of validity in tests of English as a world language: Whose standards? *World Englishes, 12*(1), 95–106.

Matthew, R. (2012). Understanding washback: A case study of a new exam in India. In C. Tribble (Ed.), *Managing change in English language teaching: Lessons from experience* (pp. 193–200). London: British Council.

Ministry of Education. (1966). *Report of the Education Commission 1964–1866.* New Delhi: Government of India.

Modiano, M. (2003). Euro-English: A Swedish perspective. *English Today, 19*(2), 35–41.

Mollin, S. (2006). *Euro-English: Assessing variety status.* Tübingen: Gunter Narr Verlag.

Murray, D. E. (2005). ESL in adult education. In E. Hinkel (Ed.), *Handbook of research in second language learning* (pp. 65–84). Mahwah, N.J.: Lawrence Erlbaum.

Murray, D. E. (2010). Changing stripes––chameleon or tiger? In D. Nunan & J. Choi (Eds.), *Language and culture: Reflective narratives and the emergence of identity* (pp. 164–169). New York: Routledge.

Murray, D. E. (2011). Vocational ESL. In E. Hinkel (Ed.), *Handbook of research in second language teaching and learning* (Volume II, pp. 75–88). New York: Routledge.

Paikeday, T. M. (1985). *The native speaker is dead*. Toronto: Paikeday Publishing.

Patel, M. (2012). The ETeMS project in Malaysia: English for the teaching of mathematics and science. In C. Tribble (Ed.), *Managing change in English language teaching: Lessons from experience* (pp. 109–113). London: British Council.

Seidlhofer, B., Breitender, A., & Pitzl, M.-L. (2004). English as a lingua franca in Europe. *Annual Review of Applied Linguistics, 26*, 1–34.

Wedell, M. (2011). More than just "technology": English langauge teaching initiatives as complex educational changes. In H. Coleman (Ed.), *Dreams and realities: Developing countries and the English language* (pp. 275–296). London: British Council.

Yano, Y. (2001). World Englishes in 2000 and beyond. *World Englishes, 20*(2), 119–131.

Yano, Y. (2009). English as an international lingua franca: From societal to individual. *World Englishes, 28*(2), 246–255.

Chapter 4

The Technological Context

VIGNETTE

A colleague and I are working with an English language development center in Thailand that is charged with providing instruction in English for specific workplace settings, with the goal of making Thai professionals competitive in the world where English is often the medium of communication. While some instruction has been and may continue to be delivered face-to-face, the goal is to provide access to all the center's English language courses to all Thai citizens any time, any place. Therefore, online delivery of the course material is essential. The center employs highly experienced English language teachers and lecturers from the top universities in Thailand to write its face-to-face English language courses. However, it is recognized that these teachers will need special training in how to both adapt and create online course material. In our planning meeting, we jointly design the two-week training program. Teachers will be introduced to the basic concepts in online course development, instructional design, and types of online activities. The session will then look at the course syllabus and materials from the existing English for Doctors course and work on ways to effectively adapt the material for online delivery. By the end of the two weeks, teachers will be able to see material for which they have adapted and written online instructional design. [Murray, research notes]

Task: Reflect

1. In what ways do you think the syllabus for online delivery might be different from that for face-to-face (f2f) delivery in the English for Doctors course?
2. In what ways do you think designing materials for online delivery is different from that for print materials?
3. What types of applications do you think could be used for online English courses? What types of teaching/learning activities would each be used for?

Introduction

> Teachers in L2 education cannot realistically meet their students' needs if they ignore these developments [new electronic literacies] or seek to force-fit the use of electronic media to traditional modes of communication or pedagogy.
>
> (Pennington, 2004, p. 87)

The 21st Century, like the latter decades of the 20th Century, has seen new uses of computer technology, especially the growth and development of the Internet, computer-mediated communication (CMC), and social media. These technology applications have added new communication tools and uses of language to the repertoire of English. Therefore, the teaching of English needs to include the teaching of this new language and these new and emerging media. For language learners to be able to function in the 21st Century globally requires them to be as familiar with these uses of English as with traditional forms of communication, such as letters or telephone conversations. Additionally, some learners may be required to take online tests and so will need digital literacy skills to be successful (Pierce, 2013). These new media provide new platforms for delivering language instruction. Therefore, language programs need to address both the use of technology as a tool for language learning and technological applications as varieties of language use that form part of the content of language teaching.

Task: Reflect

Directions: Think about your own language learning. What technologies were used to facilitate instruction?

Key Definitions

Although the term technology is bandied around indiscriminately, it is often used to refer solely to computers. However, technology is any item that extends human capacity, a definition that includes technologies as diverse as bicycles, blackboards, eyeglasses, writing tools (and in fact writing itself), and computers. Recognizing that computers and technology are not synonymous terms, we will nevertheless use them interchangeably in this volume. Even if we confine technology to computers, we find numerous terms used in ELT to refer to the teaching of language using computers in some way in instruction. By instruction, we exclude its use by teachers for lesson preparation or grading, for example. Table 4.1 provides a list in common usage.

TELL is used more in Europe than in North America while telecollaboration was used by Warschauer and Kern (2000) to identify uses where leaners were networked together. This term was subsequently taken up by some other educators for this specific aspect of computers for instruction. In this volume, we will use the term CALL for all aspects of computer use in language instruction because it is the term most commonly used, including for the names of professional associations dedicated to the study of computer use in language instruction

Table 4.1 Terms for Use of Computers in Language Instruction

Term	Acronym
Computer-assisted instruction	CAI
Computer-assisted language learning	CALL
Cyberspace	none
Computer-based instruction	CBI
Computer-based testing	CBT
Computer-based training	CBT
e-learning	none
Intelligent CALL	ICALL
Information and communication technology	ICT
Technology enhanced language learning	TELL
Telecollaboration	none

(see *Task: Expand* at the end of this chapter). We recognize that the use of this term reifies the computer, placing it before learning; we also recognize that for many people, the mental image will be of a stand-alone desk-top or lap-top computer. However, we will use the term to encompass all the current devices that are digital and used for instruction, including smart phones, and tablets.

Roles of Technology in Curricula

There are a number of ways to view the role of technology. We will explore each perspective: whether it is used as a tool or tutor, the historic stages of CALL, the delivery mechanism, the characteristics of CALL, integrating technology into the curriculum, and language use in technology.

Technology as a Tool or Tutor

Technology can be used as either a *tool*, a *tutor*, or a *tutee* (Taylor, 1980). Taylor was the first to differentiate between these three uses of computers in education. For Taylor, when the computer is used as a tutor, it temporarily takes the place of a teacher by providing instruction and guidance. When used a tool, it has no teaching attributes but facilitates instruction. Such uses include presentation programs, email, wikis, and Learning Management Systems (LMSs). As tutee, the student programs the computer. While the latter has been used in general education, it has rarely been used in language teaching. While the difference between tool and tutor is distinct and useful, many educators refer uncritically to the computer as a tool, much in the same way they might consider a pair of scissors a tool for cutting up a reading for a jigsaw activity.

Historic Stages of CALL

In addition to choosing the role of technology as tool or tutor, educators need to make choices as to what types of technology to use and how big a role they will play. Warschauer (2001) posited three stages of how technology has been used historically for CALL.

Table 4.2 Stages of CALL

Stage	1970s–1980s Structural CALL	1980s–1990s Communicative CALL	21st Century Integrative CALL
Technology	Mainframe	PC	Multimedia and Internet
English-teaching paradigm	Grammar-translation and audio-lingual	CLT	Content-based, ESP/EAP
View of language	Structural (a formal structural system)	Cognitive (a mentally-constructed system)	Socio-cognitive
Principal use of computers	Drill and practice	Communicative exercises	Authentic discourse
Principal objective	Accuracy	And fluency	And agency

Adapted from Warschauer, 2001, p. 6. Reprinted with permission of the author.

Since this article was written in 2001, the technology has changed considerably, with the explosion of handheld devices and social media, neither of which are captured fully in Warschauer's depiction of the third stage. Multimedia and Internet include an array of applications that can be and are being used in language teaching. We would argue that handhelds and social media emphasize the social, constant connectivity, and any time, any place access. The English teaching paradigm is communities of practice (Anderson, 2008; Khalsa, 2012; Wenger, 1998), an essential aspect of constructivist approaches to learning. Constructivist approaches are learner centered. Learners play active roles in interpreting, processing, and generating knowledge through shared, purposeful activity, such as projects. The view of language is as a social semiotic (Halliday, 1978). The principal use of computers (in their various guises) is for authentic discourse to connect people to achieve collaborative tasks. The principal objective is less concerned with accuracy than with collaboration. A further criticism of Warschauer's model is that it seems to endorse an inevitable, positive development over time.

Another way of viewing the role of computers in language instruction is the extent to which the curriculum is delivered online, an issue we discuss in the next section.

Delivery Mechanism

With the Internet becoming more widely available in the 21st Century, CALL has moved from being largely computer language programs on CDs to networked, online delivery, whether used as tool or tutor. A number of terms have been used to describe the various permutations and combinations of online and f2f instructional delivery. Courses that are considered fully *online* may include some residential component, but have at least 80% delivered online, according to the Sloan Consortium, which studies online higher education in the U.S. (Allen & Seaman, 2011). Courses that make substantial use of email, chat, discussion boards, or some other Internet activity or material as supports to the classroom are often referred to as *blended learning* or *hybrid learning*. Sloan uses these terms interchangeably for courses where 30–79% is delivered online. They defined *web-facilitated* as being 0–29% delivered online. These web-facilitated courses are essentially f2f courses, where there may be an LMS used or web pages used to post the syllabus or assignments. Bauer-Ramazani (2006) distinguishes between a hybrid course, which "may have some face-to-face class time but a large proportion of the course would take place online" (p. 197), and a blended course, which "would meet face-to-face but offer online threaded discussions and file-sharing" (p. 197).

Online delivery has its roots in distance education (DE), which was introduced to help learners who were not able to attend brick-and-mortar classrooms because of distance or time constraints. DE has been a boon for people living far from large population centers with educational institutions. For example, Australia has many immigrants in regional and remote areas who are not able to leave their home to attend language schools in a town. The Adult Migrant English Program (AMEP) has, therefore, always made available a DE curriculum, *It's Over to You*, which traditionally was delivered via print and audiotape (18 lessons), with tutors who telephoned learners (Department of Immigration and Citizenship, 2013). Over time, many immigrants who had time constraints also took advantage of the DE program. Some were mothers with young children who were not willing to attend regular classes; others were people whose work schedule did not allow them to attend classes. In the first decade of the 21st Century, they have included online delivery of some aspects of the course in a blended model.

While online delivery still provides learning opportunities for those who cannot attend f2f classrooms because of time or distance constraints, quite often it is being used for other reasons. For example, many of the for-profit online language courses are designed to increase enrollment in already existing language centers. In some cases, administrators consider they are less expensive than f2f courses or that offering online courses will make them more competitive.

We believe that in the curriculum design process, technology needs to be considered as *one* of the possible resources for instruction. It needs to be chosen carefully in order to meet learners' needs. In some situations, administrators mandate a particular delivery mechanism (as in the vignette). However, the curriculum and learners' needs still need to be addressed. For example, Whittaker describes a redesign of a blended English language learning program for the Armed Forces of Bosnia-Herzegovina (Whittaker, 2012). She found that the curriculum's success depended on recognizing both the contextual and personal drivers for change that shape the curriculum design. It was essential to engage the officer instructors and teachers throughout the process. Further, they adopted an iterative approach, taking time by designing and redesigning the course over a three-year period. Others have also tried to provide frameworks for using technology in English language classrooms.

Characteristics of CALL

Because CALL is often challenging for teachers, a number of educators have proposed guidelines for developing CALL curricula. These educators all agree that an online course, for example, is not just a course where all the f2f materials are put on the web. For example, in the vignette, my colleague and I were planning professional development for the Thai instructors so that they would be able to adapt and develop online CALL curricula. We established the essentials of this training to be:

- introducing teachers to the basic concepts in online course design (selection of content, cognitive load implications, scaffolding, etc.)
- introducing teachers to the types of effective online learning activities (e.g., drop-down boxes, rollovers, drag-and-drop)
- discussing and assessing (throughout the training) how particular types of activities can best facilitate the intended learning outcomes
- introducing teachers to the nature and function of instructional design (ensuring coherence and cohesion in overall course content, choosing appropriate activity types, communicating with web designers), and guiding teachers in effective instruction writing to web designers, and
- adapting a portion of an existing course—English for Doctors—for online delivery, using instructional design concepts.

Another lens on a "successful technology-enhanced language learning environment" is provided by Butler-Pascoe and Wiburg (2003), who list 12 attributes that cover all types of delivery mechanism—online, hybrid, blended, or web-facilitated. Such a successful environment:

1. Provides interaction, communicative activities, and real audiences.
2. Supplies comprehensible input.
3. Supports development of cognitive abilities.
4. Utilizes task-based and problem-solving activities.
5. Provides sheltering techniques to support language and academic development.
6. Is student centered and promotes student autonomy.
7. Facilitates focused development of English language skills.
8. Uses multiple modalities to support various learning styles and strategies.
9. Supports collaborative learning.
10. Meets effective needs of students.
11. Fosters understanding and appreciation of the target and native cultures.
12. Provides appropriate feedback (pp. 15–19).

Yet another lens is provided by Chappelle (2001), who focused on the CALL *tasks*. She described six criteria for the appropriateness of tasks:

1. Language learning potential, that is, whether and to what level the task affords a beneficial focus on form.
2. Learner fit, the extent to which the task is appropriate for the learners in terms of language level, learning styles, and learning strategies.
3. Meaning focus (rather than only form focused).
4. Authenticity, the degree of resemblance of the CALL task to the language and situations the student may encounter in an L2 situation.
5. Positive impact, that is, whether the task creates motivation, increases interest in the L2 culture, and helps develop metacognitive learning skills.
6. Practicality—how easy it is for both teacher and student to use the task.

In a rather different approach, Levy and Stockwell (2006) begin with the technology rather than the curriculum, focusing instead on CALL design. They note that CALL design needs to integrate elements from both technology and pedagogy in a principled way and provide guidelines and examples from a variety of different language teaching contexts.

To ensure appropriate use of and facility with technology in ELT, the TESOL International Association developed technology standards for both learners and teachers (Healey et al., 2011). These standards provide an elaborated framework for teachers, institutions, and administrators. For learners, there are three goals, for teachers, there are four. Each goal is then elaborated through several standards, each of which has a number of performance indicators (see Chapter 22 for an in-depth discussion of standards in education). Goal 2 for teachers is particularly relevant for curriculum design: "Language teachers integrate pedagogical knowledge and skills with technology to enhance language teaching and learning" (p. vii). The focus is on teaching and learning, not merely on using technology because it is there. The standards for this goal are:

Standard 1: Language teachers identify and evaluate technological resources and environments for suitability to their teaching context.

Standard 2: Language teachers coherently integrate technology into their pedagogical approaches.

Standard 3: Language teachers design and manage language learning activities and tasks using technology appropriately to meet curricular goals and objectives.

Standard 4: Language teachers use relevant research findings to inform the planning of language learning activities and tasks that involve technology (p. vii).

For curricula where the computer is tutor, it is essential that instruction and guidance be provided. The instruction needs to be scaffolded (Hammond & Gibbons, 2001). Scaffolding is achieved through careful sequencing, with each component building on previous ones; with provision of linguistic models and then explicit instructions for learners to practice the language themselves; and with effective feedback. Feedback is the most difficult aspect of online tutor courses. Research has shown that language is best learned through interaction. When the computer is used as tool, this interaction can be achieved through human-to-human interaction using discussion lists, email, VOIP (voice over internet protocol), or video conferencing. When the computer is used as tutor, *interactivity* (Murray, 2008) is used to provide feedback that is timely, specific, and multimodal. This feedback needs to provide more than "correct" and "incorrect" as responses to student language use. The feedback needs to explain why the answer is correct or not.

Task: Explore

1. Conduct an online search and select two English language courses that are delivered online.
2. Analyze these two courses to determine to what extent they meet Chappelle's six criteria.

3. Analyze these two courses to determine to what extent they meet the 12 criteria established by Butler-Pascoe & Wiburg.
4. Analyze these two courses to determine to what extent they meet TESOL's technology Goal 2.
5. Would you recommend these courses to your students? Why? Why not?

Integrating Technology into the Curriculum

While a particular technology does not determine a particular curriculum approach, the two are interrelated. Different technological affordances facilitate particular approaches. Therefore curriculum designers need to make informed decisions about which technologies support their preferred approaches. As already stated, we believe that it is the curriculum and the needs of learners that should drive the adoption of various technologies in the language classroom. Even when, institutionally, the decision has been made to convert an entire course to online, decisions need to be made about what tasks to use, what multimedia technologies to use, whether to choose synchronous or asynchronous CMC, whether or how to have group or project work, and what LMS to use. These decisions depend on the curriculum objectives and the characteristics and needs of the learners. For example, if learners are in widely different time zones, synchronous CMC would be a burden on teachers and learners who might have to link up in the middle of the night or during a period of religious observance. Learners with limited bandwidth or even access to regular electricity supplies might find it impossible to stay online for any long periods of time, obviating regular collaborative class time. Teachers might have to send emails with attachments for students who cannot access certain websites either because of government censorship or filters in their local library where they go to use computers. Or they may mail a CD with the video components to learners. Even when using an LMS, teachers might find they need to supplement with other tools such as Skype or Adobe Connect (a web-based asynchronous conferencing tool).

If the decision is to choose a blended design, or a f2f design with some CALL support, decisions also need to be made about whether to have a self-access language learning laboratory where learners can practice using commercial software, surf the web to complete course assignments, and so on. Decisions depend on curriculum needs.

For example, when one of us (Murray) was working with colleagues to design a multimedia course in Australian citizenship for immigrants to Australia, we were aware that many of these learners had minimal literacy in their mother tongue and many were beginners in English language learning. Our overarching approach was constructivist, encouraging students to actively engage in knowledge construction rather than knowledge reproduction. Consequently, our design included visual materials such as videos and a multimedia CD. The videos were of people who had become citizens, talking about their process and reasons for doing so. The CD was situated in a government office, with which the learners were already familiar. It used learning objects that students could access by rolling a mouse over symbols and icons. They consisted of short sequences of spoken or written text linked to learning activities such that learners could access the entire syllabus by completing matching, drag and drop, and sequencing activities based on spoken and written texts drawn from the video and workbooks (Murray & McPherson, 2006). Because many of the concepts of citizenship privileges and responsibilities are highly abstract, they also provided supplementary fact sheets in multiple languages.

Language Use in Technology

As indicated in the introduction, not only can technology be used as a tool or tutor in ELT, but also it provides another dimension of language in use as content for language teaching. While in many contexts, young people are more adept at technology than their teachers, it does not mean that they necessarily have the language to use it in English, or that they have the sociocultural expertise to know what to use, with whom, and when. The TESOL Standards (Healey et al., 2011) address this issue with a goal for learners: "Language learners use technology in socially and culturally appropriate, legal, and ethical ways" (p. vi). The two standards for this goal are:

> Standard 1: Language learners understand that communication conventions differ across cultures, communities, and contexts.
>
> Standard 2: Language learners demonstrate respect for others in their use of private and public information (p. vi).

Different technologies adapt language and each focuses on particular linguistic choices that are best suited for the technology, such as the abbreviations used in Twitter and texting (for example, Crystal, 2008). Communicators then move among the different media, depending on the context. While it might be appropriate to apply for some jobs via Twitter or email, for other applications, it is inappropriate. Similarly, there has been considerable research on the structure of webpages (for example, "Eyetrack study," 2000) and the need to include web reading and navigation in English language instruction (Murray, 2008). We need more research of this kind that clearly shows how different registers and genres operate in the new technologies. In language instruction, the curriculum needs to expose learners to the different language uses, helping them identify what is appropriate for different audiences and contexts, just as we might for varieties based on social class, ethnicity, or region.

Conclusion

As we indicated in Chapter 1, curricula are embedded in the sociocultural setting in which they are enacted, including the technological context. Technology use, therefore, reflects the attitudes towards and access to technology in the local community. There is "no single optimal mix. What configuration is best can only be determined relative to whatever goals and constraints are presented in a given situation" (Shaw & Igneri, 2006, p. 3).

Task: Expand

Several CALL professional associations and journals have an online presence. The following are useful sites for further exploration of issues and trends in the area of CALL.

APACALL, the Asia-Pacific Association for Computer-Assisted Language Learning, has a forum, book series, newsletter, and special interest groups (SIGs).

http://www.apacall.org

AsiaCALL has an online journal, an annual conference, and a bibliography.

http://www.asiacall.org

CALICO, Computer-Assisted Language Instruction Consortium, has a journal, conference, and SIGs.

http://www.calico.org

EUROCALL, the European Association for Computer Assisted Language Learning, has an annual conference, an online journal, and SIGs.

http://www.eurocall-languages.org/

IALLT, the International Association for Language Learning Technology, has an annual conference, a journal, and regional groups such as IndiaCALL.

http://www.iallt.org

In addition to these associations dedicated solely to CALL, ELT professional associations have interest groups that focus on CALL. The most active are:

IATEFL, the International Association of Teachers of English as a Foreign Language, has a Learning Technologies SIG:

http://ltsig.org.uk/

JALT, the Japan Association for Language Teaching, has a Computer Assisted Language Learning SIG:

http://jalt.org/groups/447

The TESOL International Association has a Computer-Assisted Language Learning Interest Section that supports an Electronic Village at the Annual Convention, as well as an online Electronic Village:

http://www.tesol.org/connect/interest-sections/computer-assisted-language-learning

Questions for Discussion

1. Explain the difference between using technology as a tool and as a tutor. Provide examples.

2. How well do you think Warschauer's motel captures the history of CALL? How would you elaborate on it?
3. How could you use social media to develop communities of practice in your classroom setting?

References

Allen, I. E., & Seaman, J. (2011). *Going the distance: Online education in the United States, 2011.* Retrieved from http://www.onlinelearningsurvey.com/reports/goingthedistance.pdf

Anderson, T. (2008). Teaching in an online learning context. In T. Anderson (Ed.), *The theory and practice of online learning* (pp. 343–366). Edmonton, AB: AU Press, Athabasca University.

Bauer-Ramazani, C. (2006). Training CALL teachers online. In P. Hubbard & M. Levy (Eds.), *Teacher education in CALL* (pp. 183–200). Amsterdam: John Benjamins.

Butler-Pascoe, M. E., & Wiburg, K. (2003). *Technology and teaching English language learners.* New York: Allyn & Bacon.

Chappelle, C. (2001). *Computer applications in second language acquisition: Foundations for teaching, testing and research.* Cambridge: Cambridge University Press.

Crystal, D. (2008). *Txtng: The Gr8 Db8.* Oxford: Oxford University Press.

Department of Immigration and Citizenship. (2013). *Fact Sheet 94: English courses for eligible migrants and humanitarian entrants in Australia.* Retrieved from http://www.immi.gov.au/media/fact-sheets/94amep.htm.

Eyetrack study. (2000). Retrieved from http://www.poynter.org/Eyetrack/previous.html

Halliday, M. A. K. (1978). *Language as social semiotic.* London: Edward Arnold.

Hammond, J., & Gibbons, J. (2001). What is scaffolding? In J. Hammond (Ed.), *Scaffolding: Teaching and learning in language and literacy education.* Sydney: PETA.

Healey, D., Hanson-Smith, E., Hubbard, P., Ioannou-Georgiou, S., Kessler, G., & Ware, P. (2011). *TESOL technology standards: Description, implementation, integration.* Alexandria, VA: TESOL.

Khalsa, D. K. (2012). Creating communities of practice: Active collaboration between students. In L. England (Ed.), *Online language teacher education: TESOL perspectives* (pp. 81–92). New York: Taylor & Francis.

Levy, M., & Stockwell, G. (2006). *CALL Dimensions: Options and issues in computer-assisted language learning.* Mahwah, NJ: Lawrence Erlbaum Associates.

Murray, D. E. (2008). From marginalisation to transformation: How ICT is being used in ESL learning today. *International Journal of Pedagogies and Learning, 4*(5), 20–35.

Murray, D. E., & McPherson, P. (2006). Let's participate: Designing a civics course for adult migrants. In M. A. Snow & L. Kamhi-Stein (Eds.), *Developing a new course for adult learners* (pp. 285–309). Alexandria, VA: TESOL.

Pennington, M. (2004). Electronic media in second language writing: An overview of tools and research findings. In S. Fotos & C. M. Brown (Eds.), *New perspectives on CALL for second language classrooms* (pp. 68–92). Mahwah, NJ: Lawrence Erlbaum Associates.

Pierce, D. (2013). Common core testing will require digital literacy skills [Electronic Version]. *eSchool News.* Retrieved from http://www.eschoolnews.com/2013/04/24/common-core-testing-will-require-digital-literacy-skills/?

Shaw, S., & Igneri, N. (2006). *Effectively implementing a blended learning approach.* Retrieved from http://wvuheducation.com/LinkClick.aspx?fileticket=7Hhk4Bw4lyg%3D&tabid=148

Taylor, R. P. (1980). *The computer in the school: Tutor, tool, tutee.* New York: Teacher's College Press.

Warschauer, M. (2001). The death of cyberspace and the rebirth of CALL. In P. Brett (Ed.), *CALL in the 21st century* (CD-Rom). Whistable, Kent: IATEFL.

Warschauer, M., & Kern, R. (2000). *Network-based language teaching: Concepts and practice.* Cambridge: Cambridge University Press.

Wenger, E. (1998). *Communities of practice: Learning, meaning, and identity.* New York: Cambridge University Press.

Whittaker, C. (2012). Redesigning a blended learning course in Bosnia and Herzegovina: Introducing new technologies for ELT. In C. Tribble (Ed.), *Managing change in English language teaching: Lessons from experience* (pp. 135–139). London: British Council.

Part II

Key Processes in Curriculum Design

While there are many models of curriculum design for English language teaching (for example, Graves, 1999; Nation & Macalister, 2009), we present in Part II a model that we have used extensively ourselves in a variety of different teaching contexts.

As indicated in Chapter 1, there is general agreement that curriculum includes planning, implementation, and evaluation. These three aspects of curriculum are not stages to be considered in a linear fashion; rather, the process is cyclical. For example, during implementation, evaluation may occur and changes made to the original intended curriculum. However, to simplify the presentation of a complex process, we will focus on each in separate chapters. Chapter 5 focuses on planning, Chapter 6 on implementation, and Chapter 7 on evaluation. We say "focuses" because the other aspects of curriculum design will be referred to in the other chapters, but they will not be the focus of the chapter. In Chapter 7, we discuss all issues around program quality assurance as they relate to the curriculum.

References

Graves, K. (1999). *Designing language courses: A guide for teachers*. Boston, MA: Heinle and Heinle.

Nation, P., & Macalister, J. (2009). *Language curriculum design*. London: Routledge.

Chapter 5

The Cycle of Curriculum Design

VIGNETTE

My colleagues and I have been charged with setting up a new department. Part of our task is to develop a curriculum to prepare learners to enter Freshman Composition.[1] All students take an English placement test and, depending on their score, can take Freshman Composition or are required to take one or two courses prior to that. Our research has shown us that these learners are largely immigrants or children of immigrants. They have graduated from US high schools but have not yet mastered the English required of them at the university level. Many are very proficient orally, but they lack academic English. Although Freshman Composition is essentially a writing course, our research has shown us that these learners have poor reading skills, especially of academic subjects. While they take these preparatory courses, they will also be taking General Education courses[2] in a variety of subject areas. We also know that to be successful in Freshman Composition, they need to pass a final examination. This exam is a timed essay based on a reading passage, often of literature. Our overall approach to teaching is to start with learners' background knowledge and build on this in a constructivist approach. Therefore, with all these needs in mind, we described the curriculum content as: "This course develops students' ability to use English for academic purposes. The focus is on literacy at the college level, with the use of oral language to support and reinforce the development of reading and writing. Emphasizing the connection between reading and writing, the course will include naturally sequenced, culturally relevant reading selections and writing assignments that challenge students to examine and reinterpret their own experience and background knowledge. Recognizing the connection between oral and written language, the course will include peer discussion of reading assignments and essay drafts. Issues in the structure of English, both at the sentence and the text level, will be examined in the context of reading and writing assignments." To ensure students can respond to the timed essays in Freshman Composition, the curriculum includes timed essays and the final exam for the course is a timed essay, but uses readings of relevance to the particular learners. [Murray, research notes]

Task: Reflect

1. Think about your own learning to read and write academic English. What sort of instruction did you receive?
2. How do you think academic English differs from everyday English?
3. Why do you think it's important to begin instruction with what learners already know?
4. Have you evaluated peer writing? What was this experience like?

Introduction

Designing curricula is an iterative process. We will present a model for this process, recognizing that, in reality, curriculum developers often enter the process at any of the stages. Most models of curriculum development include *planning, implementing*, and *evaluating*. However, these are usually presented as three stages. In reality, the process is complex, iterative, and dynamic, and cycles through its various components. We will focus on planning in this chapter, exploring implementing further in Chapter 6 and evaluating in Chapter 7.

Task: Explore

Directions: Interview an administrator in an ELT center. Use the following questions to guide your interview:

1. Please describe the curriculum in use in your center. What is the focus? What is the pedagogical philosophy of the center?
2. Who designed the curriculum?
3. How did they determine what your students needed?
4. How often is the curriculum reviewed? What is the process used for curriculum review?
5. How are new teachers helped to interpret the curriculum?

Curriculum Design Process

In this chapter, we provide a design process that we have used in our own ELT work. While it includes planning, implementing, and evaluating, it elaborates on these aspects. The center of our process is student learning and student performance as a result of learning. Although this process is presented as linear stages, as already indicated, in reality the process is cyclical. What is important is that all the components of the process are addressed. These components are provided in Table 5.1. We then describe each stage, providing examples from a variety of different ELT contexts.

We do not refer to "method" or "methodology" in the above process. Although method and methodology have been variously described by ELT professionals (see Kumaravadivelu, 1994 for a critique of method), here methodology is the activities, tasks, and learning experiences used by the teacher within the teaching and learning process. Teachers choose methodologies based on their assumptions

Table 5.1 Process of Curriculum Design

Stage	Sample Questions to Ask
Understanding the context	
Determining theoretical framework	What is the broad sociocultural context of learning? What beliefs about language and language learning are to be articulated through the curriculum?
Conducting stakeholder analysis	Who are the stakeholders? What do they expect learners to be able to do? What expertise already exists in the institution? How committed are various stakeholders to curriculum development/renewal?
Conducting needs analysis	What do learners already know and what are they able to do? What do they need to know and be able to do?
Developing curriculum relevant to the context	
Determining outcomes/goals	What are the intended goals of the curriculum? What will learners be able to do as a result of the curriculum? What will learners have to do to achieve those goals?
Selecting approach to curriculum design	What approach to curriculum design is most appropriate for the outcomes and goals? Are teaching staff educated in using this approach? If not, can professional development be conducted? What would it entail?
Selecting content (scope)	What content needs to be taught so learners can achieve these goals?
Sequencing content	How should the content be organized? Should there be a number of courses to reach the goals?
Selecting learning materials and activities	What materials help learners acquire the content? What activities help learners achieve the course objectives? What roles do teachers and learners take?
Assessing learning	How will learners be placed in different courses? How will we determine what learners have achieved? What do we do with this information?
Evaluating the curriculum (impact study)	
Tying instruction to context	Does instruction reflect the theoretical framework? Are teachers teaching to the curriculum? Are learners engaged in the curriculum? What impact does the curriculum have on instruction?
Tying learning to context	Does student learning achieve the goals/objectives of the curriculum? Does this learning meet student needs? Does this learning meet stakeholder needs? What impact does the curriculum have on learning?

Adapted from Murray, D. E., & Christison, M. A. (2011). *What English Language Teachers Need to Know Volume II: Facilitating Learning* (p. 10). New York: Routledge.

about: (a) language; (b) second language learning; (c) teacher and learner roles; (d) effective learning activities; and (e) preferred instructional materials. We will refer to these specifics rather than a method or methodology because many different activities and so forth can be used within the same general methodology.

Understanding the Context

Understanding the context requires an examination of the beliefs about language and language learning, of the stakeholders and their specific interests and roles, and the goals and needs expressed by the learners themselves.

Determining a Theoretical Framework

In the vignette, Murray and her colleagues chose a curriculum that was based on both a stakeholder analysis and their own views of language and language learner. What initiated the need for a new curriculum was university administrators' desire to help ESL students be successful in both Freshman Composition and in their other university courses. However, quite often the driver for curriculum innovation is particular views of language and/or learning. Often these views have changed with the advent of new administrators with different understandings or with their learning about new approaches from other institutions or countries. For example, the worldwide trend of teaching English in primary schools has grown exponentially as different governments have worried that their citizens might be left behind in globalization. Whatever the impetus for designing a new curriculum, it is essential to have a common understanding of language and language learning. However, often the understanding of language and language learning is mandated by administrators, without consultation with educators. This was not the case in the vignette. The expertise of the ELT professionals engaged in the curriculum design was solicited and respected. It may not be the case in other contexts.

In the early 21st Century, Thailand, like many other countries, embarked on an ambitious reform agenda across all sectors and subjects, including the English language. One (of many) theoretical frameworks was based on the American Council for the Teaching of Foreign Languages (ACTFL) model in the U.S., largely because some key stakeholders had experience with this model while studying in the U.S. This model has five interconnected areas around which the standards are written:

- Communication: communicate in languages other than English.
- Cultures: gain knowledge and understanding of other cultures.
- Connections: connect with other disciplines and acquire information.
- Comparisons: develop insight into the nature of language and culture.
- Communities: participate in multilingual communities at home and around the world (American Council for the Teaching of Foreign Languages, 1996).

The crucial question is whether curricular models or even aspects of a curriculum from one context can be imported (or exported) to a very different context. In the Thai situation, not all of these areas are relevant to all Thai learners. The literature has many other examples where such translations, while having some impact on some of the players, were not able to sustain an innovation (see, for example, Canagarajah, 2001; Chick, 2001; Katz, Beyrkun, & Sullivan, 2008).

Conducting a Stakeholder Analysis

In one sense, the stakeholder analysis is part of an overall needs analysis. However, we have divided this concept into two parts: a stakeholder analysis and a needs analysis from learners. We have done this to emphasize the importance of both. A stakeholder analysis will identify the roles of different groups with a vested interest in English language learning in the specific context. In many contexts, changes in national language policy have led to top-down curriculum renewal, such as the teaching of English at primary school level. Local implementation may resist, reject, circumvent, adapt, or subvert curricular change if those expected to implement the curriculum are not engaged in its development (see Kennedy, Doyle, & Goh, 1999, for examples from China, Hong Kong, and Malaysia). These implementers include principals or directors, heads of departments, professional development personnel, school superintendents, teacher educators, and teachers. Teachers are ultimately the agents of change or not (Fullan, 1991) because they enact the curriculum.

One such case is the English Language Syllabus 2001 in Singapore, a top-down, large-scale curriculum change. It was a language *use* curriculum with the goal of teaching learners to communicate effectively in English so that they could use language meaningfully and appropriately. However, teachers reinterpreted the curriculum based on their own previous teaching experiences and their understandings of their students' needs. They interpreted their students' needs through the lens of the final national English language examination, which focused on reading, writing, and grammar[3] (Singapore Examinations and Assessment Board, 2005–2013). Hence, the teaching of speaking and listening was neglected (see Goh & Yin, 2008 for a full description of the design process).

The stakeholder analysis is vital to curriculum development. It is necessary not only to identify the stakeholders, but also to determine what roles they need to play in the process. In the Singapore example, teacher expertise and ability to work with the new curriculum was not sufficiently considered. Nor was the role of the Singapore Examinations and Assessment Board considered in order to ensure alignment between the national exam and the new curriculum.

In vocational and workplace English language instruction, the needs analysis of necessity includes a specific work-task needs analysis, usually conducted on site. "Task analyses are generally used in curriculum development as educators observe and record their observations of the discrete steps included in workplace tasks such as setting up the salad bar for a cafeteria or making change for a customer at the cash register" (Burt & Saccomano, 1995). Stakeholders such as management and unions need to be consulted and participate in the curriculum development process. In addition to the specific workplace language requirements, both Australia and Canada have vocational systems that provide detailed competencies for different vocational skills nationally, many of which are communication skills. Such taxonomies need to be considered in vocational or workplace ELT curriculum development. There is, however, sometimes a mismatch between employers' and employees' needs. While employers want to focus on their specific workplace communication, workers may be more interested in general English that will transfer outside the workplace.

In addition to these directly involved stakeholders are stakeholders in the wider community. So, for example, in many countries, governments have established generic or employability skills required of all citizens. Where these exist, they may need to be included in the English language curriculum. Then, there is the role of English in the broader community. In Chapter 3 we explored Kachru's (1986) three circles of Englishes and how and why different varieties are valued. Therefore, the stakeholder analysis needs to explore these issues for the particular context. Is it used for wider communication in the community or a subject of study in schools? Are all varieties of English valued? Which is considered the appropriate language for instruction? What does the wider community expect from English language education? Is it to support individual development or national economic development in a global world?

Conducting a Needs Analysis with Learners

For curricula to be effective they need to be based on the language learning needs of the specific learners in their specific contexts. However, this is not always the case, as indicated by a teacher from a university in Thailand, who said: "We just thought 'this' is what our students have to learn" (Burton, Daroon, Raimaturapong, & Siripong, 2008, p. 62). There are two aspects of learner needs: objective needs based on biographic data and subjective needs in terms of wants and desires (Nunan, 1985). While the latter are more difficult to ascertain, it is possible to uncover some of the learners' subjective needs as they relate to what and how they want to learn.

Given the wide range of contexts in which English is taught (see Chapter 3), learner needs are dependent on the context of learning. Thus, many of these needs come from the stakeholder analysis. However, curriculum designers also need to conduct a needs analysis of their actual learners. In the vignette, we had researched the types of students who entered the university needing ELT preparation prior to Freshman Composition. We had conducted a survey of students to uncover their language use and preferences (Murray, Nichols, & Heisch, 1992). Such a survey or questionnaire needs to uncover learner identities, experiences, and goals. Our students were able to respond to the survey themselves. In other cases an interview may be appropriate. For beginners, a simple agree/disagree survey or a survey in their home language may be more appropriate.

The following list provides some sample questions for a learner needs analysis. This is not a questionnaire for a specific group of learners; rather it includes sample items for different types of learners. For example, 10c and 10d would be appropriate for an academic curriculum, while 2, 3, 10e, and 10f might be appropriate for adult immigrants; and 10g and 10h would be appropriate for an ESP course in the tourism or hospitality industry. Question 6 would be somewhat irrelevant in compulsory education unless English is offered as an elective. These questions are provided to illustrate the types of questions to ask for your particular context.

1. What is your age?
2. What is your occupation?
3. What is your marital status? If married, do you have children?
4. How many and which languages do you speak?
5. How long have you been learning English?

6. Where did you learn English?
7. What will you do when you finish this course/program?
8. With whom do you use English?
9. Why are you learning English?

    a. To pass a school subject?
    b. To pass a gatekeeping examination?
    c. To settle in an English-dominant country?
    d. To work for a multinational company?
    e. To study in an English-medium university?
    f. Other

10. How difficult are these tasks for you in English?
    very difficult   OK   easy

    a. Asking questions in class
    b. Participating in group work in class
    c. Reading a subject matter textbook
    d. Writing reports
    e. Reading labels on food
    f. Talking to the doctor
    g. Writing emails in response to a travel inquiry
    h. Answering questions from a hotel guest
    i. Reading newspapers
    j. Reading webpages in English

11. Which skills are most important for you?

    a. Listening
    b. Speaking
    c. Reading
    d. Writing

12. How do you like to learn? Rank your choices.

    a. In groups
    b. By reading
    c. By writing
    d. By thinking by myself
    e. By being told by the teacher
    f. By memorization

13. How important is English to you?   very   a little   not at all

---

Task: Explore

These sample questions cover identity, experiences, and goals. Rearrange the list so it is categorized under these three aspects. What other questions could you add for each category? How do you think these questions might influence curriculum?

In addition to a learner-response survey, it is also necessary to conduct a placement assessment, so learners can be placed in appropriate classes and also to determine where to start teaching.

Developing Curriculum Relevant to the Context

The context, explored through values and beliefs about language and language learning, and through stakeholder and learner needs analysis, provides the impetus for developing the goals and objectives, the curricular approach, and the materials and activities for the curriculum.

Determining Outcomes and Goals

Goals and objectives need to be measurable in order to measure student learning. By aligning objectives and assessment, we can determine the extent to which learners have mastered the curriculum goals and objectives. Most curricula have a small, limited set of goals (usually around five or six) for which specific sets of objectives are developed. Objectives may include specific language objectives of what learners know and are able to do with the language. They may also include learning how-to-learn strategies, that is, the extent to which learners have become independent learners. Learners can reflect on their own learning process and develop strategies appropriate for the curriculum and that align with their own learning preferences to become more effective language learners. Table 5.2 provides sample goals (both language and learning-how-to-learn) and some possible specific objectives.

Selecting a Curricular Approach

In Chapters 8 through 21 we discuss the most common curricular arrangements in ELT. While all curricula need to include all aspects of language, have subject matter around which the language is taught, and consider the learner and learning, each curriculum has a particular orientation, a particular starting point. For example, in Turkey's Hotel Management and Tourism vocational high schools (discussed

Table 5.2 Sample Goals and Objectives

Goals	Sample Related Objectives
Language To develop English language competency for professional purposes, applying English to real-life situations	Learners will be able to • respond appropriately to common personal information questions • interpret wages, wage deductions, benefits, and timekeeping forms • follow, clarify, give, or provide feedback to instructions
Learning-how to-learn Learners will take responsibility for the management of their own learning	• organize workbooks and folders • evaluate the usefulness of specific activities and resources • work effectively in groups • learn from mistakes

in more detail below), the curriculum choices could begin with functions (see Chapter 9): What language functions do hotel staff need to engage in? So, the curriculum might be designed around functions such as "Apologizing," "Making a polite request," or "Making an offer." Equally, the curriculum choices could begin with content: a hotel employee manual, a national park brochure, or an airline website. The rationale for the choice of approach should emerge from the Theoretical Framework, Stakeholder Analysis, Learner Needs Analysis, and the Goals and Objectives. This is not always the case, however. Sometimes, the choice is made for reasons suggested earlier, such as changes in administration, or new ideas.

Selecting Content

Language teaching is somewhat different from other teaching because content includes both the language to be taught and the subject matter in which the language is embedded. The scope (see Chapter 1) determines what and how much language and subject matter. When determining the scope of language for the curriculum, all the following aspects of language need to be considered:

* language structures
* language skills
* genres
* registers
* speech acts/functions
* sociocultural appropriacy
* process/product
* generic skills, and
* non-language outcomes.

For example, in the vignette, although the curriculum was to prepare learners for Freshman Composition, the curriculum did not focus on writing only. It included the other three skills. Reading was considered essential as part of preparation for academic success, and listening and speaking were considered as both starting points and vehicles for instruction. Writing instruction included process and product, academic genres, and the language structures that came out of readings or written assignments. We include non-language, such as body language, in this list because different cultures have different conventions of body language use and learners need to understand what is appropriate for English in their particular context.

Although language structures can be taught as a subject matter, in teaching language in use, it is necessary to provide contexts of use as referred to in Table 5.2 above. The subject matter content needs to be chosen based on curricular goals and objectives and the curricular approach. So, for example, in Turkey's Hotel Management and Tourism vocational high schools, subject matter would be around hotel management and tourism. For beginning immigrants, the content might be around *survival* topics such as visiting the doctor or shopping.

Sequencing Content

Once the scope has been determined, the next issue is how to sequence the language and subject matter content. Sequencing is more complicated in language instruction than in subject areas such as arithmetic, where there is a logical progression. Additionally, sequencing depends on what learners acquire along the way. The sequencing also differs depending on the curricular approach chosen. For a structural approach (Chapter 8), the most common progression is from what is considered to be more simple to what is considered more complex. For a content-based course such as survival skills for new immigrants (Chapter 14), the progression is often based on what language they need immediately and what can wait. In an adjunct approach (Chapter 14), the content depends on the subject matter of the course to which the language course is attached. Some questions to ask when deciding on sequencing are:

- What subject matter knowledge builds on other knowledge?
- What language functions build on other functions, texts, and grammar?
- What grammar needs to be included so learners have the language to create texts or engage in tasks?

Once the scope and sequence have been determined, materials and activities that facilitate learning can be chosen.

Selecting Learning Materials and Activities

Materials and activities need to translate the goals and objectives into learning experiences for students. Often, materials or activities are chosen because the teacher thinks learners will enjoy them or they have just seen the activity demonstrated at a conference. In other situations, materials and activities are chosen because a particular textbook has been mandated by the program, institution, state, or country. Materials and activities need to be aligned to the goals and objectives of the curriculum and chosen because they will help learners achieve those goals. As a result, usually they are developed once the curriculum goals and objectives have been established. And, as mentioned previously, individual teachers choose their methodologies for implementing the curriculum.

In a project in Turkey a rather different approach was used. The curriculum goal was rather general: To improve the language skills of students in Turkey's Hotel Management and Tourism vocational high schools. Rather than writing a new curriculum, the project trained a core of excellent teachers from around the country in current Content and Language Integrated Learning methodologies (see Chapter 14 for an in-depth discussion of this curricular approach), materials design, and course design. This core group of teachers then wrote the textbooks, with guidance from the project leaders. Teachers were trained in using the materials and the materials were piloted, and revised. The rationale for this approach was that "[m]aterials have an immediate impact on classroom teaching, pushing teachers to reflect on the innovation and encouraging them to change their methodology and content" (Scholey, 2012). It was, therefore, hoped that as the materials were adopted, all teachers would change their teaching methodologies.

Assessing Learning

Teachers and other stakeholders only know whether learners have learned and are able to use language through assessment. Assessment must be aligned to the goals and objectives of the curriculum. Assessment can be both formative and summative (see Volume II, Chapters 12 and 13 for full discussions of assessment). Formative assessment provides teachers and others, including learners, with ongoing information about how to adjust instruction. When the summative examination is not aligned to the objectives and goals, the examination often becomes the de facto curriculum, as in the case of the English Language Syllabus 2001 in Singapore discussed above. In some workplace and ESP curricula the most appropriate form of assessment is observation of the learners in their actual workplace or other setting. For example, a curriculum to teach managers in the electronics industry how to give presentations can be assessed by observing them giving a presentation in their workplace. Or, in an ESP curriculum designed to prepare learners for undertaking a degree in accounting, the assessment might entail an assignment co-evaluated by both language and accounting instructors.

Evaluating the Curriculum

Evaluating the curriculum is a large topic in itself. Therefore, we have devoted Chapter 7 to this topic. Here we just acknowledge that it is an essential part of the iterative curriculum design process.

Conclusion

Curricula are embedded in the sociocultural, political, and historic settings in which they are used. Therefore curricula need to reflect the beliefs and values about language and language learning of the stakeholders. As a result, curricula are best designed for local use, rather than adopted from outside contexts. If teachers have the opportunity to design their own curriculum, either by themselves or with colleagues, they will need to use the dynamic process we have described as a guideline. Depending on their current context, they may be entering the process at any stage. Having assessed whether learners are achieving the goals and objectives, teachers then need to go back to the curriculum and adjust where needed.

Task: Expand

In this chapter we have briefly addressed a broad range of issues related to the process of curriculum design. We were not able to go into detail on many topics. The following resources will expand your knowledge of some of these topics:

Murray, D. E., & Christison, M. A. (2011). *What English language teachers need to know Volume I: Understanding learning*. New York: Routledge.

This volume has chapters on identity and context, language awareness, and theories of language learning.

Murray, D. E., & Christison, M. A. (2011). *What English language teachers need to know Volume II: Facilitating learning*. New York: Routledge.

This volume has chapters on selecting and adapting materials, planning activities and managing classroom interaction, and assessment.

Questions for Discussion

1. Explain the different stakeholders that need to be considered when designing curricula. What role does each play?
2. What is a needs analysis? How can it be conducted? Why is it important in planning instruction?
3. Who do you think should be involved in the various stages of curriculum design? Why?
4. Explain the relationship between language and subject matter in English language teaching.
5. How could you avoid the problem that Singapore teachers had when trying to implement their new curriculum?

Notes

1. Most US universities require students to take one or two courses in composition, unless they test out of the requirement. These courses are usually referred to generically as *Freshman Composition*.
2. Most US universities require students to take a broad range of courses outside their major. At this university, these courses are labeled "General Education" (GE).
3. The Primary School Leaving Examination now includes listening and oral components.

References

American Council for the Teaching of Foreign Languages. (1996). *National standards for foreign language education*. Retrieved from http://www.actfl.org/i4a/pages/index.cfm?pageid=3392

Burt, M., & Saccomano, M. (1995). *Evaluating workplace ESL instructional programs*. Washington, DC: Center for Adult English Language Acquisition.

Burton, J., Daroon, Y., Raimaturapong, A., & Siripong, S. (2008). Professional renewal and educational policy: Some examples of theorizing practice in TEFL in Thailand. In D. E. Murray (Ed.), *Planning change, changing plans: Innovations in second language teaching* (pp. 62–84). Ann Arbor, MI: The University of Michigan Press.

Canagarajah, A. S. (2001). Critical ethnography of a Sri Lankan classroom: Ambiguities in student opposition to reproduction through ESOL. In C. N. Candlin & N. Mercer (Eds.), *English language teaching in its social context* (pp. 208–226). London: Routledge.

Chick, J. K. (2001). Safe-talk: Collusion in apartheid education. In C. N. Candlin & N. Mercer (Eds.), *English language teaching in its social context* (pp. 227–240). London: Routledge.

Fullan, M. G. (1991). *The new meaning of educational change* (2nd ed.). London: Cassell.

Goh, C. C. M., & Yin, T. M. (2008). Implementing the English Language Syllabus 2001 in Singapore schools: Interpretations and re-interpretations. In D. E. Murray (Ed.), *Planning change, changing plans: Innovations in second language teaching* (pp. 85–107). Ann Arbor, MI: University of Michigan Press.

Kachru, B. B. (1986). *The alchemy of English: The spread, functions and models of non-native Englishes*. Oxford: Pergamon Press.

Katz, A., Beyrkun, L., & Sullivan, P. (2008). Challenges in translating change into practice: Textbook development in Ukraine. In D. E. Murray (Ed.), *Planning change; changing plans: Innovations in second language teaching*. Ann Arbor, MI: University of Michigan Press.

Kennedy, C., Doyle, P., & Goh, C. (Eds.). (1999). *Exploring change in English language teaching*. Oxford: Macmillan Heinemann.

Kumaravadivelu, B. (1994). The postmethod condition: (E)merging strategies for second/foreign language learning. *TESOL Quarterly, 28*(1), 27–48.

Murray, D. E., Nichols, P. C., & Heisch, A. (1992). Identifying the languages and cultures of our students. In D. E. Murray (Ed.), *Diversity as resource: Redefining cultural literacy* (pp. 63–83). Alexandria, VA: TESOL.

Nunan, D. (1985). *Language teaching course design: Trends and issues.* Adelaide, Australia: National Curriculum Resource Centre.

Scholey, M. (2012). Materials design and development in English for the world of work in Turkey: Policy, strategies and process. In C. Tribble (Ed.), *Managing change in English language teaching: Lessons from experience* (pp. 115–121). London: British Council.

Singapore Examinations and Assessment Board. (2005–2013). Primary School Leaving Examination. Retrieved from http://www.seab.gov.sg/psle/2013subjectInfo.html

Chapter 6

Using Curriculum to Connect Lessons, Courses, and Programs

VIGNETTE

Recent budget cuts, as well as new requirements for K–12 public school licensure for pre-service teachers (PSTs) have greatly affected the composition of my teacher education classes at the university. The membership in my classes couldn't be more diverse. Not only do I have graduate and undergraduate students in the same class, but I also have content area, English as a second language (ESL), and foreign language teachers who have a primary interest in working with learners of majority languages other than English, such as Spanish, Chinese, and Arabic. Even though all students are beginners in terms of content and language integrated models of second language (L2) classroom instruction and curriculum development, they have very different backgrounds and profiles. Some students are only interested in US K–12 public schools while others want to work outside of the U.S. in both private and public sectors. They also want to work with different learner populations, from young learners to adults and from academic to non-academic contexts. These different backgrounds and profiles translate into very different needs.

My brain has been churning for days as I try to figure out how to adjust my instruction to accommodate the varying needs of the students in my course. What could they possibly have in common with one another? Last week I collected samples of student "work." This work consisted of a written lesson plan for a previously taught lesson or a lesson for a future class. I also asked students to provide a written explanation or diagram of how the lesson fit into the course they taught or planned to teach and how the course fit into a specific curriculum. As I was looking over the sample materials that I had collected, I realized that one theme had begun to emerge. Few of the materials that I looked at seemed to provide evidence of students' abilities to make the appropriate connections at either the instructional level in terms of course objectives and instructional tasks in the classroom or at the curricular level in terms of courses, programs, or schools. In some cases the required connections should have even been extended beyond a school or program. Although I realize that I have my work cut out for me in terms of meeting the needs of this diverse group of PSTs, I realize that all of them can benefit from specific instruction on making curricular connections.
[Christison, research notes, October 2009]

Task: Reflect

1. Why do you think the teacher in the vignette above asked for a sample lesson plan from her students?
2. Why do you think the teacher in the vignette also asked her students for an explanation of how their lesson plans fit into their courses and how the courses fit into the program or school curricula?
3. When you prepare a lesson plan, where do you begin? Why?

Introduction

In Chapter 5 we introduced the cycle of curriculum development in which three specific stages in the process were identified—understanding the context, developing curriculum relevant to the context, and evaluating the curriculum (see Table 6.1). Within each stage there are specific activities that must be undertaken, such as conducting stakeholder and needs analyses, determining goals, selecting and sequencing content, selecting learning materials and tasks, assessing learning, and tying instruction and learning to the context. These activities are referred to as the component parts of the cycle of curriculum development. Because an effective curriculum must be connected through its component parts, Chapter 6 will focus specifically on how these component parts are connected to one another. A key principle in making curricular connections is that each of the component parts in the cycle of curriculum development must be addressed regardless of the approach to curriculum design that one selects.

General Approaches to Curriculum Design

There are two processes that influence how individuals approach curriculum design. In order to understand the tensions that frame curriculum design (i.e., how can a process be both linear and iterative?), we discuss both of these processes briefly. We use the term *technological process* (Tyler, 1950) to describe how connections are made within a curriculum. The term as Tyler originally used it describes a curriculum development approach in which terminal outcomes (i.e., what learners are expected to know and be able to do) are articulated early in the process and then steps are identified to achieve those outcomes. In this sense, the curriculum design process that we propose in Chapter 5 with its component parts presented in a linear fashion is a technological process. Regardless of the level at which curriculum design occurs or the connections that one is making, developing curriculum relevant to the context begins with outcomes and goals and, then, considers the additional component parts—determining the content or scope, sequencing the content, selecting the learning materials and tasks, and assessing learning—in relationship to outcomes.

The teacher educator in the vignette above came face-to-face with the political and contextual realities of creating and implementing curricula as she experienced a shift in learner needs. In the context of the real world, the process of developing curriculum relevant to the context must be flexible, recursive, and iterative. We use the term *naturalistic process* (Glatthorn, Boschee, & Whitehead, 2006) to refer to the features of the curriculum design process that must be responsive to the context; therefore, it is concerned with the implemented curriculum, rather than the planned one.

In some contexts, beginning with outcomes that derive from an appropriate theoretical framework that keeps learners' and stakeholders' needs in mind may be desirable but unrealistic. For example, one of us taught English as a second language (ESL) in a non-academic, life skills program for adults for a number of years. We learned that we had been given funding in one week and were told that the program had to begin almost immediately; there was little opportunity for lengthy, advanced planning. We were suddenly overwhelmed with students, but there were no materials for teachers and no curriculum guides; consequently, teachers entered the curriculum design process by focusing on the creation of learning materials and activities. There was no time to do otherwise. However, as the program continued and teachers and administrators were able to focus on the other components of the curriculum development process in addition to tasks and materials and, eventually, articulate outcomes for the students that were based on learner and stakeholder needs, as well as on an evaluation of the curriculum (see also the vignette in Chapter 21 for another example). As these examples demonstrate, curriculum planning and implementation are recursive and iterative, but they must also be linear in the sense that they address terminal objectives. In almost any context, there will be tensions between the technological and naturalistic processes.

Types of Connections

Language educators and curriculum designers are always challenged with the task of making useful and appropriate connections within a curriculum regardless of the approach they take. The teacher educator in the vignette identified the inability to make connections as a common problem for all of her students (both pre-service and in-service teachers) in her course. Making connections that are integral to the development of learner knowledge and skills takes careful planning, extensive knowledge on the part of teachers and curriculum designers, and teacher and learner participation in an ongoing assessment process.

The curriculum design process includes different types of connections depending on whether one is making connections within lessons, across lessons, across courses within a specific program, or across programs within a language-teaching center. Teachers who are implementing the curriculum design process at the level of an individual lesson plan may be concerned with, for example, how to make connections between the specified outcomes for the lesson and the tasks students are asked to do. In a content and language integrated curriculum (see Chapter 14), teachers must also be concerned with making connections between selecting and sequencing content and the creation of content objectives, and with making connections between content and language objectives.

As soon as teachers move beyond one individual lesson to a series of lessons for a course, other types of connections are needed. For example, the curricular focus may shift to include how the tasks in which students participate in one lesson prepare them to meet the objectives for another lesson. Teachers who are responsible for teaching different courses within a program must be concerned with how the individual courses are connected to one another. For example, how do writing tasks in one course prepare learners to complete the writing tasks for a project in a subsequent course? Administrators of English language centers, which may include several different programs, must consider how the programs within the center are connected. For example, how are several very different programs connected to the center's goals and objectives?

In Chapter 6, we provide examples of how connections can be actualized at different levels of the curriculum design process, for example within lessons as well as within courses and programs. The types of connections one makes in the curriculum design process are similar metaphorically to the *matryoshka* dolls (Russian nesting dolls) that fit neatly inside one another (Figure 6.1).

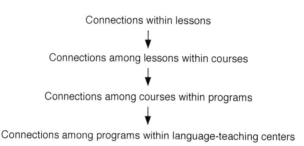

Connections within lessons
↓
Connections among lessons within courses
↓
Connections among courses within programs
↓
Connections among programs within language-teaching centers

Figure 6.1 Types of Connections in Curriculum Design Process

Making Connections within Lessons

There are a number of important connections that need to be made within lessons. These connections include creating lesson objectives for both content and language, selecting and sequencing content, identifying essential or key questions, developing learning tasks, and assessing learning. From a technological process point of view, lesson planning begins with the articulation of terminal learning objectives, and many L2 teacher educators suggest beginning with the articulation of terminal objectives even though they recognize that the process of planning a lesson is not a linear one. There are several reasons for this preference in ordering. First, learning objectives are statements that represent what learners need to know and be able to do at the completion of a lesson; as such, they serve as natural connectors between who is doing the learning, what is being learned, and how the learning is taking place (see Murray & Christison, 2011 for more information on writing objectives).

Teachers often arrive at learning objectives by asking key or essential questions. These are broad questions that learners should to be able to answer at the culmination of instruction, rather than after one activity or one class period. One of us (Christison) recently observed a third grade teacher in the U.S. who was working with 17 English language learners (ELLs) in a class of 30 children. She was working on a theme called "Living Things" with a series of topics and sub-topics. The topic covered during the class was flowering plants (i.e., angiosperms) with sub-topics of monocots and dicots. The key questions she wanted students to be able to answer were the following: *What are the properties of angiosperms (flowering plants)? How do monocot and dicot plants differ?* In order to answer these questions, students needed to cover multiple lessons on cotyledons, floral parts, leaves, pollen, stems, vascular bundles, monocots, and dicots, as well as participate in a plant dissection activity. The focus for learning objectives needs to be on measurable performances that collectively lead learners to outcomes for a course or program.

Learning objectives and course content must also be connected. The connection is an obvious one: the content selected is based on what learners are expected to know and be able to do. The learning activities and tasks should also be aligned with corresponding learning objectives to facilitate the fulfillment of course goals (Fink, 2003). Finally, the procedures that are used to evaluate the extent to which the corresponding learning objectives (i.e., the assessments) have been met are used to reinforce course and program outcomes and should mirror the content and learning tasks used as a part of the instructional process.

Connections within lessons revolve around three important concepts—the input that learners receive, the tasks and activities used to acquire new skills and knowledge, and the way in which learner output is assessed (Figure 6.2).

Input ◄──► Tasks or activities ◄──► Output (assessments)

Figure 6.2 Connections within Lessons

Making Connections among Lessons

Lessons should be connected in obvious ways to courses. The most common way for lessons to be connected to one another is through outcome statements. Outcome statements are more commonly referred to as course or program goals. Goals typically define the purpose or end product of learning for a course or program and provide answers to the following questions: *What is the overall purpose of the course or program? How will the learner be changed as a result of participation on the course or program?* Each lesson should contribute to the goal of the course. For example, if the course goal is to assist English learners in the development of academic writing skills, then each lesson should be focused on some aspect of academic writing and contribute towards the achievement of the course goal. A lesson that focused on writing in non-academic contexts would likely not contribute directly to the achievement of that course goal.

Lessons can be linked through the careful sequencing of content (see Chapter 14 for a discussion of content connections in planning curriculum and Murray & Christison, 2011). Lesson content is linked through content topics; topics are linked to themes, and threads are used to link themes (Grabe & Stoller, 1997). In addition to content, lessons can be linked through a series of instructional tasks that support the completion of a project, such as lessons focused on writing a five-paragraph essay by completing a series of tasks that are part of the writing process. Lessons can be connected to one another in other ways as well, such as through the development of specific vocabulary, grammar skills, or job skills, or through the use of standards. There are several options for making connections among lessons. It does not matter so much what options curriculum developers and teachers choose; the important principle to remember is that there must be an obvious connection.

Making Connections among Courses

Programs are made up of a series of courses, and the courses within a program must also be connected to one another in a logical and useful way. Building a cohesive set of courses for an English language program in any context begins with careful planning and the development of maps or templates (Jacobs, 2004). These maps or templates serve as tools for the creation and the assessment of the courses. In practice, curriculum designers of English language programs have conceptualized the connection of courses within programs in traditional ways, such as through language skills (e.g., listening, reading, writing, and speaking or pronunciation), grammatical structures (see Chapter 8 on the structural syllabus) for different levels of language proficiency, or academic skills (see Chapter 10 on academic functions), such as outlining, taking notes, or writing an essay. While these different ways of connecting courses are useful for helping teachers make logical connections in a general sense, they are less useful in the assessment process.

A less common approach to connecting courses within programs is the use of curriculum maps or templates. In this approach, we are suggesting that the components that teachers use to make connections within lessons (i.e., key or essential questions, objectives, content, tasks, assessments) are mapped across courses using a map or template such as the one in Table 6.1.

In English language programs, courses are often connected at different proficiency levels. Curriculum maps or templates can be created for each proficiency level and reviewed by instructors, supervisors, curriculum designers, program directors, and other key administrators. By looking at each of the components horizontally and across courses, it is possible to determine how the components can be linked together.

Task: Explore

Work with another teacher. Create a curriculum template using the components for your course that are identified in Table 6.1. What connections do you see between your courses? What changes would you need to make in the curriculum template in order to have stronger connections between the two courses?

Making Connections among Programs

English language-teaching centers are administrative units that are made up of different types of programs. For example, a center may oversee a program that

Table 6.1 Curriculum Map or Template for Connecting Courses

	Course 1	Course 2	Course 3	Course 4
Key or essential questions				
Objectives				
Content				
Tasks and activities				
Assessments				

focuses on providing English language instruction for adults working for local businesses. In addition, the same center may offer an academic writing program for students who have been admitted to the university, as well as specific content and language integrated programs (see Chapter 14) for specific departments within the university, such as engineering or business administration. How are these seemingly different programs connected? Centers that have clearly articulated goals and objectives make decisions to accept or reject programs based on how they support the center's overall goals and objectives. Before adding new programs or when making a determination to continue a program, centers must determine the overall fit of the programs for the center.

Making Connections beyond Programs or Language-teaching Centers

There are connections or levels of coherence that go beyond lessons, courses, programs, or centers. For some programs and centers, there is also a need to make connections with a specific discipline, for example, math, social studies, or history. These connections are often articulated in terms of standards (see Chapter 21) or benchmarks (see, for example, *Wisconsin's Model Academic Standards for Social Studies* (Wisconsin Department of Public Instruction, 1998)). In addition to the coherence in a curriculum provided by the internal organization of lessons, units, courses, programs, and centers, a curriculum may also derive coherence from a discipline or across fields by focusing on issues, themes, or real-life phenomena that are manifested in standards or competencies. Making connections beyond programs or centers is important for learners who must pass standardized tests or exams and will be in competition with students from other centers for jobs and other career opportunities.

Conclusion

In this chapter we have focused on the importance of coherence in curriculum design through a discussion of how both technological and naturalistic approaches are valuable in making connections. We have also discussed the different types of connections that teachers and curriculum designers must consider from the connections teachers make within lessons when they consider how to connect instructional tasks to learning objectives to the connections that administrators make in connecting courses and programs. We also provided a brief discussion of connections that go beyond specific programs and centers to connect with disciplines or fields of study through the use of standards.

Task: Expand

Visit one of the following websites that seems most appropriate for the context in which you work or see yourself working in the future. Review the standards. What types of connections do you see in the standards you reviewed? For what context would they be useful? Share your results with a peer.

1. www.wida.us/standards
2. www.cambridgeenglish.org/exams-and-qualifactions/young-learners

3. www.pearsonpte.com/PTEyounglearners
4. www.tesol.org/standards (select from any of the standards documents—pre-K–12, technology, P–12 teacher education programs, standards for adult education, or the link on teaching to the standards for the Common Core.)

Questions for Discussion

1. In your own words, explain the differences between the technological and naturalistic processes in curriculum design and the importance of each in the process.
2. Give an example from your own experience of how curriculum design is both linear and iterative.
3. Discuss the different types of connections that curriculum designers must consider.
4. In your own words, explain Table 6.1 to a peer.
5. If you were a program or center administrator, would you encourage the use of curriculum maps or taxonomies for connecting the components of the curriculum? Why? Why not?

References

Fink, L. D. (2003). *Creating significant learning experiences: An integrated approach to designing a college course.* San Francisco: Jossey-Bass.

Glatthorn, A. A., Boschee, F., & Whitehead, B. M. (2006). *Curriculum leadership: Development and implementation.* Thousand Oaks, CA: Sage Publications.

Grabe, W., & Stoller, F. L. (1997). Content-based instruction: Theoretical foundations. In M. A. Snow & D. Brinton (Eds). *The content-based classroom* (pp. 5–21). White Plains, NY: Longman.

Jacobs, H. H. (2004). *Getting results with curriculum mapping.* Alexandria, VA: Association of Curriculum Development.

Murray, D. E., & Christison, M. A. (2011). *What English language teachers need to know Volume II: Facilitating learning.* New York: Routledge.

Tyler, R. W. (1950). *Basic principles of curriculum and instruction.* Chicago: University of Chicago Press.

Wisconsin Department of Public Instruction (1998). *Wisconsin's Model Academic Standards for Social Studies.* Retrieved from http://www.sdb.k12.wi.us/curriculum/standards/state/SocialStudies/SS%20Standard.pdf

Chapter 7

Quality Assurance and the Curriculum

VIGNETTE

I am working with colleagues in an English language program in Australia to develop a quality assurance system for the center. We begin by identifying the different functions of the center, from course design and delivery to teacher selection and development to student movement from marketing to graduation. For each function, we have staff responsible for the function delineate what the process of that function is, creating a reiterative process map or flow chart. So, the for example, the course design and delivery function includes: market research, academic research, choice of delivery modes, curriculum development, materials development, assessment and testing, accreditation, syllabus and lesson planning, course delivery, continuous improvement, and back again to market research and so on. Process maps for all functions include continuous improvement. Within each aspect of the function are listed its component parts around which decisions are made, including who is responsible for that particular component. So, for example, delivery mode includes internal, external, onshore, offshore, online, on campus, and multi campus. We are discussing continuous improvement for course design and delivery and have agreed that it should include student feedback, stakeholder feedback, convener (the person who coordinates multiple sections of the same course) reports, Academic Coordinator reports, tracking studies of students after they leave the program, self-assessment by teachers, all of which are currently conducted. Our next step will be to develop quality standards for these activities. We are guided to some extent by our external accreditation body. However, we also engage in some additional quality control activities, such as the moderation of student assessment. All student final examinations/projects are graded by two teachers, and the grades are compared. We wonder how we can measure improvement in this activity. How great should be the variation between teachers? How can we achieve this moderation more efficiently without increases in teachers' workloads? [Murray, research notes]

> **Task: Reflect**
>
> 1. Why do you think it is important to delineate the functions and processes of an organization?
> 2. How might this group of teachers come to closer agreement on grading?
> 3. How might this group of teachers analyze the feedback they receive for continuous improvement?
> 4. Do you agree with the list of continuous improvement methods? What would you do differently? Why? Share your ideas with a colleague.

Introduction

Quality assurance (QA) became popular in manufacturing and industry where the importance of quality products can mean the success or failure of a company. It has, however, been taken up in educational circles, especially as governments and other stakeholders have demanded accountability of educators. This does not mean that educational enterprises had previously ignored quality, but rather that many of them did not feel the need for external evaluations of their quality. Internally, their own expertise told them what was and what was not quality. This attitude can be seen across the curriculum—from decisions about who to hire, to what should be included in instruction, to how learners are to be evaluated. Parallel to this self-assurance were systems for accrediting professional programs, such as law and medicine and program reviews that are often with an external reviewer. As we saw in the vignette, some language programs are externally accredited. In this chapter we define what is meant by quality in English language education, outline some approaches to QA, examine the methods for collecting data on quality, provide guidelines for the process of developing quality standards, and discuss the role of curriculum evaluation in the QA process.

> **Task: Reflect**
>
> Think about your own organization. How is quality defined? How is it measured? What is measured? How is this information disseminated? To whom is it disseminated?

Defining Quality

In the educational literature, there is no agreement about what constitutes quality or even what aspects of an institution need to ensure quality. It is considered an elusive and intangible concept by many (Sallis, 2002). Some even question the integrity of student satisfaction as a measure of quality, concerned that students may not be the best judges of program quality (McNaught, 2009). "In language program contexts, quality becomes a function of student perceptions, student satisfaction, and the degree to which an institution can match or exceed stakeholder expectations" (Mercado, 2012, pp. 117–118). So, although teachers and administrators may believe that they know quality when they see it, they also need to examine quality from the perspective of their stakeholders. However, this does not negate their professional expertise or that of other professionals in the field. Parsons (1994), for example, considers three components of quality: client, professional, and management. By professional, he means whether the program meets the needs of clients as they are perceived by professionals. Management quality refers to the efficient use of resources to meet the goals of the organization. The Sloan Consortium, on the other hand (Moore, 2005), identifies five pillars of quality in online higher education: learning effectiveness, cost effectiveness and institutional commitment, access, faculty satisfaction, and student satisfaction. From these disparate views of quality, we can see general agreement that quality refers to perceived effectiveness of the institution in achieving its goals, vague as this definition is. Trying to operationalize quality is where it becomes more tangible, less elusive, and measurable. The next section describes some of the different approaches to operationalizing quality.

Approaches to Quality Assurance

Many approaches to QA are focused on systems, processes, and documentation, rather than continuous improvement. The former is the most common approach in accreditation schemes and in the International Standards Organization (ISO), while the latter is the hallmark of Total Quality Management (TQM). As already indicated, many institutions undertake generic accreditation, rather than accreditation specific to ELT. For example, in Australia, universities are subject to regular auditing by the Australian Universities Quality Agency (AUQA), which does not apply its own standards of quality, but rather audits whether institutions have standards of performance and a process for monitoring compliance. ELT programs within the university are subject to this system, but are also required to meet the standards of the ELT accrediting agency, the National ELT Accreditation Scheme (NEAS), if they wish to enroll international students or immigrants. In contrast, in the U.S., many educational institutions seek regional accreditation from their regional Accrediting Commission for Schools (ACS), such as the Western Association of Schools and Colleges (WASC). The ACS works with public, independent, church-related, and proprietary pre-K–12 and adult schools. WASC organizes its standards around four areas: organization for student learning, curriculum and instruction, support for student personal and academic growth, and resource management and development. Curriculum and instruction has three sub-areas: what students learn, how students learn, and how assessment is used. Each has a standard for the institution to meet. For example, the standard for what students learn states:

> The school provides a challenging, coherent and relevant curriculum for each student that fulfills the school's purpose and results in student achievement of the expected school wide learning results through successful completion of any course of study offered.
>
> (Western Association of Schools and Colleges, n.d.)

These institutions may also seek voluntary accreditation for their ELT programs through the Commission on English Language Program Accreditation (CEA).

Although voluntary, institutions that wish to accept international students can choose CEA accreditation (among others) so that they can enroll such students.

Some educational institutions seek accreditation from agencies with a more focused remit, such as the Distance Education and Training Council (DETC). DETC has standards such as curriculum delivery, organization of instructional materials, and student evaluation of courses, which are determined by an Examining Committee as "Meets Standard," "Partially Meets Standard," and "Does not Meet Standard." Another approach is that taken by the organization Quality Matters, which focuses on quality in online and blended courses in both higher education and K–12 education. For higher education, they have eight general standards, with 41 specific standards. The general standards' areas are:

1.   Course overview and introduction.
2.   Learning objectives (competencies).
3.   Assessment and measurement.
4.   Instructional materials.
5.   Learner interaction and engagement.
6.   Course technology.
7.   Accessibility.

Although focused on quality in online and blended courses, it is clear from this list that for Quality Matters, technology does not drive either the curriculum or quality. In fact, a useful aspect of their approach is the concept of alignment. By this they mean that standards 2, 3, 4, 5, and 6 "work together to ensure students achieve desired learning outcomes" (Quality Matters, 2011–2013).

We provide more details of accreditation in the ELT field and then provide a brief discussion of TQM. The agencies we discuss for ELT are NEAS and CEA, as representative of ELT accreditation.

ELT Accreditation

ELT accreditation is offered in a number of countries, in addition to NEAS and CEA. For example, the U.K. has Accreditation UK, which is managed as a partnership between the British Council and the industry association, English UK. In Canada, Languages Canada is responsible for QA, while in New Zealand the New Zealand Qualifications Authority (NZQA) is responsible. The latter oversees QA in a range of areas.

CEA. Although US-based, CEA's mission is to "promote excellence in the field of English language administration and teaching through the accreditation of English language programs and institutions worldwide" (Commission on English Language Program Accreditation, n.d.). As well as accrediting language programs within colleges and universities, it also accredits stand-alone ELT programs. CEA has 11 standards areas, with 44 total standards. The 11 areas are those required by the Secretary of the U.S. Department of Education for accrediting agencies who wish to be approved by that Department. Such approval allows the agency to accredit institutions that can accept international students. The areas include: curriculum, faculty, facilities, equipment and supplies, administrative and fiscal capacity, student services, recruiting, length and structure of program of study, student achievement,

---

Curriculum Standard 1:
The curriculum is consistent with the mission of the program or language institution, appropriate to achieve the organization's goals and meet assessed student needs, and available in writing.

Curriculum Standard 2:
Course goals, course objectives, and student learning outcomes are written, appropriate for the curriculum, and aligned with each other.

Curriculum Standard 3:
The instructional materials and methodologies are appropriate and contribute to the mastery of course objectives.

Figure 7.1 Commission on English Language Program Accreditation Curriculum Standards

student complaints, and program development. The standards for curriculum are (Commission on English Language Program Accreditation, n.d.) are shown in Figure 7.1.

The standards are evaluated through a self-study by the institution, followed by a site visit by three trained evaluators who visit classes, conduct a tour of facilities, and interview administrators, faculty, and students in order to verify the contents of the self-study report. The self-study is an opportunity for the institution to reflect on its own practice and provide data to demonstrate how it meets the standards.

NEAS. Like CEA, NEAS accredits English language programs in universities, and stand-alone ELT programs. However, it also accredits ELT programs in vocational colleges, and in schools. Like CEA, it also has a global mission. NEAS has eight standard areas: management and administration, premises, specialist staff, student services, English language programs and assessment, educational resources and equipment, promotion and student recruitment, and younger students.

The standard for English language programs and assessment requires that "The ELT centre's programs and assessment procedures are clearly documented, relevant, based on TESOL theory and practice and designed to meet the English language needs of students. Programs, assessment procedures and assessment tools are regularly reviewed" (National ELT Accreditation Scheme, 2008, p. 13). For each standard, there are detailed criteria for how the standard is to be met. This standard includes criteria for program delivery, program design, program documentation, assessment procedures, pre-program assessment, formative assessment, summative assessment, and review and evaluation of courses and assessment tools. Two of the aspects of program design, for example, are:

- The ELT centre demonstrates that for each course there is a set of specific objectives based on the needs of learners and described in terms of learner outcomes.
- The ELT centre allows for an appropriate range of teaching methods and learning activities to be provided to address the learning styles of the students (p. 13).

These two examples show that, although a range of methods and activities are promoted in the NEAS system, the approach to curriculum design values specific objectives, which would permit most of the approaches we describe in Chapters 8–21. However, it would be quite difficult for a negotiated curriculum approach (Chapter 16) to meet the criteria.

Neither CEA nor NEAS focuses on continuous improvement, although NEAS does have a system of evaluation and review as part of each criterion. TQM is the approach most often associated with continuous improvement.

Total Quality Management (TQM)

TQM focuses on continuous improvement, customer satisfaction, and the responsibility for quality resting with all involved in the enterprise, whether as suppliers, the workforce, or management. The goal is for employees to identify areas that need to improve and ways of improving. Employees are seen as a team who are all working together to improve customer satisfaction. In education, several writers have expressed caution about implementing a TQM approach. They note that team work has not been traditional in either universities or schools, and also, as indicated earlier, that students may not be the best judges of satisfaction. In fact Bogue (1998) goes so far as to say students can state they are highly satisfied in a survey and yet remain uneducated. He also argues that for systems to develop quality, they need to go beyond accreditation and assessment and include values and ethics. "Quality can only be defined in relation to the articulated values and purposes and the desired processes and outcomes of a particular program or service" (McNaught, 2009, p. 161).

For example, in the vignette, we described how one of us (Murray) worked with staff and faculty to develop a QA system for an English language program. As part of this process, we developed a Customer Service Charter, which was placed in prominent places where students and other stakeholders interacted with our staff. The Charter listed our mission and goals and so on, but also delineated our service standards as:

When you contact Aristotle Language Centre,[1] you can expect an innovative institution, which is well-resourced, offers a pleasant and safe environment, and maintains the highest standards. Our staff are dedicated professionals who are friendly and approachable. You can also expect us to:

- be courteous, efficient, and responsive to your needs
- be culturally sensitive and value the diversity of our customers
- provide up-to-date information about our products and services
- exercise the utmost integrity in providing services and programs, and
- not disclose any information about you without your consent, except as permitted by law (Murray, research notes).

Despite the possible limitations of TQM in education, the language center in the vignette did develop a continuous improvement process, which we will now describe.

Developing a Continuous Improvement Quality System

As indicated in the vignette, we first mapped out flow charts for the various activities of each unit in the organization. We had an overall QA leader and QA lead people in each unit. They developed the format for the mapping exercise. In the case of the English Language Programs unit described in the vignette, maps were developed for each of the activities. As indicated for course design in the vignette, the mapping showed the processes within that activity. They also identified who was responsible for the activity and established a goal for the activity. Below are the six activities and the goal for each:

- student movement (Goal: To ensure the most efficient and effective processing of students towards the achievement of their academic goals.)
- physical facilities and environment (Goal: To ensure the provision of professional facilities and a safe environment in which ELP will achieve its goals.)
- teacher selection and development (Goals: (i) To recruit qualified teachers with a diversity of skills and experience, while maximising professional opportunities for all staff. (ii) To achieve the strategic goals of ELP and the individual professional goals of all staff members by providing a range of high quality professional development programs and research opportunities.)
- course design and delivery (Goal: To develop and ensure high quality delivery of innovative academic programs based on careful identification of student needs and current ELP and TESOL research.)
- independent learning center (Goals: (i) To facilitate the independent development of English language and study skills by providing a comprehensive collection of ESL and other relevant resources and services for students and teachers. (ii) To maintain a close liaison with teachers and to regularly disseminate information about available resources.), and
- English for academic purposes (Goal: To assist undergraduate students of non-English speaking background to achieve their academic goals and to integrate into the academic community by providing courses in English language and academic study skills and other support services.).

English for academic purposes (EAP) was mapped separately because the EAP courses were credit-bearing for the university, unlike the other language courses which prepared students for university or were stand-alone language courses. Within these activities some of the individual activities required their own maps. For example, teacher selection and development contained eight areas, two of which, induction of new teachers and professional development, had their own goals and their processes mapped. Having mapped our activities, we then examined how we could obtain data in order to improve quality on an ongoing basis.

Major Methods for Continuous Improvement

The major methods we devised were:

- formal and informal feedback

- surveys, consultations, focus groups
- self-evaluation
- course evaluation by students
- complaints handling
- system monitoring/data analysis
- work redesign[2]
- staff meetings
- teacher action research
- professional development, and
- mentoring.

Because curriculum is the central focus of an ELT institution, evaluating the quality of the curriculum is an essential component of QA. Mercado (2012), for example, suggests the following methods for continuous improvement of the curriculum:

- classroom observation
- teacher input, such as offering suggestions or posing questions
- exploratory scanning studies (focusing on specific aspects of the program) through:

  o   observation
  o   student language samples
  o   test results, and
  o   action research.

- academic quality markers, such as:

  o   why students choose the program
  o   what students consider when making their selection, and
  o   what students consider to be quality practices and service.

- training reports, such as during professional development, and
- environmental scanning, that is, assessing trends and issues outside the institution.

While the methods used by the center in the vignette and by Mercado at the Instituto Cultural Peruano Norteamericano (ICPNA) provide ways of getting feedback from various stakeholders, from students to staff to funding bodies, the questions asked in surveys or focus groups and the focus of professional development and so on all require a clear understanding of what the institution aims to achieve. While the goals can act as overarching areas for feedback, the issue remains as to how an organization knows when it has or has not achieved its goals. Thus, there is a need for quality standards.

Developing Quality Standards

Quality standards may derive from a number of different sources, including:

- accreditation requirements
- legislation and regulations
- strategic and other plans

- position descriptions, organizational charts, and awards
- contracts, agreements, and schedules
- professional association guidelines
- research and best practice
- national standards associations, and
- education and training.

When developing quality standards, all of the above sources need to be examined to determine which are binding standards (e.g., legislation or accreditation). In practice, accreditation agencies include any obligatory legislation or regulations. However, in some contexts, there are no accrediting agencies and then legislation and regulation provide the overarching standards. In the section on accreditation above we provided samples of standards from two ELT accreditation agencies, samples that can be used by institutions whether they seek accreditation or just wish to evaluate the quality of their programs.

Feedback Loops

Many, if not all, of the standards in most accreditation schemes focus on either having a QA system in place (e.g., AUQA) or the components of quality (e.g., CEA), rather than on ensuring continuous improvement as in the TQM model. To ensure continuous improvement, the language center described in the vignette included continuous improvement in all its maps. We conducted audits, based on the goals and standards, leading to recommendations for improvement in each area. Each recommendation was accompanied by the name/title of the person responsible for implementing the improvement and the date by which it was to be completed. For example, in the teacher selection and development activity, some of the recommendations were that:

- the techniques of lesson planning be incorporated in the ELP Teacher Professional Development program, and
- the curriculum framework be continually revised and refined to maximize the advantages for teachers and students.

These recommendations, and when, how, and with what effect they are achieved then become the basis for determining whether improvement has been realized.

Task: Explore

If you are teaching, explore how QA is handled in your institution. How is it similar to or different from that discussed in this chapter? How would you develop a plan to introduce a rigorous, viable QA system in your organization?

Conclusion

This chapter has examined QA, whether it is to meet accreditation requirements or develop an institution committed to continuous improvement. For accountability, it is vital for institutions to be able to demonstrate their quality in all aspects and processes. In Chapter 5 we described the various components of the curriculum design process. Each component needs to be part of the quality process. Mercado (2012) indicates that QA is not just a good in and of itself, but it leads to student (and other stakeholder) satisfaction, which in turn leads to the reputation and in turn the durability of the program.

Task: Expand

Chalmers, D., Lee, K., & Walker, B. (2008). *International and national quality teaching and learning*. From http://www.olt.gov.au/resources/3899,6108 ?solrsort=sort_title%20asc/

This research report provides a comparison of quality assurance systems in higher education in 16 countries around the world.

McNaught, C. (2009). Ensuring quality programs. In M. A. Christison & D. E. Murray (Eds.), *Leadership in English language education* (pp. 156–171). New York: Routledge.

This chapter provides an excellent overview of quality assurance models and their application to English language teaching.

Mercado, L. A. (2012). Guarantor of quality assurance. In M. A. Christison & F. L. Stoller (Eds.), *A Handbook for language program administrators* (2nd ed., pp. 117–136). Miami Beach, FL: Alta Book Center.

This chapter also provides an excellent overview for ELT QA.

The major accreditation/QA agencies that accredit ELT programs in the English-speaking world all have their own websites:

In Australia, National ELT Accreditation Scheme (NEAS) program evaluation standards are available at:

http://www.neas.org.au/home/

Information about Accreditation UK can be found at their website:

http://www.britishcouncil.org/accreditation.htm

Languages Canada standards are available at:

http://www.languagescanada.ca/en/accreditation-quality-assurance

New Zealand Qualifications Authority (NZQA) standards are available at:

http://www.nzqa.govt.nz/

Questions for Discussion

1. Explain the relationship between QA and accreditation.
2. Why do you think the Sloan Consortium included access in its five pillars of quality?
3. Why do you think continuous improvement is important?
4. Why do you think some people are critical of TQM?
5. What do you think is missing from CEA's curriculum standards?

Notes

1. This is a pseudonym.
2. Work redesign was a formal process developed in consultation between university management and the union. This process was used when there were major changes in staff assignments or management structures.

References

Bogue, G. E. (1998). Quality assurance in higher education: The evolution of systems and design models. *New Directions for Institutional Research, 99*, 7–18.

Commission on English Language Program Accreditation. (n.d.). Leading by advancing standards. Retrieved from http://www.cea-accredit.org/

McNaught, C. (2009). Ensuring quality programs. In M. A. Christison & D. E. Murray (Eds.), *Leadership in English language education* (pp. 156–171). New York: Routledge.

Mercado, L. A. (2012). Guarantor of quality assurance. In M. A. Christison & F. L. Stoller (Eds.), *A Handbook for language program administrators* (2nd ed., pp. 117–136). Miami Beach, FL: Alta Book Center.

Moore, J. C. (2005). *The Sloan Consortium quality framework and the five pillars*. Retrieved from http://sloanconsortium.org/publications/books/qualityframework.pdf

National ELT Accreditation Scheme. (2008). Standards and criteria for English Language Teaching (ELT) centres. Retrieved from http://www.neas.org.au/wp-content/uploads/2013/05/NEAS-Standards-2008.pdf

Parsons, C. (1994). *Quality improvement in education: Case studies in schools, colleges and universities*. London: David Fulton.

Quality Matters. (2011–2013). Higher ed program rubric. Retrieved from https://www.qualitymatters.org/rubric

Sallis, E. (2002). *Total quality management in education*. London: Kogan Page.

Western Association of Schools and Colleges. (n.d.). WASC Focus on Learning Schoolwide Criteria. Retrieved from http://www.acswasc.org/about_criteria.htm#FOLB

Part III

Linguistic-based Curricula

In Part III, we present six different approaches to curriculum design that are linguistic-based in origin. By linguistic-based, we mean that these approaches to curriculum design are based on certain features of language (e.g., grammatical structures, language functions, or text types) that are given prominence for the purposes of organizing and designing curriculum. Chapter 8 presents the most common type of linguistic-based curriculum, a structural approach. It is based on the presentation and sequencing of grammatical structures and on an approach to teaching grammatical structure (i.e., to the form, meaning, and use) within a communicative framework.

The content of Chapters 9 and 10 is focused on language functions. In Chapter 9 we look at a notional-functional approach. It is based on what learners communicate through language. The starting point for this approach is based on social language functions, such as asking for directions, asking for help, greeting information, or giving personal information, but it also includes referential language to include metalinguistic notions. Chapter 10 narrows the focus of language functions to academic language functions. These are the language functions that L2 learners need to master to become successful learners in academic environments.

Chapter 11 features a genre or text-based approach to curriculum design with text types, both written and spoken, serving as resources for making meaning. In this approach, the features of the particular text being taught determine the selection of grammatical structures and other linguistic features for instruction. Vocabulary is fundamental in the language learning process; consequently, it plays a major role in the design of curriculum. Chapter 12 focuses on the complex process of constructing a curriculum that promotes the acquisition of vocabulary and understanding the role that vocabulary plays in designing curriculum across various approaches.

The last chapter in Part III is Chapter 13. It takes a look at approaches to curriculum design that are based on the four language skills—listening, speaking, reading, and writing. The chapter considers the specific contributions of traditions in teaching each of the four skills, as well as the development of multiple skills in an integrated approach.

Chapter 8

The Structural Approach

VIGNETTE

I have been hired to start an international program at a small college in the western U.S. and to design a curriculum for an intensive English program (IEP) to provide academic support for the new international students who are non-native speakers of English. One of the first tasks that I face in designing the curriculum for the new IEP is to create the scope and sequence for the teaching of grammatical structures at four different proficiency levels. This task is an expectation of the college and the faculty who are focused on academic English. Because the IEP is new, all of the courses will need to be approved by the College Curriculum Committee, and the committee has requested supporting documents, such as the complete grammatical syllabus for all four proficiency levels. I have never created a grammatical syllabus, and I am feeling completely overwhelmed by the task at hand. As a survival technique, I hope to employ the grammar textbooks that I taught from in a previous IEP and use them to help identify potential structures for each proficiency level. [Christison, research notes]

Task: Reflect

If you were assigned to teach an English grammar class to beginning proficiency level English language learners, what ten grammatical structures would you teach? Which ten grammatical structures would you select for advanced proficiency level learners? Why would you categorize the structures in this way?

Introduction

The most common type of linguistic-based curriculum for second and foreign language teaching is the structural curriculum (also known as the grammatical syllabus). Structural approaches to curriculum design are based on the grammatical structures of a given language. The ordering or sequencing of these grammatical structures for the purposes of teaching them to L2 learners is based on the perceived complexity or simplicity of the structures by proficient users of the language, and this order may be different from the order in which second language (L2) learners actually acquire the structures. In addition, individual variability and natural language background affect the acquisition orders (Larsen-Freeman, 1975, 1978) (see Volume I, Chapters 11 and 12 for more information on orders of acquisition and developmental sequences in second language acquisition). This chapter will explain the structural approach to curriculum design, the procedures for creating this type of curriculum, its strengths and weaknesses, its influence on textbook design, types of classroom activities that support it, and provide an example of a structural syllabus (see Appendix A) that was prepared for students, so the structures are given using example sentences rather than the grammatical terms used for describing structures, such as present tense, present progressive, subject relative clause, and third-person singular–*s*.

Defining Grammar

The structural approach is generally characterized as teaching *grammar*. Technically, grammar is defined as the underlying structure of a language that native speakers know intuitively. It includes the sounds, words, and sentences of a language. The grammar of a language also encompasses how sounds, words, and sentences combine to create meaning and includes semantics and pragmatics. In a restricted sense, the term grammar in a structural approach is used to reference the study of word structure and how words combine to form sentences. Depending on one's approach to studying grammar, grammar can be *prescriptive* with a focus on the rules for the conventions of use for language structures, *descriptive* with a focus on how language is used in context, *generative* with a focus on how a series of rules can be generated to account for the production of an infinite number of sentences (Chomsky, 1957), or *systemic functional* with a focus on language as making meaning for a particular purpose or to carry out critical functions (Halliday, 1973, 1975).

The Grammatical Syllabus

A *grammatical syllabus* is the term most frequently used to describe what is to be taught in a structural approach. In order to develop a grammatical syllabus, curriculum developers must identify the language structures that are to be taught. The author of the vignette acknowledged that creating a grammatical syllabus for each of the proficiency levels for the new IEP she was directing was an expectation of both the college administration and the faculty (see Appendix A for an example of a grammatical syllabus). Her task was to identify the discrete units of language structure that learners would study and determine at what proficiency level the structures were to be taught. Grammatical structures are most frequently graded according to the perceived grammatical complexity or simplicity of the items, for example *present tense* is thought to be one of the easiest structures for language learners, while *indirect object relative clauses* are thought to be one of the most difficult. In addition, there are other factors that affect decisions about how structures are to be sequenced in a grammatical syllabus, such as the frequency of the structure in the input, their contrastive difficulty in relation to a learner's first language, the situational need for the use of the structures, and their pedagogic convenience, such as when the structures might be introduced in the textbooks chosen for the courses or if the structures are known to the teachers.

Issues with a Structural Approach

As with all approaches to instructional design, there are issues with a structural approach. We will frame these issues in terms of perceived strengths and weaknesses. A structural syllabus can be attractive for many language learners because it presents language in an organized way and in manageable chunks. It can also help learners build their confidence with the language as they concentrate on mastering specific components of the language in a classroom setting before encountering them in real-life contexts. An understanding of grammar creates the core of language knowledge for the development of language skills—listening, speaking, reading, and writing. A structural syllabus is often popular with teachers, especially new and inexperienced teachers who are new to the field of English language teaching (ELT) because it provides teachers with an organized and balanced plan for the sequencing of lesson content that is gradual and systematic, making it possible for both language learners and teachers to have similar expectations for learning. In English language programs with multiple sections of the same course taught by different teachers, a structural syllabus contributes to quality assurance, making it more likely that all sections cover the same content regardless of the teacher. Through the study of grammar English language learners notice specific language structures in the input, thereby giving them the opportunity to develop skills for self-monitoring and self-correction so that they can continue to improve and develop their language skills (Fotos, 2001; Nassaji & Fotos, 2004).

Some teachers and researches see that there are also weaknesses associated with teaching from a grammatical syllabus. Language in real-life contexts can be quite different from some language in classroom contexts, specifically if the language used in a classroom is motivated by the mastery of the grammatical forms in a structural curriculum. Activities that focus on form may be manageable and pre-dictable, but they can also be mundane and boring for learners. When language is used for the purposes of communication, it includes many different structures that are motivated by language use and not by their sequence in a grammatical syllabus. In addition, there is no one-to-one relationship between a specific form and its function. For example, while the present continuous tense in English can be used to describe something that happens at the moment (especially in sports commen-tating), it is also often used for complaining (e.g., *He's always playing video games*), among other functions. In reality, a form can realize more than one function and a function can be realized by more than one form.

Curriculum developers and L2 teachers must realize that the presentation of structures that is based on perceived complexity in a grammatical syllabus is some-what arbitrary. The perceived complexity of structures for proficient users of a language may not represent learners' perceptions. Even though English present tense is frequently taught to beginning language learners, the third-person singular −s marker for present tense is a difficult structure for most English language learners and is often one of the last structures to be acquired. Most English language teachers who have taught this structure to beginning level students recognize that there is a difference between how students perform relative to the use of the structure in class and their ability to use it correctly in real-life situations outside of class. The facility with which language learners acquire structures is determined by how difficult language learners find the structures to process psycholinguistically, rather than how simple or complex native speakers perceive them to be (for example, Pienemann, 1998; see also Volume I, Chapters 11 and 12). Formal instruction may have little effect on the acquisition of a structure in real-life communicative encounters.

Teaching Grammatical Structures

In a structural approach, classroom instruction revolves around the language structures identified in the grammatical syllabus. Given that most English language learners are studying English in order to use it in real-life situations, an eclectic approach to studying grammatical structure seems to be the most practical one (Richards & Rodgers, 2001). An eclectic approach to teaching grammar includes both a focus on form and opportunities for communication. Classroom instruction that includes a focus on form and a focus on classroom interaction is more effective than instruction that does not focus on form or does not provide opportunities for communication and interaction (Larsen-Freeman, 2001; Lightbown & Spada, 1998).

Larsen-Freeman (2001) offers a model for teaching grammar that includes three dimensions for each structure taught—a focus on form, meaning, and use. Using this model, a five-stage lesson plan—introduction/staging, presentation, practice, evaluation, and summary—(see Chapter 2 for more information on lesson planning) would include a presentation, practice, and evaluation stage for each structure taught for form, meaning, and use (Christison, 2014). Included in this lesson-planning model are practice and presentation stages for form, meaning, and use).

Stages in Planning. Grammar Lesson
Stage 1: Introduction/staging
Stage 2a: Presentation of form
Stage 3a: Practice of form
Stage 2b: Presentation of meaning
Stage 3b: Practice of meaning
Stage 2c: Presentation of use
Stage 3c: Practice of use
Stage 4: Evaluation
Stage 5: Summary/application

In addition to the structure of the lesson plan, there are other important considerations for curriculum designers relative to grammar in the classroom. For example, curriculum designers must decide whether form, meaning, and use are to be taught *inductively* or *deductively* (Savage, Bitterlin, & Price, 2010). An inductive approach to teaching form offers learners many examples of the structure first before presenting the grammar rule. In a deductive approach, the grammar rule is given first and is followed by examples of the structure. Research has shown that explicit teaching of the grammar rule is important for optimizing learning (Norris & Ortega, 2000) in both approaches.

Guided practice is important for each structure for form, meaning, and use. Curriculum designers must think about how to structure grammar practice activities so that learners can be successful in understanding and using the structures. Many teachers believe that drills are important as a fundamental starting place for structures because they assist learners in committing the structures to memory (Azar, Folse, & Swan, 2009). Drills are controlled for vocabulary, task-types, and language structures. Learners memorize an appropriate response or supply missing information based on a grammar rule. Learners are limited in the types of responses they can give that are considered correct and appropriate. As grammar practice activities progress along the continuum of guided practice, learners are expected to control a greater range of structures, vocabulary, and task-types. Curriculum designers must pay careful attention not only to sequencing the structures themselves but also to sequencing guided practice for each structure.

In addition to drills, other grammar practice activities include conversation cards (see Diaz, 2002), dialogs, grids and charts, Find Someone Who (Moskowitz, 1978), Jigsaw, interviews, Information Gap, and sentence scrambles. Resources for grammar practice activities include Bassano and Christison (2013), Christison and Bassano (1995), Christison (2014), Nunan (2005), Savage, Bitterlin, and Price (2010), and Ur (2009). Some resources provide a description of activity proto-types as well as descriptions of the activities and examples of how to use them. Many more resources are readily available. In fact, it is safe to say that the structural approach has had a huge impact on textbook design. Until the mid-1970s and early 1980s the main organizational principle for textbooks was language structures. Eventually, teachers began to embrace communicative language teaching and experiment with activities that encouraged student–student interaction and real-life communication. They began looking for textbooks that offered their students more than the presentation and practice of structures. In addition to language structures, other organizational principles began to be included in textbook design, such as task-types and language functions; nevertheless, there are still many English language-teaching textbooks that use language structure as the chief organizational principle.

Task: Explore

Use online and/or other resources. Identify five more grammar practice proto-type activities as well as the structures you might use them with.

Conclusion

In this chapter, we have considered the structural approach to curriculum design and considered its strengths and weaknesses. Finally, we have recommended an eclectic approach that considers form, meaning, and use (Larsen-Freeman, 2001) for the teaching of language structures. We also provide an example of an English grammatical syllabus (Appendix A). While the identification and sequencing of language structures (i.e., the grammatical syllabus) provides the foundation for the structural approach, curriculum designers working in this approach have additional factors to consider. This chapter has also reviewed some of these factors, such as incorporating grammar in lesson planning and sequencing grammar practice activities.

Task: Expand

Work with a partner. Using the Internet, see if you can find 20 additional resources (including books, articles, and websites) beyond those identified in the chapter for teaching English grammar to second language learners. Prepare a written version of your document. Exchange your document with at least two other partnerships. Which of your resources are the same as the ones identified by the other partnerships? Which ones are different? Update your own document to include the resources you obtained from your exchanges with the other partnerships. How many resources do you have in total?

Questions for Discussion

1. What is an eclectic approach to teaching grammar?
2. How are inductive and deductive approaches to teaching grammar different? How might these different approaches affect the development of curriculum?
3. Do you think grammar drills should be included when teaching grammar in communicative language teaching? Why? Why not? Explain your response.
4. Work with another teacher or a peer in your class. Outline a lesson plan for teaching a language structure using the eclectic approach.

References

Azar, B., Folse, K., & Swan, M. (2009). Teaching grammar in today's classroom. Panel discussion at the 42nd TESOL Annual Convention, New York, April 2–5, 2008. Retrieved from www.azargrammar.com

Chomsky, N. (1957). *Syntactic structures.* The Hague: Mouton.

Christison, M. A. (2014). *Learning to teach languages.* Ann Arbor, MI: University of Michigan Press.

Christison, M. A., & Bassano, S. K. (1995). *Look who's talking.* Burlingame, CA: Alta Book Publishers.

Diaz, C. J. S. (2002). *Cathy's cards.* Burlingame, CA: Alta Book Publishers.

Fotos, S. (2001). Cognitive approaches to grammar instruction. In M. Celce-Murcia (Ed.), *Teaching English as a second or foreign language* (3rd ed., pp. 267–284). Boston, MA: Heinle & Heinle.

Halliday, M. A. K. (1973). *Explorations in the functions of language.* London: Edward Arnold.

Halliday, M. A. K. (1975). *Learning how to mean.* London: Edward Arnold.

Larsen-Freeman, D. (1975). The acquisition of grammatical morphemes by adult ESL students. *TESOL Quarterly, 9,* 409–430.

Larsen-Freeman, D. (1978). An explanation for the morpheme acquisition order of second language learners. *Language Learning, 26,* 125–134.

Larsen-Freeman, D. (2001). Teaching grammar. In M. Celce-Murcia (Ed.) *Teaching English as a second language* (3rd ed., pp. 251–266). Boston, MA: Heinle & Heinle.

Lightbown, P., & Spada, N. (1998). *How languages are learned* (2nd ed.). Oxford: Oxford University Press.

Moskowitz, G. (1978). *Caring and sharing in the foreign language classroom.* Rowley, MA: Heinle & Heinle. (Reprinted 1991, New York: Harper Collins)

Nassaji, H., & Fotos, S. (2004). Current developments in research on the teaching of grammar. *Annual Review of Applied Linguistics, 24,* 126–45.

Norris, J. M., & Ortega, L. (2000). Effectiveness of L2 instruction: A research synthesis and quantitative meta-analysis. *Language Learning, 50,* 417–528.

Nunan, D. (2005). *Practical English language teaching: Teaching grammar.* New York: McGraw-Hill.

Pienemann, M. (1998). *Language processing and second language acquisition: Processability theory.* Amsterdam: John Benjamins.

Richards, J., & Rodgers, T. (2001). *Approaches and methods in language teaching.* New York: Cambridge University Press.

Savage, L. K., Bitterlin, G., & Price, D. (2010). *Grammar matters: Teaching grammar in adult ESL programs.* New York: Cambridge University Press.

Ur, P. (2009). *Grammar practice activities* (2nd ed.). Cambridge: Cambridge University Press.

Appendix A

Example Grammatical Syllabus

Proficiency Levels
   Beginning – Levels One and Two
   Intermediate – Level Three
   Advanced – Level Four

Level One Structures

1. The boy is/'s happy.
2. He/she is happy.
3. Is the boy happy? Yes, he is.
4. He is not happy (isn't).
5. Is the man short or tall?
6. They are happy.
7. Are they happy? No, they aren't.
8. They are not happy.
9. Who is happy?
10. He is a student.
11. They are students.
12. He is Korean. He is from Korea.
13. He is not a student. They are not students.
14. The young man is a good student.
15. I/we/you am/are tall/good students.
16. Are you good students?
17. We are (we're) not good students.
18. John and Bill are good students.
19. What is a wall? Those are walls.
20. Is that a wall? Yes, it is. Are those walls? Yes, they are.
21. That is not a wall. Those are walls.
22. What is it? What are they? It is a door. They are doors.
23. This is a wall. These are walls.
24. This attractive picture/these interesting books are here.
25. My/your/his/her/our/their book. John's/the students' books.
26. This is not my book.
27. Whose book is green?
28. Whose books are those?
29. What color is the book?
30. The books are on the table. Are my books on the table? Where are they?
31. Mine/yours/his/hers/ours/yours/theirs/John's is red.
32. This pen is mine/. . . Is this pen yours/. . .?
33. What kind of book is this?
34. There is a chair in the room. There is chalk in the room. There is some chalk. There are some chairs.
35. Is/are there any . . .? There isn't/aren't any . . .? No, there isn't/aren't. Yes, there is/are.

36. My office is in/on/at . . .
37. The boy is reading. Is the boy reading? The boy is not reading.
38. What is the boy doing?
39. He is eating a sandwich.
40. They are eating breakfast now.
41. He is working in a department store this year.
42. The teacher is listening to him.
43. Whom is John listening to?
44. John is eating breakfast, and I am too.
45. John is not working, and I am not either.
46. I am not eating, but John is.
47. We are going to read. Are we going to read?
48. Where is John going to be tomorrow?
49. When is the boy going to watch television?
50. John is going to be at home in/on/at . . .

Level Two Structures

51. Does John write a letter every day?
52. John does not write a letter every day.
53. John writes a letter in his room every day.
54. When does the boy watch television? Does the boy watch television?
55. What does John do every night?
56. How often does . . .? John gets a haircut twice a month.
57. John usually gets a haircut twice a month.
58. Do you ever study in the library?
59. He knows the words now. He is studying the words now.
60. I feel happy today.
61. John does not eat eggs, and I don't either.
62. John eats eggs, and I do too.
63. I am/was sick today/yesterday.
64. I was here last night/two weeks ago/in 1995/at 8:30 PM/on July 4th.
65. How long were you in California? I was in California for three months/from
    . . . to . . .
66. John read/did not read a newspaper yesterday. Did John read . . .?
67. I sent John/him the package. I sent the package to him. I sent it to him.
68. John didn't hear the bell, and I didn't either.
69. John heard the bell, but I didn't. John didn't hear the bell, but I did.
70. Who saw the movie?
71. They liked that movie.
72. How did you go to Boston? How did she speak? How did John write . . .?
73. How long is the room? How long did you stay in Boston?
74. How much coffee did you have? How many books did you buy?
75. many/a few/a lot of/some/any books – much/a little/a lot of/lots of/some/
    any milk/a book.
76. I was reading the book at home last night.

Level Three Structures

77. John can speak French. John cannot speak French. Can John speak French?
78. Who can drive a car?
79. The Greens have been in Boston for two years.
80. The Greens have been living in Philadelphia for two years.
81. The Greens have been living in Philadelphia since 2003.
82. He is still in Boston. He isn't in Boston anymore.
83. The Browns have been in Japan already. They haven't been here yet.
84. We have always/often/rarely/seldom/frequently taken the train.
85. I have finally/just/at last/read that book.
86. I/we... could/was/were able to drive a car.
87. I will/won't go.
88. Maybe/perhaps/probably they will leave early.
89. The boy with the big nose is giving the book to the girl.
90. The boy wearing the funny hat took the girl to the party.
91. The boy who speaks French fluently gave the book to the girl.
92. The boy gave the book that fell on the floor to the girl.
93. The man whom I met last night took the book home.
94. The man took the book that I found under the desk.
95. The girl whose sister is in your class spoke to the man.
96. The girl whose sister you met at the party spoke to the man.
97. You can speak to John or Tom, whoever is at the desk.
98. You can take the novel or the play, whichever is available.
99. You can speak to John or Tom, whomever you see at the bank.
100. You can take the novel or the play, whichever you prefer.
101. Pre-articles: another/other/others/whichever/all/while
102. You can/could take the subway.
103. Bill could have gone by car.
104. Bill has to get up early.
105. They must apply for a passport.
106. Do you have to go to the dentist?
107. John does not have to wear glasses.
108. Bill had to get up early.
109. Bill did not have to wear glasses.
110. John should be studying now.
111. Mary ought to be more careful.
112. John should not watch TV.
113. Should I take an umbrella today?
114. John should have studied.
115. John ought to have studied.
116. John should not have watched TV.
117. Should you have asked John for the answers?
118. John had better slow down.
119. John had better not speed.
120. John must not talk so loudly.
121. Bob is as old as Tom.
122. Bob is not as old as Dick.

123. Bob is the same age as Tom.
124. Bob has as many children as Tom.
125. Bob has as much education as Tom.
126. Tom is older than Bob.
127. Dick has more children than Bob.
128. Dick is a more efficient worker than Tom.
129. Tom is a less efficient worker than Dick.
130. Dick drives more/less carefully than Tom.
131. Dick is the oldest of the three children. Dick is the tallest man in the room.
132. Dick has the most/least children of the three.
133. Tom is the most/least efficient worker of the group.
134. Joe drives a car the most/least carefully of the three.
135. [the irregular comparative and superlative form, for example, good, better, best]
136. Joe may/might be working now.
137. I may/might not be there.
138. John may/might have read this book. John may/might not have read this book.
139. John could be tired. He could walk to his house.
140. John could be waiting for someone.
141. The Browns could have gone to Canada.
142. Jerry couldn't have taken the book.
143. Mary must need glasses.
144. The Browns must not be home.
145. Bill must/must not have done it.
146. They should/ought to be here soon.

Level Four Structures

147. John says that he is tired.
148. Mary asks whether you are tired.
149. Do you know where John went?
150. John said that he was tired.
151. Mary asked/asked me whether I was tired.
152. Mary asked me where John was.
153. Mary told John that she was hungry.
154. John told Mary to close/not to close the window.
155. How long/whether/that/the fact that John was tired did not affect my decision.
156. It is obvious that John is tired.
157. The man insisted that John close the door.
158. I enjoy studying English at this school.
159. He did not advise singing.
160. The doctor suggested my seeing/my not seeing a specialist.
161. He approved of writing it.
162. He is afraid of failing the test.
163. In addition to reading the story, I answered the questions that followed.
164. John wants to speak to the teacher.

165. Tom did not want to sing. Tom wanted not to sing.
166. Mary permitted me to drive her car.
167. John decided what to do. John decided where to go.
168. The teacher showed me how to study for the test.
169. It's difficult to learn English.
170. John is too tired to go to the movies.
171. The room is big enough. Kathy is leaving early enough. I have enough time.
172. John hasn't gone yet, but he wants to.
173. I would rather have a cup of tea.
174. I would rather not talk to him now.
175. I would prefer going to a play.
176. I would prefer not to stay home tonight.
177. I prefer coffee to tea.
178. I would like Italian food tonight.
179. The tower was designed by the city's leading architect.
180. It was mentioned that Mary had been late.
181. Mr. Green considers his wife a genius.
182. They elected Bob president. Bob was elected class president.
183. Mr. Green's wife is considered a genius.
184. I am going to have my eyes examined. Bob got his car washed.
185. Barbara listens to the radio when/whenever/while she cleans the house.
186. Tom is going to study chemistry before/after he studies biology.
187. Tom waited until Bob arrived.
188. Tom is going to leave as soon as he gets the money.
189. I have studied English since I arrived in the United States.
190. Tom cannot attend the party because he has a cold.
191. I put the book where it belongs.
192. Tom has such a bad cold that he cannot attend the party.
193. Tom left early so that he would be in class on time.
194. I am calling Joan to invite her to the party.
195. You may take this book even though/although/though/in spite of the fact that/despite the fact that I need it.
196. If John had studied, he would have passed the test.
197. If John were tired, he would take the bus.
198. Tom works for a newspaper, and, in addition, he is writing a book.
199. Tom seems to work hard, but he doesn't accomplish much.
200. John was unable to get to the party; nevertheless/however/on the contrary/yet/on the other hand/all the same/just the same he sent a telegram.
201. We can leave the sandwiches on the table, or we can put them in the refrigerator.
202. We can leave the sandwiches on the table; otherwise, we can put them in the refrigerator.
203. Tom cannot attend the party for he has a bad cold.
204. Tom has a bad cold; therefore, he cannot attend the party.
205. Tom left; then/next/later/after/afterwards/after/subsequently, John arrived.

Chapter 9

The Notional-Functional Approach

VIGNETTE

I was attending the Third AILA World Congress in Copenhagen, Denmark and presenting a paper on language testing. AILA (Association Internationale de la Linguistique Appliquée) is an international professional association of applied linguists, so attendees at the conference were applied linguists like myself from all over the world. Being at an international conference in a city I had never been to before was very exciting, and it was equally exciting to attend the AILA conference and network with other applied linguists. Even though I considered myself primarily a language tester even then, I also had a wide range of interests in other areas of applied linguistics; consequently, I attended papers on many different topics during the AILA week (August 21–26, 1972). One of the most interesting papers for me was a paper given by British linguist David Wilkins on the notional-functional syllabus. I had heard about Wilkins's idea of moving away from a purely grammatical syllabus that focuses on language structures to one that focuses on language functions. As the grammatical syllabus at that time was almost sacrosanct for language teachers, Wilkins's suggestion of replacing it with a notional-functional syllabus was garnering him much attention at AILA and elsewhere in the world of applied linguistics. The ideas Wilkins expressed in his paper at AILA were well conceived and well received. Wilkins was promoting a view of curriculum design that was so exciting in terms of my own beliefs about communicative language teaching, and I immediately began thinking about what these ideas would mean for the work that I did as a language tester. I was eager to talk about his ideas with others and genuinely wondered where these ideas would take the profession. I also thought just how timely Wilkins's ideas were in coming to light. A purely grammatical syllabus with its focus on form has its limitations for language learners who have primary goals that are related to achieving success in communicating and interacting in contexts outside of the classroom and for teachers who recognized this fact. I have many great memories from the AILA conference—from the beautiful venue in Copenhagen and the interesting linguists I met to the intellectual stimulation that I felt. If you had asked me then to predict what I would remember most about the AILA conference 40 years later, I would likely have said that it would be the Wilkins paper and my introduction to the notional-functional syllabus. [Interview with A. Palmer, April 2013]

Task: Reflect

1.   What is a notional-functional syllabus?
2.   Why do you think the person being interviewed in this vignette said that Wilkins's idea for a notional-functional syllabus was timely?
3.   What type of syllabus do you think the person in the vignette was most familiar with before he attended the AILA conference?
4.   Can you think of two reasons why a functional syllabus may be preferable to a grammatical syllabus?

Introduction

A notional-functional approach is concerned with analyzing language in terms of its communicative uses in specific contexts. As you learned in the vignette, British linguist David Wilkins (1976) outlined the basic tenets of this approach almost 40 years ago. You can tell from the reactions of the interviewee in the vignette that the notional-functional approach to curriculum design is quite different from a purely structural approach with its focus on language structures. The structural approach is often thought to be a *synthetic* approach because it is made up of separate, pre-selected, and ordered units of language (see Chapter 8, Appendix A, for example). The notional-functional approach as Wilkins conceived it was intended to be an *analytic* approach because it was not meant to rely totally on linguistic controls but to present language globally and in context.[1] In an analytic approach, semantic demands determine linguistic content.

Understanding the distinction between *synthetic* and *analytic* approaches to curriculum design is particularly useful when curriculum development is viewed from the standpoint of language learners. Synthetic and analytic are terms used to describe what learners do. In a synthetic approach language is taught in parts with the belief that learners will be able to synthesize or integrate the separate parts, such as when language forms are taught separately from a specific context. In an analytic approach, language learners work with samples of language that have not been controlled for structure. It is assumed that learners will be able to analyze the language to which they have been exposed and come to an understanding of its structure.

Synthetic and analytic approaches to curriculum design are the endpoints on a curriculum design continuum. Larsen-Freeman's (2001) eclectic model within a structural approach considers meaning and use in addition to form, thereby adding features of an analytic approach to a typically synthetic one. Similarly, a notional-functional approach that also includes explicit teaching of language structures within a specific context incorporates features of a synthetic approach into a typically analytical one.

Notional-functional approaches are based on answers to the question, "What is it that learners communicate through language?" In order to make this determination, the needs of learners must be analyzed in order to determine what needs to be included in lessons, courses, and programs. The starting point for this approach to curriculum design is based on the communicative functions, such as asking for directions, asking for help, greetings, and giving personal information.

The chapter will explain this approach, providing examples from lessons and language courses.

Defining Notional-Functional

A notional-functional approach is based on what people do with language or what ideas they want to convey. The basic idea behind a notional-functional approach is to transfer *functions* and *notions* to acts of communication. Notions and functions form the basic organizational components of a notional-functional approach.

Notions and Functions

A notion is basically a concept or an idea. A notion can be very specific so that it is synonymous with a vocabulary word (e.g., *food*, *cat*, *car*). Consequently, we can say that notions are expressed through nouns, pronouns, verbs, prepositions, conjunctions, adjectives, and adverbs. Notions may also be very general. In this sense notions can be thought of in terms of such basic ones as *quantity*, *location*, *time*, *size*, *movement*, or *emotion*, to name a few. For example, the notion of time is important for all language learners and each language has its own agreed upon way of marking time. Becoming a competent and effective user of any language requires an understanding of the notion of time. Curriculum designers must consider how and when the curriculum will help learners develop skills in working with time. The notion of *time* may be further specified as past time, and lessons may be structured to include structures such as the past tense and words and phrases typically used to express past time, such as *in 2010*, *last year*, *two weeks ago*, and temporal clauses, such as *before . . .* and *after . . .*

The notional-functional approach is also made up of language functions. A language function is a type of communicative act that is used to achieve a purpose and most often involves at least two people. Example language functions include *requesting help*, *giving suggestions*, *making promises*, and *offering apologies.*

Context

Another critical component of a notional-functional approach for curriculum designers is context. Context determines the relative importance of specific notions and functions. When context changes, the people, the location, the time, or even the activity may change, thereby affecting how language is used. For example, the language one uses to request help from a close friend may be quite different from the language one uses to request help from a boss or a superior at work.

Major Characteristics of a Notional-Functional Approach

Barnett (1980) offered a list of characteristics of a notional-functional approach. These characteristics include the fact that there is a functional view of language (see also Chapter 10 on functional views of language) with a focus on doing something with language as opposed to simply studying language structures;

consequently, a notional-functional approach is semantically based. The focus of a notional-functional approach is learner centered, and the curriculum design process begins with an analysis of learner needs. It is learner needs that determine learning goals, content selection, the sequencing of content, the methodology chosen, and how learning is evaluated. Because the notional-functional approach focuses on doing something with language, the learning activities are driven by authentic language use and how learners operate in a given language context. In a structural approach, the sentence forms the basic unit for language teaching, however in a notional-functional approach, discourse (i.e., sentences in combination) is the basic unit for language teaching. With a notional-functional approach, there is less focus on grammatical accuracy than in a structural approach. Fluency and whether learners can achieve their communicative goals are more important than accuracy.

Implementation

The Notional-Functional Syllabus

As a first step in the development of a notional-functional syllabus, curriculum designers should identify the following general components:

1. Situation. The situations in which the English will be used must be ascertained. A situation will always include the following: the participants, the place or location, and the time.
2. Topics. The topics and what the learner will be able to do with them must be clarified. For example, topics related to everyday interactions, such as buying food, giving directions, and offering advice may be quite different from topics generated by academic situations, such as identifying main ideas, asking for clarification, or arguing for a specific point of view.
3. Language activities. The language activities in which the learner will engage must be identified and related to the situations in which the language is to be used.
4. Notions. The general notions that the learner will be expected to handle should be clarified. Examples of notions are time (time relation: past tense, present tense; duration: until, since), quantity (countable, uncountable), space (dimensions, locations, motion) and so on.
5. Language functions. The language functions that the learner will perform should be identified and classified.
6. Language forms. The language forms the learner will be expected to use should also be identified. These forms are most often referred to as *exponents*— language utterances or statements that stem from the notions, language function, the situations, and the topics.
7. Skill levels. The degree of skill the learner will be required to display.

Functional Categories

There are different taxonomies for organizing language functions within a notional-functional syllabus. One of the most common organizational frameworks stems from general language use. There are five general categories for language functions that curriculum designers should consider.

1. Language is often used for personal means to express one's feelings (e.g., love, joy, pleasure, happiness) and to talk about everyday needs and wants (e.g., hunger, thirst, fatigue, sleepiness). This is one of the most common uses of language.
2. Language can be used for interpersonal purposes to establish and maintain desirable social and working relationships (e.g., greetings and leave takings, introducing people to others, expressing pleasure at another's success, interrupting, or asking for clarification). Language used for interaction is known as *phatic* language, and it is important for most language learners whose goals are related to effective and successful communication with others (i.e., goals beyond reading and translating written text).
3. Attempting to influence the actions of others, such as persuading someone to change their plans or warning someone about an action you see as dangerous; these are examples of directive language. Directive language is typical in academic contexts and with higher-order thinking skills that require one to evaluate or make a judgment.
4. Language can also be used referentially, such as for talking or reporting about your actions (or the actions of others) in the past, present, or future. When you use language to talk about language this is also a type of referential language known as *metalinguistic* language. Examples of metalinguistic uses of language are paraphrasing or summarizing what others say.
5. The imaginative use of language may also be important in some contexts and involves elements of creativity and artistic expression, such as using language to write poems, stories, lyrics, or plays.

Language Functions

Within each functional category there are specific language functions. Table 9.1 provides examples of how language functions such as requesting, apologizing, asking for directions, and complaining fit together with the functional categories for language use. The language functions that appear in the right-hand column of Table 9.1 are not to be interpreted as an exhaustive list. They are examples of language functions for each of the functional categories of language use. Specific academic functions are explored in Chapter 10 in this volume. For an expanded list of language functions see Appendix A.

Task: Explore

Table 9.1 presents an example of how categorical functions based on general language use work together with language functions in notional-functional syllabus design. Work with a colleague or peer. Select one or two of the categorical functions and add a third column to the table. See if you can predict what types of grammatical structures might be needed to carry out the language functions.

Table 9.1 Functional Categories and Language Functions

Functional Categories of Language Use	Example Language Functions
Personal (talking about ourselves)	Expressing emotions Clarifying one's ideas
Interpersonal (maintaining desirable relationships)	Greetings Making introductions Offering help Apologizing Sharing ideas Clarifying Making an inquiry
Directive (influencing others)	Making requests Persuading Giving and receiving instructions Accepting and refusing Complaining
Referential (using language to reference things/using language to talk about language)	Identifying items Summarizing Evaluating Analyzing Reporting
Imaginative (using language creatively)	Discussing a poem or film Writing a poem or a play Telling jokes

Instructional Materials

In a notional-functional approach learners can have free conversation about a variety of topics, such as famous people, the weather, and TV shows or debates about current affairs, politics, and the public media. Competent and effective language teachers should know how to manage all classroom resources and activities, such as facilitate free conversation and structure debates. They are also responsible for providing information to their students and engaging their students in diverse classroom activities. For experienced, proficient, and well-qualified teachers, this freedom in teaching and learning may be one of the strongest points in favor of a notional-functional approach. For new and inexperienced teachers or teachers who worry about their language proficiency level, the notional-functional approach presents a bigger challenge. Curriculum designers and textbook writers struggle with how to make the approach accessible to the latter group of teachers.

The ideas proposed by Wilkins in 1976 have had an effect on textbook design and have been realized in a number of successful textbooks for English language learners. Throughout the 1980s, one of us (Christison) used a textbook with academic language learners who were young adults in which language functions served as the chief organizing principles (Jones & Von Baeyer, 1983). This text represented a direct attempt to implement the notional-functional approach. The text replaced a grammar-based text that I had been using for several years, so I was both nervous about the change and eager to make it. The language functions were introduced through dialogs and carried out and practiced through numerous language practice activities, both guided and unguided. In terms of the organization of the chapters, the book was very similar to the grammar book I had used previously, in that each chapter began with a dialog and included different types of language practice activities, including discussions. The grammatical structures had been replaced by language functions.

In the 1980s and early 1990s, we consulted regularly for international English language programs on curriculum design and language teacher education. Several of these programs were using texts that were not purely notional-functional in their approach to design, but were clearly a departure from other learner texts of the late 1970s and the 1980s with their focus on language structure (see Swan & Walter, 1984, 1985; Viney & Hartley, 1978, 1979, 1982). It was easy to see that these writers were influenced by concepts from the notional-functional approach, addressing language use, semantics, and a focus on meaning even though they may not have used the terminology proposed by Wilkins (1976). Similarly, most competency-based approaches (see Chapter 20) define competencies in notional-functional terms.

Issues in a Notional-Functional Curriculum

A notional-functional approach has both strength and weaknesses. In terms of its strengths, it emphasizes the communicative purposes of language, so learners are introduced to sociocultural situations, as well as grammatical and cultural knowledge. The approach also recognizes that there is real purpose for using language and that learners' needs are at the very core of what is to be taught; consequently, it is likely that learners will be more motivated to learn than they would be with a decontextualized approach.

There are also a number of weaknesses associated with a notional-functional approach. Anyone who has ever tried to separate notions and functions will find that in practice the concepts are not as easy to separate and define as they seem to be based on simple definitions. In addition, it is hard to decide which functions or notions require more coverage or frequency than others, and it is difficult to determine how to sequence the functions. In the sense that notions and functions can be broken down into discrete components that can be taught separately, the notional-functional approach can be similar to a structural approach.

In an ideal setting, language functions are identified through a needs analysis. In reality, language functions and notions are often identified in advance and a notional-functional curriculum is similar in this regard to the identification of grammatical features in the structural approach. Although a needs analysis is a critical component of a notional-functional approach, it is not always easy to carry out a needs analysis with learners in real life. For example, open entry/open exit programs create considerable variation in attendance, thereby making it almost impossible to identify specific learners' needs as the population of learners is never stable.

In terms of combining language functions with language structures there are also some challenges for curriculum designers who use this approach. The grammatical structures that are derived from the functions are not offered to learners in a systematic order. Many grammatical structures that are perceived to be important in terms of the context and the number of occasions of use may not be elicited by the language functions that are selected for inclusion.

Conclusion

A notional-functional approach to curriculum design places a major emphasis on the communicative purposes of language. The focus for both teachers and curriculum designers must be on what learners want and need to do with the target language (i.e., the language functions) and the ideas or concepts they need to know (i.e., notions) in order to communicate successfully with others. In this chapter, we have highlighted the basic tenets of a notional-functional approach and provided clarification of its key components—notions, functions—as well as the role of context. In addition, we outline the key characteristics of a notional-functional approach and provide guidance to curriculum developers on the design of a notional-functional syllabus by demonstrating how functional categories and language functions work together. Lastly, the chapter discusses issues related to a notional-functional approach and offers some insight into its influence on classroom teaching, including textbook design.

Task: Expand

Finocchiaro, M., & Brumfit, C. (1983) *The functional-notional approach*. New York: Oxford University Press.

Both the theoretical basis of functional-notionalism and its practical classroom applications are discussed in this text. Featured in the text are: (1) a historical overview of language learning and teaching; (2) definitions of terms; (3) characteristics of the approach; (4) lists of functions and notions; (5) step-by-step techniques; (6) communicative activities; (7) the role of grammar; and (8) evaluation procedures. Discussion is included of general methodology and strategies that have been found most effective in helping learners use the language appropriately in a variety of real-world situations, as well as reading, writing, and grammar instructional techniques.

This is a free e-book that can be downloaded online.

www.gobookee.net/notional-functional-language/

Questions for Discussion

1. In your own words, explain the differences between an analytic and a synthetic approach to curriculum design.
2. What is the difference between a functional category and a language function?
3. Without using your book, make a list of the key characteristics of the notional-functional approach and share your list with a colleague.
4. Can you think of other strengths or weaknesses of the notional-functional approach that are not mentioned in this chapter? If so, share your list with a colleague.

Note

1. In practice, the notional-functional approach was criticized for the same reasons as the structural approach had been. It often led to teaching a list of linguistic features out of context and with no real, authentic communication.

References

Barnett, J. (1980) Notional/functional approaches. *Annual Review of Applied Linguistics, 1*(1), 43–57.

Finocchiaro, M., & Brumfit, C. (1983). The functional-notional approach. New York: Oxford University Press.

Jones, L., & Von Baeyer, C. (1983). *Functions of American English*. Cambridge: Cambridge University Press.

Larsen-Freeman, D. (2001). *Teaching grammar.* In M. Celce-Murcia (Ed.) *Teaching English as a second language* (3rd ed., pp. 251–266). Boston, MA: Heinle & Heinle.

Swan, M., & Walter, C. (1984) *The Cambridge English Course Book 1,* Cambridge: Cambridge University Press.

Swan, M., & Walter, C. (1985) *The Cambridge English Course Book 2*, Cambridge: Cambridge University Press.

Viney, P., & Hartley, B. (1978). *Streamline departures.* Oxford: Oxford University Press.

Viney, P., & Hartley, B. (1979). *Streamline connections.* Oxford: Oxford University Press.

Viney, P., & Hartley, B. (1982). *Streamline directions.* Oxford: Oxford University Press.

Wilkins, D. A. (1976). *Notional syllabuses.* London: Oxford University Press.

Appendix A

Language Functions	Examples (Pronouns will change depending on the speaker (e.g., *You should do it; I should do it*) and the particular example.)
Agreeing	*I agree.* *That is a good point.* *You are absolutely right.*
Apologizing	*I am really sorry.* *I can't tell you how sorry I am.* *Please forgive me.* *Please accept my apology.*
Asking for help	*Excuse me, could you …* *Could you give me a hand?* *Could you help me please? I'm …* *When you have a minute, could you …*
Clarifying	*Is this true?* *Could you explain?* *Could you say that again?* *Are you certain that is the case?*
Disagreeing	*I cannot agree with your position.* *Impossible.* *I don't agree.* *I think you're mistaken.* *I think you might be mistaken.* *I'm not so sure about that.* *I take your point, but …*
Drawing conclusions	*It follows that …* *This means that …* *It seems to be the case that …*
Expressing anxiety	*I'm very worried about …* *It seems to be taking a long time.* *Do you have any idea about …*
Expressing certainty	*I'm certain that …* *There seems to be no doubt that …* *I'm sure that …*
Expressing obligation	*You should obey …* *You have to …* *You must …* *You have got to …* *You had better …* *I've got an obligation to …*
Expressing pleasure	*I feel great.* *I think this is great.* *I'm really pleased.* *How wonderful!* *How marvelous!* *This gives me great pleasure.*
Expressing sympathy	*I'm so sorry to hear that.* *Please accept my deepest sympathies.* *I'm truly so sad for you.*

Expressing wants	*I'd rather …* *I feel like …* *I wouldn't mind …* *I would like to …*
Giving advice	*If I were you, I would …* *The best thing for you to do is …* *I think you should …* *You'd better …* *I think you'd better …*
Giving directions	*First go … then …* *Do you have a map?* *Do you know where … is?* *Take a left at … then take a right at …* *Go straight … turn … then …*
Giving opinions	*In my opinion, I think that …* *I believe that …* *As I see it …* *My point is that …* *My view is that …*
Giving suggestions	*What about …* *I suggest that you …* *Why don't we …* *Why not …* *Have you ever thought about …* *Let's …* *You can …* *You could …*
Making a concession	*OK, I'll do it.* *If you say so.* *I can't argue with that.* *You've got a point.* *I take your point.*
Making requests	*Would you help me, please?* *Could you help me, please?* *Would you …* *I'd be grateful if you would …* *I wonder if you would please …*
Making statements of probability	*It will rain later.* *Perhaps I will see you this evening/later/next week/ tomorrow.* *I might …* *It might …* *It will probably …*
Offering congratulations	*That's wonderful.* *Congratulations!* *I'm so pleased for you.* *It's wonderful that you …*
Persuading	*Can't I persuade you to …* *It would be great if you …* *Please …*
Refusing	*No, thank you.* *I refuse.* *Sorry. I don't feel like it.*

Language Functions	Examples (Pronouns will change depending on the speaker (e.g., *You should do it; I should do it*) and the particular example.)
Stating or accepting blame	*You're to blame for …* *You must take the blame …* *It's my fault that …* *It's your fault that …*
Stating approval	*Well done.* *I really enjoyed it.* *Great job!* *I've never done/heard/seen/tasted anything like this before.* *I think it's lovely.*
Stating intentions	*He is planning to …* *I've decided to …* *I've made up my mind to …* *I propose to …* *I mean to …* *I plan to …*
Stating preferences	*I'd rather …* *I'd prefer to …* *It would be better if …*

Chapter 10

The Academic Language Functions Approach

VIGNETTE

I am observing a science class in a middle school. The middle school houses Grades 6–8, children between the ages of 11–14. The students in the Science 2 class that I am observing are all in Grade 7 and about 12 or 13 years old depending on the month in which they were born. About 60% of the students are mother tongue (L1) speakers of English and about 40% are English language learners (ELLs) who have varying levels of English language proficiency. For the past two weeks, the students have been studying the carbon cycle. Today the teacher has been reviewing important vocabulary, such as "atmosphere," "photosynthesis," "carbon dioxide," "greenhouse gases," "factory emissions," and "fossil fuels" in preparation for a problem solving activity that she has designed called "Walk About"—an activity that will require students to make predictions. At the moment, students are working in partnerships with small whiteboards. The teacher points to a list of words on the overhead projector and asks, "Which of these words means to change light energy to chemical energy?" Students have 30 seconds to conference, write the word on the whiteboard, and hold it up. After each 30-second conference, she circles the word she is looking for on the overhead. She can see students' responses on the whiteboards, and students can check their answers and get immediate feedback from the overhead. She also repeats words and states her prompts in slightly different ways so that her learners must stay engaged in the process and cannot choose words by a process of elimination. The teacher then moves to a short problem solving activity, still using the conferencing teams. Her questions are directed at trying to get the students to understand how changing key components in the cycle affects outcomes. In other words, she is trying to get learners to make predictions. The teacher asks, "What would happen if there were not enough sun? What would happen if there were too many auto and factory emissions? What if many plants and trees died?" There are charts around the room labeled "Let me hear you say ..." On these charts are printed numerous prompts for making predictions, such as "It would ..." "There would be ..." "I might ..." "Perhaps they would need to ..." The teacher walks to one of the charts and says, "Use these phrases to help you make predictions." She waits while the students conference with one another. [Christison, research notes]

Task: Reflect

1. How does the lesson excerpt described in the vignette help the ELLs work with difficult content while learning language?
2. What scaffolding techniques does the teacher use to help English language learners?
3. What academic language functions are used in this lesson?
4. What activities does the teacher use to help learners develop skills in using the academic language functions?

Introduction

English language learners (ELLs) in many different contexts from secondary schools to institutions of higher education are expected to engage with difficult and challenging content. In order to refer to learners in different contexts with some clarity and remain consistent with the literature and sensitive to research done in specific contexts, we use the term English language learners to refer to learners in K–12 public school contexts and the term second language (L2) learner, L2 user, or L2 writer to refer to learners in all other contexts, including tertiary contexts for learners who have and have not satisfied institutional admissions requirements for English language proficiency, or to refer to all L2 learners collectively.

The example vignette was meant to focus on ELLs in a public school in a US context, but it could just as easily have focused on learners in a public school in another *inner circle country* such as Australia, Canada, New Zealand, or the U.K. (see Chapter 3 in this volume for a discussion of inner circle countries—Kachru, 1986 and Kachru & Nelson, 1996) or in an institution of higher education in the U.S. or any of the other inner circle countries where L2 learners must engage with challenging academic content. In fact, the need for ELLs to work with challenging academic content at the same time they are acquiring English is becoming increasingly more common in K–12 secondary school contexts in *outer* and *expanding* circle countries as well. For example, content and language integrated learning (CLIL) has emerged as a trend in Europe for teaching English (Dalton-Puffer, 2011). Its focus is on academic content with both content (e.g., science, math, or geography) taught together with English in foreign language contexts (see Chapter 14 in this volume for more information on CLIL). The secondary school ELLs in the vignette were working with difficult and challenging content in their science class, and they were also competing, in a sense, with L1 speakers of English. In these contexts, ELLs in inner circle countries must do "double the work" of L1 users by acquiring not only academic English but also difficult subject matter (Short & Fitzsimmons, 2007).

Similar issues exist in tertiary educational contexts. Even though most institutions of higher education require that students achieve a certain score on an English proficiency test (e.g., TOEFL or IELTS) prior to admission, most institutions have found that learners who achieve the requisite cutoff score for admission, in fact, often need additional assistance with academic English. English for Specific Purposes (ESP) courses focus specifically on academic English and are typically designed to prepare L2 learners for the language demands of disciplinary contexts, such as courses in business administration, geology, and engineering. As such, "instruction represents a highly pragmatic approach to learning, encompassing needs analyses, evaluation, academic skills, disciplinary content, and tasks" (Carkin, 2005, p. 85). English for Academic Purposes (EAP) courses focus on helping L2 users develop general academic language and skills, such as note-taking and summarizing. EAP courses include a range of academic language functions that must be mastered in order to understand text and communicate one's ideas clearly, particularly in academic writing.

The type of language that is needed in these different contexts to interact successfully with difficult academic content is referred to as *academic language*. Academic language is the specific language through which school subjects are taught and assessed (Schleppegrell & O'Hallaron, 2011). Academic language includes various disciplinary registers that require complex language and present difficulties for learners in all contexts. Academic language cannot simply be picked up from daily interactions and casual communication. There are many ELLs and L2 learners who struggle with academic English even after years in an English academic environment. Language learners need specific, explicit, and intensive instruction to develop the competency levels with academic language that are needed for academic success (Schleppegrell, 2004).

In K–12 environments in the U.S., the academic achievement success rates of English language learners fall well below the norms for school children whose primary language at home is English. For example, in the U.S. only 4% of eighth grade ELLs and 20% of students classified as "formerly ELL" achieve scores at proficient or advanced levels on the National Assessment of Educational Performance (NAEP) (Perie, Grigg, & Donahue, 2005). NAEP is the only ongoing assessment in the U.S. that is based on learner performance in the content areas. The most recent PISA (The Programme for International Student Assessment) results for Australia show no significant difference in literacy, math, or science for NESB (non-English-speaking background) students but significantly lower scores for indigenous students. PISA is a worldwide evaluation of 15-year-old school children's scholastic achievement. For a comparison of performances across the 17 OECD (Organization for Economic Co-operation and Development) countries (i.e., countries that have large numbers of immigrant students) see http://www.oecd.org/pisa/pisaproducts/pisa2003/36664934.pdf. Performance levels vary across countries.

The focus of much educational research in recent years has been directed towards understanding the challenges and difficulties L2 learners face in achieving a level of competency with academic language that supports literacy development and academic achievement in content areas, particularly in math and science.

The academic functions approach to curriculum design is based on the specific academic language functions that L2 learners need in order to become successful in academic environments. In this chapter, we will explain the importance of an academic functions approach in contexts where school or academic subjects are taught in the target language. The chapter also offers several workable taxonomies for identifying academic functions and provides examples of a curriculum design process designed to target language demands in an academic functions approach.

Defining Academic Language

Academic language is the term used to represent the literacy-based/language demands of schools. Academic language is the language used in textbooks, essays, research articles, classroom discussions referencing academic content, and tests. It is different from the language used every day in informal social situations. Cummins (2001) has identified two different types of language proficiency that are necessary for success in schools—BICS (Basic Interpersonal Communicative Skills) and CALP (Cognitive Academic Language Proficiency). BICS is basically the social language of schools. It is the language used informally in daily communication. It is informal, grounded in the here and now, and includes many contextual clues, such as facial expressions, gestures, physical objects, and actions that can be observed. The language functions introduced in Chapter 9, such as greetings, requesting information, giving information, and expressing feelings, are associated with Cummins's notion of BICS. The language functions introduced in Chapter 9 for referential language (i.e., using language to reference things or ideas or using language to talk about language—*metalinguistic* functions) are associated with Cummins's notion of CALP. Academic language is abstract and governed by conventions that are specific to particular disciplines or content areas. It contains technical vocabulary and the use of a wide variety of accurate descriptors rather than non-technical slang. Academic language contains more connective devices than social language, such as transition words like *nevertheless, moreover,* and *however.*

The language of school can be viewed along a continuum with social language and academic language occupying the end points. Social language is best represented by natural face-to-face communication and informal interpersonal exchanges. Academic language is best represented in the skills needed to comprehend, discuss, and evaluate academic text and to use specific text structures successfully in writing for academic purposes. In between these two end points, we can place tasks that share features of both social and academic language, such as writing email messages to peers or instructors, asking for specific information related to a class, clarifying a process for completing an instructional task, leaving notes for friends, making lists, telling a friend about a new movie or book you read, explaining how to do a task or what you know about a topic, or evaluating a classroom activity.

Cummins's distinction between the two different types of language proficiencies (1996) has helped non-language specialists (i.e., content area teachers and mainstream faculty in institutions of higher education) develop a more sophisticated understanding of the academic language needs of L2 learners. L2 learners generally develop BICS in a relatively short period of time so that they can interact with their peers and teachers quite effectively. Non-language specialists who interact successfully with L2 learners for social language purposes are often fooled into believing that L2 learners are proficient users of English in academic contexts, attributing lack of learner academic success in school to laziness or intellectual slowness, thereby disadvantaging and labeling the learners. The more likely profile is that L2 learners have developed BICS but not CALP because CALP takes much longer to develop—over seven years for ELLs in K–12 contexts who do not already have academic language in a home language (Thomas & Collier, 1997, 2003, 2009). L2 learners in higher education often develop academic language in English much more quickly because they benefit from the academic language expertise they have already developed in their native languages. Some ELLs who were educated in K–12 English schools never acquire CALP; hence, tertiary institutions often include language development courses in their service-oriented/conditional admit/pre-admission curricula.

Academic language is the specific language through which academic subjects are taught and assessed. This language includes the specialized vocabulary, grammar, discourse, textual markers, and functional language skills associated with academic instruction and the mastery of academic materials and tasks. Academic language requires that L2 learners have sufficient background knowledge in general English so that they can successfully apply that knowledge to specific disciplines. For example, the words *division* and *product* have very different meanings in the disciplines of math and business. Academic language development tasks must be incorporated into all subjects and content areas; consequently, all content area and mainstream teachers need an extensive knowledge of academic language in their content areas (Schleppegrell & O'Hallaron, 2011).

Defining Academic Language Functions

Academic language functions are the specific tasks, purposes, or uses of language in academic environments, excluding the social uses of school language, which are similar to the social uses of language outside of the language classroom. Academic language functions include comparing, classifying, analyzing, persuading, synthesizing, and evaluating (see Table 10.2 for additional examples of academic language functions).

Researchers have used other terms to refer to the concept of academic language functions. In the Cognitive Academic Language Learning Approach (CALLA), Chamot and O'Malley (1994) used the term *learning strategies*, while Oxford (1990) used the term *language learning strategies* in her research. Doyle (1983) and Nunan (1989) prefer *academic tasks* (see also Chapter 18 in this volume). Institutions of higher education often use the term *academic skills* (see, for example, the teaching and learning support unit at the University of Southern Queensland: www.usq.edu.au/learnteach/). In this chapter, we use the term *academic language functions* to reference literacy-based tasks, such as defining, sequencing, comparing attributes and content concepts, summarizing text, and sequencing (Dutro & Levy, 2008; Dutro & Moran, 2003).

Table 10.1 Social and Academic Language Functions

Social Language Functions	Academic Language Functions
Asking for help	Classifying
Asking personal questions	Comparing/contrasting
Describing	Defining
Expressing feelings	Describing
Giving information	Negotiating
Greetings	Persuading
Leave takings	Sequencing
Requesting information	Summarizing

In order to clarify the meaning of academic language functions, we list some social language functions and some academic language functions in Table 10.1. Examples of social language functions are presented in the left-hand column while examples of academic language functions are presented in the right-hand column. The language functions in the left-hand column are typical of social language, while the ones in the right-hand column are typical of academic language. Neither list is meant to be exhaustive. For a list of additional academic language functions, see Table 10.2.

Table 10.2 Typical Academic Language Functions for Secondary School Contexts

Academic Language Functions

Analyze	Infer
Argue for/against	Inquire
Classify	Interpret
Compare	Label
Contrast	Negotiate
Critique	Organize
Define	Persuade
Describe	Predict
Enumerate	Represent
Evaluate	Re-tell
Explain	Sequence
Generalize	Summarize
Hypothesize	Symbolize
Identify	Synthesize

Academic Language Functions in the Classroom

One of the important benefits for learners in working with academic language functions is that they can apply the skills they developed from working with social language functions, such as describing—a language function that can occur in both social and academic contexts—to an academic setting. For example, let's say an L2 learner wants to describe a car he has just purchased to one of his friends. If he is to be successful in this endeavor, he will need to talk about specific features of the car that would make the purchase a good one when "evaluated" by peers (e.g., the make and model, color, speed potential, engine, gas consumption) and realize that determining features and then providing details about the features are keys to describing. If learners know how to describe in one context, they can apply that skill to another context, such as describing a picture of the human brain in an anatomy class or a proposed model of efficiency in a business class.

Curriculum developers and teachers working in the tradition of an academic language function approach must identify the most common academic language functions, and then operationalize the general academic language functions by focusing on the language with which learners need to engage. Table 10.2 offers a list of some of the most common academic language functions that operate across content areas in most contexts.

Teaching academic English or designing curricula from the perspective of academic language functions requires teachers and curriculum designers not only to identify the academic language functions, but also to operationalize each function by specifying the language demands associated with each of the functions. Table 10.3 presents a selected number of academic language functions—classify, predict, persuade, sequence, and synthesize. For each of these functions the language demands, instructional tasks, specific words and phrases, and appropriate language samples have been specified.

Task: Explore

Using Table 10.3 as a guide, select two additional academic language functions from Table 10.2 and specify the language demands, instructional activity, tasks, words, discourse markers, and phrases. Then, provide example formulaic expressions. Share your work with others. Then, combine your work with Table 10.3 so that you have an expanded list of academic language functions with their specified language demands.

Table 10.3 shows the curriculum design process for connecting academic language functions to the specific language demands associated with the instructional activity and the specific tasks in which learners will participate. In addition, useful words, phrases, discourse markers, and sentences can be targeted to the specific context.

Managing Language Demands and Cognition

Another taxonomy that teachers and curriculum developers have found useful in designing curriculum within an academic language functions approach is Bloom's Taxonomy (Bloom, 1956; Bloom & Krathwohl, 1977). This taxonomy is useful in managing cognition and language demands. The taxonomy assists teachers and curriculum designers in thinking about instructional tasks and the language demands of those tasks in terms of demands on cognition. Bloom presented six different levels of cognitive demand—knowledge, comprehension, application, analysis, synthesis, and evaluation. Knowledge, comprehension, and application are the lower-order thinking skills and require less demand on cognition than analysis, synthesis, and evaluation, which are known as higher-order thinking skills (see http://www.officeport.com/edu/blooms.htm for definitions of each level and descriptions of tasks associated with each one; see also Volume I, Chapter 10 and Chapter 14 in this volume for information on using the taxonomy within a content and language integrated approach). Figure 10.1 presents each of the levels in Bloom's Taxonomy with a list of academic language functions for each level. This information is useful for teachers and curriculum designers because it offers a system for managing cognitive and language demands. While English language teachers certainly want to challenge their students, they also want to find a way to create a balance for learners. When both language and cognitive demands are too high for extended periods of time, learners experience anxiety that can interfere with learning. When language and cognitive demands are insufficient so that

Table 10.3 Curriculum Design Process for Specifying Language Demands

Academic Language Function	Language Demand	Instructional Activity and Appropriate Language Frames
Classifying	Learners use words, phrases, or sentences to place an object, action, event, or concept in the category to which it belongs	Instructional activity: Group objects or ideas according to their characteristics or identify the rules that govern class or category membership Tasks: Create a collaborative poster that features categories and offers examples of each one, participate in word sorts, or sort and label in pairs Words: sort, categorize, select, belongs to, fits into, features, traits of, qualities of Phrases and discourse markers: _____ consists of [quantity] categories. Formulaic expressions: The [quantity] categories of _____ are _____ , _____ , and _____ We can classify _____ according to _____ _____ and _____ are types of _____ because _____ The most salient characteristics of this group are _____ These _____ are arranged according to _____
Persuading	Learners use phrases or sentences to present ideas, opinions, and/or principles with the intent of convincing others of a position or conviction	Instructional activity: State reasons for an action, make a decision and explain why, state your point of view and provide support, convince others of your position Tasks: Participate in an anticipatory chart/set, conduct a Socratic seminar, participate in a debate Words: although, because, defend, show, rationalize, argue, convince, influence, sway, urge, claim, evidence for, have to, ought to, should, appeal Phrases and discourse markers: moreover, furthermore, for this reason, in my opinion, it seems to me Formulaic expressions: My primary reason for thinking this is _____ It is vital to consider _____ The advantages of _____ outweigh the disadvantages of _____ These facts/reasons/data strongly suggest that _____

Predicting

Learners use words, phrases, or sentences to express a notion or idea about an action in the future based on evidence available in the present time frame

Instructional activity: Make inferences from selected information, hypothesize, and make predictions

Tasks: Make guesses and check correctness, apply the scientific method, find patterns, and make predictions structure and visuals to make predictions about the text

Words: guess, estimate, speculate, conclude, conclusion

Phrases and discourse markers: in light of, due to, since, maybe, perhaps, obviously, evidently

Formulaic expressions:

I predict that _____

Given _____, I hypothesize that _____

If I use _____ then I predict _____

I foresee _____ because _____

Based on _____, I infer that _____

My conjecture is that _____

I anticipate that _____

Sequencing

Learners use words, phrases, or sentences to express the order of information: *first, next, then, and finally*

Instructional activity: sequence objects, ideas, or events

Tasks: describe or make a timeline, develop a continuum, create a cycle, explain a process or retell a narrative sequence

Words: first and other ordinals, next, then, and finally, simultaneously, initially

Phrases and discourse markers: at which point, at this time, simultaneously, subsequently.

Formulaic expressions:

First, _____ and second, _____

While _____ was _____, _____ was _____

Finally _____ completed _____

Previously, _____ had decided to _____

Initially _____

Some time later _____

In the first step/stage _____

(Continued overleaf)

Table 10.3 (Continued)

Academic Language Function	Language Demand	Instructional Activity and Appropriate Language Frames
Synthesizing	Learners use phrases or sentences to express, describe, or explain relationships among two or more ideas	Instructional activity: combine or integrate ideas to form a whole group Tasks: collaborate on a poster, create a compare/contrast matrix, create and use mnemonics, write summaries, solve a problem by proposing multiple solutions, write a short paper from an outline, defend a point of view Words: combine, contain, entail, merge, form, put together, consist of, combination Phrases and discourse markers: partitives, such as a part of, a segment of, almost all, hardly any Formulaic expressions: From my perspective, _____ means _____ The main point(s) is/are _____ The point that _____ makes is related to _____ in that _____ The concept of _____ can be expressed as _____ I think that _____ and _____'s viewpoints are related in that _____

learners do not feel challenged, they become bored, and this feeling can also interfere with learning (Csikszentmihalyi, 1997). Using a tool, such as Figure 10.1, can guide teachers and curriculum designers in selecting cognitive and language tasks that are balanced. For example, with new concepts and language, a teacher may want to begin instruction by using tasks associated with the lower levels of cognition, such as knowledge and comprehension, until learners become familiar with the concepts. At that time, they are likely ready to be challenged with more difficult tasks and better prepared to handle the additional demands.

Lower-order thinking skills

Level 1 Knowledge: arrange, define, duplicate, label, list, memorize, name, order, recognize, relate, recall, repeat, reproduce, and state.

Level 2 Comprehension: classify, describe, discuss, explain, express, identify, indicate, locate, recognize, report, restate, review, select, and translate.

Level 3 Application: apply, choose, demonstrate, dramatize, employ, illustrate, interpret, operate, practice, schedule, sketch, solve, and use.

Higher-order thinking skills

Level 4 Analysis: analyze, appraise, calculate, categorize, compare, contrast, criticize, differentiate, discriminate, distinguish, examine, experiment, question, and test.

Level 5 Synthesis: arrange, assemble, collect, compose, construct, create, design, develop, formulate, manage, organize, plan, prepare, propose, set up, and write.

Level 6 Evaluation: appraise, argue, assess, attach, choose, compare, defend, estimate, evaluate, judge, predict, rate, core, select, support, and value.

Figure 10.1 Using Academic Language: Bloom's Taxonomy

Hammond and Gibbons (2001) propose a scaffolding model for managing demands on cognition and increasing motivation. In this model, two factors are considered: the amount of challenge presented by the academic task and the amount of support or scaffolding[1] that the teacher provides to the students in order that they may accomplish the goals of the task. If the challenge is high and the support is too low, the chances for failure are very high. If the challenge is not high enough and the teacher offers no support, boredom will result and behavior problems will most likely result. If the teacher is providing support for the learners, but the challenge is low, learning is not likely to occur even though the teacher may be attempting to engage the students in learning. An ideal situation for English learners is for the challenge of the task to remain high and the support to remain high. In this way, teachers are able to extend learning capability (see also Csikszentmihalyi, 1997 and his model for explaining *flow*—optimal learning experiences; and Cummins, 2001 for learning quadrants that result from the intersection of two continua—degree of cognitive demand and context embeddedness).

Task: Expand

Visit any or all of the following websites. Select an idea that you think would be helpful for you in designing materials or a curriculum that focuses on academic language functions.

http://www.coun.uvic.ca/learn/program/hndouts/bloom.html
http://www.teachers.ash.org.au/researchskills/dalton.htm
http://www.kcmetro.cc.mo.us/longview/ctac/blooms.htm
http://chiron.valdosta.edu/whuitt/col/cogsys/bloom.html
http://faculty.washington.edu/krumme/guides/bloom1.html

Conclusion

In this chapter we have provided an introduction to an academic language functions approach to curriculum design and provided background information across academic contexts where language learners are required to work with difficult and complex academic content while learning English. We also provide background information to explain why there is concern about academic language across many different contexts. In addition to defining academic language, we have provided examples of academic language functions, and introduced a process for curriculum design that attaches language demands to academic language functions. Bloom's Taxonomy and a scaffolding framework have also been offered as useful tools for managing cognitive and language demands.

Questions for Discussion

1. What is academic language? How is it different from social language?
2. In your own words, explain the difference between Cummins's two types of language proficiency.
3. What is an academic language function?
4. How can teachers and curriculum designers tie academic language functions to the language demands of learners?
5. Why is it important to manage cognitive and language demands in the curriculum design process?

Note

1. Scaffolding theory was first introduced in the late 1950s by cognitive psychologist Jerome Bruner, who first used the term in a lecture to describe the support that parents give to young children's oral language development when they first start to speak. The term was first used in the literature when Wood, Bruner, and Ross (1976) described how tutors interacted with pre-schoolers to help them solve a problem. Vygotsky (1978) later used the term to refer to the support given by experts when assisting novices. Cazden (1983) defined a scaffold as "a temporary framework for the 'construction' in progress." More recently, Ovando, Collier, and Combs (2003) defined scaffolding as "providing contextual supports for meaning through the use of simplified language, teacher modeling, visuals and graphics, cooperative learning, and hands-on learning" (p. 345), and this is a term consistent with its use in the scaffolding model described by Hammond and Gibbons (2001).

References

Bloom, B. S. (1956). *Taxonomy of educational objectives, handbook I: The cognitive domain*. New York: David McKay.

Bloom, B., & Krathwohl, D. (1977). *Taxonomy of educational objectives, handbook I: Cognitive domain*. White Plains, NY: Longman.

Carkin, S. (2005). English for academic purposes. In E. Hinkel (Ed.), *Handbook of research on second language teaching and learning* (pp. 85–98). Mahwah, NJ: Lawrence Erlbaum Associates.

Cazden, C. B. (1983). Adult assistance to language development: Scaffolds, models, and direct instruction. In R. P. Parker & F. A. Davis (Eds.), *Developing literacy: Young children's use of language* (pp. 3–17). Newark, DE: International Reading Association.

Chamot, A., & O'Malley, M. (1994). *The CALLA handbook: Implementing the Cognitive Academic Language Learning Approach*. Reading, MA: Addison Wesley.

Csikszentmihalyi, M. (1997). *Finding flow: The psychology of engagement with everyday life*. New York: Basic Books.

Cummins, J. (2001). *Negotiating identities: Education for empowerment in a diverse society* (2nd ed.). Sacramento, CA: California Association of Bilingual Education.

Dalton-Puffer, C. (2011). Content and language integrated learning: From practice to principles. *Annual Review of Applied Linguistics, 31*, 182–204.

Dutro, S., & Moran, C. (2003). *Rethinking English language instruction: An architectural approach*. In G. Garcia (Ed.) *English learners: Reaching the highest level of English literacy* (pp. 227–258). Newark, DE: International Reading Association.

Dutro, S., & Levy, E. (2008). *Improving education for English learners: Research based applications*. Sacramento: California Department of Education.

Hammond, J., & Gibbons, P. (2001). What is scaffolding? In J. Hammond (Ed.) *Scaffolding: teaching and learning language and literacy education* (pp. 1–4). Newton, NSW: Primary Education Teachers Association (PETA).

Kachru, B. B. (1986). *The alchemy of English: The spread, functions and models of non-native Englishes*. Oxford: Pergamon Press.

Kachru, B. B., & Nelson, C. L. (1996). World Englishes. In S. L. McKay (Ed.), *Sociolinguistics and language teaching* (pp. 71–102). Cambridge: Cambridge University Press.

Ovando, C., Collier, V., & Combs, M. (2003). Bilingual and ESL classrooms: Teaching multicultural contexts (3rd ed.). Boston, MA: McGraw-Hill.

Oxford, R. (1990). *Language learning strategies: What every teacher should know*. New York: Newbury House.

Perie, M., Grigg, W. S., & Donahue, P. L. (2005). *The nation's report card: Reading 2005 (NCES 2006-451)*. U.S. Department of Education, Institute of Education Sciences, National Center for Education Statistics. Washington, D.C.: U.S. Government Printing Office.

Schleppegrell, M. J. (2004). *The language of schooling: A functional linguistics perspective*. Mahwah, NJ: Lawrence Erlbaum.

Schleppegrell, M. J., & O'Halloron, C. L. (2011). Teaching academic language in L2 secondary settings. *Annual Review of Applied Linguistics, 31*, 3–18.

Short, D. J., & Fitzsimmons, S. (2007). *Double the work: Challenges and solutions to acquiring language and academic literacy for adolescent English language learners—A report to the Carnegie Corporation of New York*. Washington, D.C.: Alliance for Excellent Education. Retrieved from www.alled.org/files/DoubleWork.pdf.

Thomas, W. P., & Collier, V. P. (1997). School effectiveness for language minority students. National Clearinghouse for English Language Acquisition (NCELA). *Resource Collection Series,* No. 9, December 1997.

Thomas, W. P., & Collier, V. P. (2003). Reforming educational policies for English learners: Research evidence from U.S. schools. *The Multilingual Educator, 4*(1), 16–19. (A semiannual journal published by the California Association for Bilingual Education [CABE], Covina, CA.)

Thomas, W. P., & Collier, V. P. (2009). *Educating English language learners for a transformed world*. Albuquerque, NM: Fuente Press.

Vygotsky, L. S. (1987). Thinking and speech. In L. S. Vygotsky, Collected works (Volume 1, pp. 39–285) (R. Rieber & A. Carton, Eds.; N. Minick, Trans.). New York: Plenum. (Original works published in 1934 & 1960.)

Wood, D. J., Bruner, J. S., & Ross, G. (1976). The role of tutoring in problem solving. *Journal of Child Psychiatry and Psychology, 17*(2), 89–100.

Chapter 11

A Genre and Text-based Approach

VIGNETTE

I am observing an adult ESL class for immigrants and refugees in Australia. The students are beginners and have a variety of language backgrounds: Burmese, Farsi, Singhalese, Dinka, and Sudanese Arabic. The previous day, the class had taken a field trip to a nearby wildlife park, where they had been able to observe many different Australian animals, pat kangaroos, hold koalas, and learn about native animal habitats, diets, and life cycles. As well as touring the exhibits, the park's Education Officer had conducted a lesson about the animals, adjusted to the students' language level. The day I am observing, the teacher is helping the class write recounts about their experiences at the wildlife park. The teacher uses the whiteboard to present a grid for scaffolding the structure and grammar of the recount, including simple metalanguage such as "recount," "spoken," "written," and "paragraphs." The teacher elicits key vocabulary such as names of animals and descriptive adjectives. She does this through "wh" question prompts such as "where," "when," and "who with." In this way, they develop a skeleton oral recount together. She then asks them to write their own individual recounts. As the students work on them, she walks around, supporting students as needed. The students are very engaged in the activity and happy to relate what they did at the park. [Murray, research notes]

Task: Reflect

1. What are the aspects of instruction that helped learners achieve success in writing their own recounts?
2. What else do you think this teacher might do to extend learners' ability to write recounts?
3. What other topics could the teacher use for teaching recount?
4. How important do you think it is for learners to understand the structure of recount? When might they use it outside the classroom?

Introduction

In Chapters 8, 9, and 10, we detailed how curricula can be organized around sentence-level structures and notions and functions. However, language occurs in extended texts, whether written or spoken. In Chapter 9 of Volume I, we have an extensive discussion of the structure of language beyond the text. In this chapter we will only discuss the way curricula have been organized around the level of text in a genre/text approach.

Defining Text and Genre

Text has been variously defined. Van Dijk (1977), for example, uses *text* for the abstract theoretical construct, with its linguistic realization being *discourse*. In contrast, Halliday (1978) asserts that language is abstract and realized in *text* (either spoken or written). Others use *text* for written language and *discourse* for spoken language (Cicourel, 1975). For our purposes here, we will use text to refer to any extended language in use, whether written or spoken. *Genre* also has many different interpretations. Although it began as a literary concept, three distinct schools of genre-based curricula have developed over the past few decades: (1) English for specific purposes (ESP); (2) Australian systemic functional linguistics (SFL); and (3) North American New Rhetoric Studies (Coffin, 2001; Hyon, 1996). For ESP researchers and practitioners, particular genres in particular contexts have a specific set of textual features to achieve a communicative purpose (Bhatia, 1993; Swales, 1990). Within ESP, "Genre refers to abstract, socially recognized ways of using language" (Hyland, 2007, p. 149). Within SFL, "genre represents the system of staged goal oriented social processes through which social subjects in a given culture live their lives" (Martin, 1997, p. 13). Both ESP and SFL approaches to genre have been influential in ELT, as well as in developing theoretical and research-based studies. In contrast, New Rhetoric scholars have focused more on theory and research, examining the relationship between text and context, with a view that discourse structures of a genre are less important than the actions it accomplishes (Miller, 1984; Orlikowski & Yates, 1994).

Each of these perspectives will be discussed in more detail in the section on the major characteristics of genre-based curricula. Because genre- and text-based curricula is a rather clumsy term, we will refer to curricula that take texts as their organizing principle as GB (genre-based).

Task: Explore

Many studies consider the business letter as a genre. Find five business letters and analyze their schematic structure and the types of syntactic structures (such as tense, connectives, and types of verbs). From this brief analysis, would you agree that the business letters have sufficient commonality of schematic and syntactic structure to be considered the one genre?

Major Characteristics of GB Approaches

Although there may be a variety of implementation options, most GB approaches use an integrated curriculum, even if used for a writing program. Common across these three genre schools is that genres are socioculturally recurring ways of using language to achieve specific purposes. Genres make use of both schematic text structure and syntactic features of language such that each genre is distinct from other texts with different social purposes and structures. Because they are culturally bound, learners from different cultural backgrounds may not be familiar with the genres of English. The starting point, therefore, for the GB curriculum is the genres learners will need for their particular purposes in learning English. The intent is for learners to engage with whole texts, not decontextualized sentences or utterances. Both ESP and SFL approaches explicitly teach the structures of genres (as the teacher in the vignette was doing), believing that learners need explicit instruction in both the linguistic features and the schematic structure of the genre (see, for example, Christie & Misson, 1998).

Common to both ESP and SFL approaches is the centrality of needs analysis, premised on the notion that curricula can only be developed if designers determine the specific skills, texts, communicative situations, and linguistic forms learners need for their occupational, educational, or professional lives (Hyland, 2007). How then are these principles and characteristics realized in actual curricula?

As indicated above, GB approaches have largely been used for ESP in Australia and the U.K. However, educators using SFL theory have influenced curricula in Singapore (Ministry of Education Singapore, 2010), Hong Kong (Firkins, Forey, & Sengupta, 2007), and Thailand (Kongpetch, 2006), among other countries. Here, we will discuss the genre approach used in ESP and then specific examples of GB curricula in Australia and Singapore.

English for Specific Purposes (ESP)

ESP includes for our purposes here English for academic purposes (EAP). By its very definition, ESP is context-specific. However, some general curricula are often developed, such as the national ESP curriculum framework developed in Ukraine (Havrylyuk-Yensen & Kurant, 2010). However, most scholars and practitioners agree that the goal of ESP is to "help learners master the functions and linguistic conventions of texts that they need to read and write in their disciplines and professions" (Hyon, 1996, p. 698). EAP is, however, often a more general framework, with Swales (1990) identifying a general model for what he calls "creating a research space" with three "moves": establishing a territory, establishing a niche, and occupying the niche. Each move has several steps, which, he claims, are common across disciplines for academics writing for their field. While others have recognized that different discourse communities may have overlapping genres (for example, Hyland, 2007), most researchers claim that different disciplines construct genres differently (Hewings & Hewings, 2001). A report in one discipline may have a quite different schematic structure and syntactic features than a report in a different discipline.

Dudley-Evans and St. John (1988) recognized both absolute and variable features of ESP:

- Absolute Characteristics

    o   ESP is defined to meet specific needs of the learner.
    o   ESP makes use of the underlying methodology and activities of the discipline it serves.
    o   ESP is centred on the language (grammar, lexis, register), skills, discourse and genres appropriate to these activities.

- Variable Characteristics

    o   ESP may be related to or designed for specific disciplines.
    o   ESP may use, in specific teaching situations, a different methodology from that of general English.
    o   ESP is likely to be designed for adult learners, either at a tertiary level institution or in a professional work situation. It could, however, be for learners at secondary school level.
    o   ESP is generally designed for intermediate or advanced students.
    o   Most ESP courses assume some basic knowledge of the language system, but it can be used with beginners (pp. 4–5).

Because of its very nature, ESP has no one curriculum type. Both the language and subject matter content vary with the discipline.

Australian SFL Curricula

GB curricula based on SFL have been the underpinning of many curricula for different groups of learners in Australia. The earliest implementations were for the disadvantaged schools project, where learners were taught explicitly the texts they would need for schooling and their other needs. The goal was to empower socially and economically disadvantaged young people (Martin & Rothery, 1980, 1986). Since then, SFL-based GB has been used in a variety of curricula across Australia, including the most recent national curriculum (ACARA, 2012). In this chapter, we will focus on the model that was also developed in Australia's Adult Migrant English Program (AMEP) and used since 1992. The curriculum developers layered a competency model over a GB model (see Chapter 20 for more details of the AMEP's competency-based model).

The competencies are expressed in terms of learning outcomes, such as these sample outcomes for the Certificate in Spoken and Written English (CSWE) II for speaking (NSW AMES [Adult Migrant English Service], 2008):

- can negotiate a spoken transaction for goods/services/to obtain information
- can participate in a short conversational discussion, and
- can participate in a short conversation involving a recount/explanation.

Each learning outcome has accompanying assessment criteria, conditions of assessment, and a sample task. For example, the learning outcome "can negotiate a spoken transaction for goods/services" has the following assessment criteria, conditions of assessment, and sample tasks.

Assessment criteria

- uses appropriate strategies in transactional exchange, e.g., opening, making requests, confirming/checking, closing
- gives contact details intelligibly
- records relevant details
- uses appropriate vocabulary
- pronounces key utterances intelligibly, and
- requests goods/services using questions or statements.

Conditions of assessment

- face-to-face/telephone
- known interlocutor, fluent in English
- contact details include name, address and telephone number
- relevant details may include price and features of goods/date and time of service, and
- time limit: two minutes.

Sample tasks

Sample tasks include learners role-playing making an appointment, arranging a service call, or buying an appliance.

The outcome is at the genre level, such as the service negotiation above or the personal recount the teacher was teaching in the vignette. As an example of genre structure, the schematic structure and syntactic features of a recount are provided in Table 11.1.

SFL Influences in Singapore's English Curriculum

Singapore's English curriculum is standards/competency-based, with learning outcomes such as: plan and present information and ideas for a variety of purposes

Table 11.1 Structure of Recounts

Schematic Structure	Syntactic Features
• Orientation to the context • Records of events, usually series of paragraphs in temporal sequence • Reorientation with a closure of the events • Optional coda with a comment on the events	• Specific participants • Past tense • Verbs of action • Temporal connectives to indicate sequence of events • Time and place phrases

Reprinted with permission from Murray, D. E., & Christison, M. A. (2011). *What English Language Teachers Need to Know Volume I: Facilitating Learning* (p. 126). New York: Routledge.

and audiences (Ministry of Education Singapore, 2010, p. 46). However, for all language skills, learners are exposed to texts and their genre features are discussed and taught. Lists of text types to be taught are provided, such as for writing and representing: personal recounts (from Primary 1); factual recounts and information reports (from Primary 4); and notes, letters, email (from Primary 1) (p. 65). Additionally, text structure is to be explicitly taught, including the following learning outcome:

- show understanding of how the purposeful use of language shapes meaning in texts

    o   cohesion in texts
    o   language features of types of texts (p. 81).

The curriculum provides the features of the different genres/texts learners are required to learn, all expressed in SFL terminology. For example, for information reports at primary level, the features are:

- adjective, adjective phrases and clauses for clarity in descriptions of participants and setting
- language for comparing, contrasting, defining and classifying to indicate relationships between facts
- third person pronouns for conveying a sense of distance and objectivity
- the simple present for indicating the timeless nature of facts, and
- action verbs, mental verbs and linking verbs for conveying a variety of meanings (p. 96).

New Rhetoric

In contrast to the explicit teaching of generic structures as proposed in SFL and ESP, the New Rhetoric school argues that "learning a new genre is not a conscious process and that genres are generated in response to a task ... [and] they assert that students acquire new genres in the process of struggling to solve a problem" (Coffin, 2001, p. 113). For New Rhetoricians, overt awareness and knowledge of schematic and other linguistic structures comes as a result of successful performance. They also emphasize the transitory nature of genres, recognizing that they change over time and place, constantly being contested (Freedman & Medway, 1994).

Task: Explore

Examine an ESL/EFL textbook used at your institution. To what extent are whole texts represented? Is their structure presented deductively or inductively? Compare your findings with those of a colleague.

Issues in a GB Approach

Some educators consider genres and their linguistic features to be "subjective, culture-bound, vaguely defined, or even irrelevant to diverse types of ESL/EFL learners" (Hinkel, 2011). They have argued that it is impossible to identify all the schemata and structures for every genre (Bottomley, Dalton, & Corbel, 1994), especially because, being sociocultural artifacts, they are constantly evolving. In fact, "full descriptions of the structures of most oral and written genres have yet to be developed" (Murray, 1994, p. 63). Even if learners copy the structures of the genres they need, they may not have the mastery that they need to make the appropriate rhetorical choices for a particular task. As already indicated, genres vary across disciplines; furthermore, they may have other genres embedded within them, or they may be genres mixed for deliberate effect, such as infomercials. Many modern texts are, in fact, multimodal (Cope & Kalantzis, 2000). Additionally, individual texts of the same genre may vary, variations that result from individual contexts of text construction. McCarthy and Carter (1994) criticize SFL genre approaches for not sufficiently accounting for such variation.

Because GB approaches include explicit teaching, many who advocate critical pedagogy criticize such explicit instruction because it prevents learner agency (Benesch, 2001), denying them the opportunity to shape their own goals and how to reach them. Proponents of GB approaches, however, assert that if learners can master the genres of power and consciously understand how power operates through language, they will be empowered (Delpit, 1995; Halliday & Martin, 1993; Luke & Dooley, 2011). Bhatia (2004) agrees, noting that genres need to be fully mastered for learners to be able to use them creatively.

While genres may be fluid, all language learners need to acquire not only the conventions of sentence-level structures, but also the conventions of text structure. There is ample research evidence to show that even if learners master English sentence-level grammar, they may not be able to use texts appropriately, whether written or oral (Hammond, 1986). In assessment, for example, learners may be able to successfully perform one task, but not another, because the required genre is not one they have mastered (Murray, 1994). In academic writing, new learners often use personal narrative when a formal information text is required.

Teaching in a GB Approach

As indicated above, New Rhetoric is less involved in curricula. Therefore, in this section we will only examine teaching using ESP- or SFL-oriented curricula, both of which use explicit teaching of genre characteristics, along with enabling linguistic structures and vocabulary.

The SFL model typically has a five-part iterative cycle for instruction:

- building the context
- modeling and deconstructing the text
- jointly constructing the text
- independently constructing the text, and
- linking the text to related texts (Feez, 1998).

This process creates scaffolding (Hammond & Gibbons, 2001) for learners to move from not being able to perform the task, to being able to do the task collaboratively, to being able to do it independently, to being able to apply that knowledge and skill to a different task.

The Singapore curriculum of 2010 provides guidelines for its approach to teaching that includes:

> systematic and explicit instruction of grammar, with a focus on word, phrase and sentence level grammar before a gradual incorporation of text level grammar at the Upper Primary and Secondary levels . . .

> the use of a variety of print and non-print resources that provides authentic contexts for incorporating the development of information, media and visual literacy skills in the teaching of listening, reading, viewing, speaking, writing, and representing.
>
> (Ministry of Education Singapore, 2010, pp. 8–9)

The SFL GB curricula all recognize multiliteracies (Cope & Kalantzis, 2000), a term designed to capture the changing nature of literacy in a world that has culturally diverse literacy practices and whose technology is changing literacy communities. For example, email, Twitter, and Facebook have all provided us with new literacies. SFL curricula have sought to capture these evolving genres by including different modes of communication.

The SFL model, because its linguistic theoretical base is an understanding of language as meaning making in context, includes the connection between context and the language system. It therefore teaches register (see Chapter 9, Volume I), that is, the varieties of language that result from characteristics of the use or function to which the language is put. Typical registers are sports announcer talk, talk about the weather, or writing about health. Genres use specific registers. So, for example, a chemistry lab report will have specific structures, but also use the register of formal chemistry.

Teaching ESP GB curricula also involves explicit instruction of the structures of genre and the language of registers. However, because "ESP makes use of the underlying methodology and activities of the discipline it serves" (Dudley-Evans & St. John, 1988), there is considerable variation in teaching ESP courses. An area that is often overlooked in ESP curricula for occupational purposes is the casual conversation needed in the workplace (Gatehouse, 2001), a language skill that has been shown to be essential for non-native speakers to be able to both adapt to and be accepted in the workplace (Eggins & Slade, 1997). Like SFL curricula, ESP curricula have recognized the need to include new technology, although not always consciously accepting multiliteracies in their broadest sense.

Conclusion

GB approaches provide learners with the texts they will need for their lives, whether educational, occupational, or social. While there are potential disadvantages to GB, these can be overcome by planning carefully and by providing learners with opportunities to explore and create, as well as by helping them understand the flexible and fluid nature of texts.

Task: Expand

Derewianka, B. (2012). Knowledge about language in the Australian curriculum: English. *Australian Journal of Language and Literacy, 35*(2), 127–146. Also available at: http://ro.uow.edu.au/sspapers/129

This article has an excellent overview of SFL and its application to curriculum.

English for Specific Purposes (formerly *The ESP Journal*)

This international journal carries articles about theory and practice of ESP, including studies of genres of different professions and disciplines. The journal began publishing in 1980.

The Asian ESP Journal

This journal has articles about ESP theory and practice, including studies of different professional and academic genres.

Questions for Discussion

1. Explain in your own words the differences and similarities among SFL, ESP, and New Rhetoric approaches to curriculum design.
2. Think of English language learning examples for the genres *personal recount* and *factual recount*.
3. How could a teacher help learners understand the fluid nature of genre?
4. Why do you think some people criticize explicit teaching as restricting learners, rather than empowering them?
5. What is your opinion of the importance of multiliteracies in ELT? What text-types would you include in any syllabus you teach? Why?

References

ACARA. (2012). *English as an additional language or dialect teacher resource.* Retrieved from http://www.acara.edu.au/verve/_resources/English_as_an_Additional_Language_or_Dialect_Teacher_Resource_05_06_12.pdf

Benesch, S. (2001). *Critical English for academic purposes: Theory, politics and practice.* Mahwah, N.J.: Lawrence Erlbaum Associates.

Bhatia, V. K. (1993). *Analysing genre: Language use in professional settings.* London: Longman.

Bhatia, V. K. (2004). *Worlds of written discourse: A genre based view.* London: Continuum.

Bottomley, Y., Dalton, J., & Corbel, C. (1994). *From proficiency to competencies: A collaborative approach to curriculum innovation.* Sydney: NCELTR.

Christie, F., & Misson, R. (1998). *Literacy and schooling.* London: Taylor & Francis.

Cicourel, A. V. (1975). Discourse and text: Cognitive and linguistic processes in studies of social structure. *Versus, 12,* 33–84.

Coffin, C. (2001). Theoretical approaches to written language—A TESOL perspective. In A. Burns & C. Coffin (Eds.), *Analysing English in a global context* (pp. 93–122). London: Routledge.

Cope, B., & Kalantzis, M. (2000). *Multiliteracies: Literacy learning and the design of social futures.* London: Routledge.

Delpit, L. D. (1995). *Other people's children: Cultural conflict in the classroom.* New York: The New Press.

Derewianka, B. (2012). Knowledge about language in the Australian curriculum: English. *Australian Journal of Language and Literacy, 35*(2), 127–146. Also available at: http://ro.uow.edu.au/sspapers/129

Dudley-Evans, T., & St. John, M. (1988). *Developments in ESP: A multidisciplinary approach.* Cambridge: Cambridge University Press.

Eggins, S., & Slade, D. (1997). *Analysing casual conversation.* London: Cassell.

Feez, S. (1998). *Text-based syllabus design.* Sydney: NCELTR.

Firkins, A., Forey, G., & Sengupta, S. (2007). Teaching writing to low proficiency EFL students. *ELT Journal, 61*(4), 341–352.

Freedman, A., & Medway, P. (Eds.). (1994). *Genre and the new rhetoric.* London: Taylor & Francis.

Gatehouse, K. (2001). Key issues in English for specific purposes (ESP) curriculum development [Electronic Version]. *The Internet TESL Journal, VII.* Retrieved from http://iteslj.org/Articles/Gatehouse-ESP.ht

Halliday, M. A. K. (1978). *Language as social semiotic.* London: Edward Arnold.

Halliday, M. A. K., & Martin, J. R. (1993). *Writing science: Literacy and discursive power.* London: The Falmer Press.

Hammond, J. (1986). The effect of modelling reports and narratives on the writing of year two children from a non-English speaking background. *Australian Review of Applied Linguistics, 9*(2), 75–93.

Hammond, J., & Gibbons, P. (2001). *Scaffolding teaching and learning in language and literacy education.* Sydney: PETA.

Havrylyuk-Yensen, L., & Kurant, L. (2010). Ukraine: English for specific purposes (ESP) curriculum reforming processes [Electronic Version]. *The Magazine of Global English Speaking Higher Education, 2.* Retrieved from http://www.anglohigher.com/magazines/magazine_detail/45/25

Hewings, A., & Hewings, M. (2001). Disciplinary variation in academic writing. In D. R. Hall & A. Hewings (Eds.), *Innovation in English language teaching* (pp. 71–83). London: Routledge.

Hinkel, E. (2011). What research on second language writing tells us and what it doesn't. In E. Hinkel (Ed.), *Handbook of research in second language teaching and learning* (Volume II, pp. 523–538). New York: Routledge.

Hyland, K. (2007). Genre pedagogy: Language, literacy, and L2 writing instruction. *Journal of Second Language Writing, 16,* 148–164.

Hyon, S. (1996). Genre in three traditions: Implications for ESL. *TESOL Quarterly, 30*(1), 693–722.

Kongpetch, S. (2006). Using a genre-based approach to teach writing to Thai students: A case study. *Prospect, 21*(2), 3–33.

Luke, A., & Dooley, K. (2011). Critical literacy and second language learning. In E. Hinkel (Ed.), *Handbook of research in second language teaching and learning* (Volume II, pp. 856–867). New York: Routledge.

Martin, J. R. (1997). Analysing genre: functional parameters. In F. Christie & J. R. Martin (Eds.), *Genre and institutions: Social processes in the workplace and the school* (pp. 3–19). London: Cassell.

Martin, J. R., & Rothery, J. (1980). *Writing project report, No. 1.* Sydney: Department of Linguistics, University of Sydney.

Martin, J. R., & Rothery, J. (1986). *Writing project report No. 4.* Sydney: Department of Linguistics, University of Sydney.

McCarthy, M., & Carter, R. (1994). *Language as discourse: Perspectives for language teaching.* London: Longman.

Miller, C. (1984). Genre as social action. *Quarterly Journal of Speech, 70*, 151–167.

Ministry of Education Singapore. (2010). *English language syllabus 2010 (primary and secondary).* Retrieved from http://www.moe.gov.sg/education/syllabuses/english-language-and-literature/files/english-primary-secondary-express-normal-academic.pdf

Murray, D. E. (1994). Using portfolios to assess writing. *Prospect, 9*(2), 56–69.

NSW AMES (Adult Migrant English Service). (2008). *Certificate in spoken and written English.* Sydney: NSW AMES.

Orlikowski, W. J., & Yates, J. (1994). Genre repertoire: The structuring of communicative practices in organizations. *Administrative Sciences Quarterly, 33*, 541–574.

Swales, J. M. (1990). *Genre analysis.* Cambridge: Cambridge University Press.

Van Dijk, T. A. (1977). *Text and context: Explorations in the semantics and pragmatics of discourse.* London: Longman.

Chapter 12

A Vocabulary Approach

VIGNETTE

I am in Indonesia conducting English language teacher education programs for the U.S. Department of State. My assignment for the week is to conduct half-day workshops for teachers at one of the largest English language teaching programs in Jakarta. The workshops for teachers go from 9:00 AM to 12:00 noon each day for five days. Then, I enjoy an informal lunch with the level supervisors and the two directors. In the afternoon I consult with the curriculum team, the level supervisors, and the two directors on an overall revision of the curriculum; however, yesterday, it seemed as if they didn't really know what to do with me in the afternoon, so today I suggested that I visit classes because knowing more about the classes, teachers, and students will help me be a better consultant for them as I develop an understanding of their curriculum in practice. The first class I visit is a Level 2 class (Level 8 is the highest) with adolescent learners. There are about 20 students in the class. When I enter the class, the students are copying vocabulary words from the board into their notebooks. I see that the words are all related to clothing and weather. Once the teacher can see that most of the students have completed the copying activity, she moves on to a dictation of the words and then to a partner dictation. Finally, students complete a cloze exercise with the vocabulary words in their workbooks. The second class that I observe is for young learners. The students are between the ages of six and eight, and there are about 15 students in the class. The teacher asks the students to join her by sitting around her on the floor while she reads a story. She then takes large colored cards from a box and asks the students, "Who can show me where the blackboard is? The teacher's chair? The bookcase? The garbage can? The door? The pencil sharpener?" Students are chosen to respond and given a colored card with the appropriate word. They take the card and tape it to the classroom item. When students finish with this activity, the items in the entire class are labeled. The teacher told me after class that she leaves cards up for a week and then takes them down using the same process only to put them up again. Although the students may not actually be reading the words, they are becoming familiar with them and learning to recognize them in conjunction with the items in the room. [Christison, research notes]

Task: Reflect

1. What do the two different lessons in the vignette have in common instructionally?
2. How do the two lesson excerpts described in the vignette help L2 learners work with vocabulary?
3. What activities does the teacher use to help learners develop vocabulary skills?

Introduction

Vocabulary is fundamental in the language learning process. One of the main barriers to student comprehension of text (both spoken and written) is low-level understanding of social and academic vocabulary. Vocabulary often plays a major role in L2 instruction and is frequently the key organizational feature of a curriculum around which other aspects of the curriculum design revolve, such as grammatical structures or instructional tasks. Given the prominence that vocabulary has played in the design of L2 courses, curricula, and textbooks, it seems logical to recognize vocabulary as an approach to curriculum design in much the same way as language structures or functions (see Nation, 2009 for an example of texts promoting a vocabulary approach). Vocabulary is often the organizing principle and the key factor in curriculum design. However, it is also true that vocabulary plays a major role in the design of curriculum across different approaches (Folse, 2004). As we look at vocabulary in this chapter, we will consider the role of vocabulary from these two vantage points.

Acquiring vocabulary involves more than looking up words in a dictionary, memorizing lists of words, and using them in sentences. It is a complex process that involves many factors, such as the activation of students' background knowledge and their ability to use vocabulary words in context. For example, no students are expected to know the technical vocabulary of biology before studying biology or taking a course in biology. However, key to understanding technical vocabulary is also making use of the vocabulary that is used to teach biology. Lower-level proficiency English learners may not know the vocabulary used to teach the important concepts that underpin biology, such as *assumption*, *predict*, *theory*, *hypothesis*, and *evaluate*, and these words are important in understanding text. Content teachers and mainstream faculty often assume that L2 students can comprehend this type of vocabulary, when, in fact, they cannot. The words and phrases that support the technical vocabulary are not frequent in informal face-to-face communication, so it is not likely they can be picked up in the same manner as everyday social language.

This chapter focuses on understanding the role that vocabulary plays in designing curriculum, particularly in academic settings. It also covers the various options available for curriculum designers who wish to focus on vocabulary, including the role of vocabulary in teaching the four skills.

Defining Vocabulary

Fundamental to any discussion of vocabulary in curriculum design is coming to an agreed upon understanding of what it means to "know" a word. Folse (2004) states that a definition of vocabulary is more than a list of single words. It also includes phrases, idioms, and phrasal verbs. To this end, vocabulary can be defined to include all of the following: (1) all the words of a language; (2) the sum of words that are used by, understood by, or at the command of a particular person or group; (3) a list of words or phrases or formulaic expressions arranged in some logical fashion; or (4) a repertoire of communication possibilities to include words and their *collocations*. A collocation can be defined as the habitual juxtaposition of a particular word with another word or words with a frequency greater than chance. These juxtapositions are determined nowadays most frequently by looking at *corpora* (i.e., samples of real-world text) that are derived through the use of an automated process. In recent years, *corpus linguistics*, which is the study of language as it is expressed in real-world samples of language, has begun to have an impact on curriculum design as teachers and curriculum designers consult corpora to find the exact collocations and the frequency with which they occur (Biber, Conrad, & Reppen, 1998; McCarthy, 2006; O'Keeffe & McCarthy, 2010).

Determining how words are used and juxtaposed with other words is an important feature of L2 vocabulary instruction. For example, while the phrases *heavy rain*, *strong rain*, and *big rain* are all technically grammatically correct combinations, an examination of corpora would confirm *heavy rain* to be the most frequently used phrase among proficient users of English; thus, it would be the appropriate collocation. The use of corpora for identifying technical vocabulary and genre-based approaches to curriculum design is becoming more common than it was in the past.

Vocabulary differs in its relative difficulty for learning, depending on the learners' orientation to the vocabulary and on whether the vocabulary word being learned is an unknown word for a known concept, an unknown word for an unknown concept, a known word for an unknown concept, a known word for a known concept, or a known or unknown word that can cover more than one concept. For example, a young English learner may study about plants in a content and language integrated course and learn about *photosynthesis* for the first time. In this case, she will be learning a previously unknown word for a previously unknown concept. Another English learner may be learning the words for clothes in English. In this case, the concepts are already known; the task is simply to learn different vocabulary for referencing clothing. The word *palm* in English means the inner surface of the hand, but it can also be used to refer a particular type of tree—a *palm tree*. In this case a known word may be used to refer to more than one concept, depending on context.

Technical vocabulary words have very specific meanings. As L2 learners gain experience in different contexts, they learn specific meanings of words. For example, a learner might assume that the word *leaf* can be used in reference to all tree foliage; however, through experience the learner may discover that a leaf on a palm tree is called a *frond*, thereby requiring the learner to refine her definition of a *leaf*. The difficulty level for learning new words is affected by all of these factors and must be considered by both teachers and curriculum designers in the selection of vocabulary.

Nation (2005) lists various aspects of knowledge that are involved in knowing a word. These aspects fit into three categories. Knowing a word involves knowing its form (e.g., knowing is spelling, pronunciation, and word parts), knowing its meaning (e.g., knowing the concept for the word, knowing what it can and cannot refer to, knowing what other words are related to it), and knowing its use (e.g., the part of speech, the sentence patterns it fits into, its collocations). Given the diversity of meanings associated with defining vocabulary, it is easy to see why designing curriculum to teach vocabulary to L2 learners has been described as a complex task.

Task: Explore

Choose a chapter from a textbook for English learners or use a lesson plan that you have created. Identify the vocabulary targeted for the lesson plan or chapter you have chosen. Categorize the vocabulary in terms of their difficulty level. Does the vocabulary target known or unknown concepts? What other factors influence the difficulty of learning a vocabulary word?

English Vocabulary

There are some general pieces of knowledge about English vocabulary that can aid curriculum designers and teachers in making choices about what vocabulary to include in a course or program and how to do it. These two important pieces of information are related to 1) English etymology, and 2) the use of frequency word lists (Nation, 2005). English vocabulary comes from two major sources—Germanic (Anglo Saxon or Old English) and Latin (primarily indirectly through French after the Norman invasion of England in 1066), and these sources interact with the frequency of words in English. For example, the main source of high frequency words in English is Anglo Saxon with Germanic words making up 97% of the most frequent 100 words in English, 57% of the first 1,000, 39% of the second 1,000 and 36% of the remaining words. While Latin words make up only 3% of the first 100, 36% of the first 1,000, and 51% of the second 1,000, they make up over 90% of the words in the Academic Word List (AWL). Academic vocabulary is, therefore, based on more Latin and Greek roots than is everyday spoken English vocabulary. Word study activities can be very helpful in acquiring this vocabulary. In addition, academic lectures and texts tend to use longer, more complex sentences than are used in spoken English.

Nation (2005) considers the above frequency counts and makes the following recommendations for vocabulary instruction. He states that there are between 1,500 and 2,000 high frequency words that are most important (West, 1953), and he recommends that these high frequency words be taught early on and included as quickly as possible in beginning level courses. He also points out that there are thousands of low frequency words that do not need to be targeted or taught. They will be acquired over time and should not take prominence in course and curriculum design. Rather, teachers and curriculum designers should focus on vocabulary learning strategies to help learners acquire the large numbers of technical and low frequency words they will encounter. Courses in which L2 learners must work with challenging academic content should include a large number of Latin words that target word study through affixation (i.e., learning the meanings of prefixes and suffixes and recognizing them in words).

Issues in Learning Vocabulary

Folse (2004) identifies several myths about teaching vocabulary that influence the choices that teachers and curriculum designers make when selecting vocabulary for inclusion in lessons, courses, and programs and determining how vocabulary should be taught.

1. The first myth that many language practitioners hold is that grammar plays a more important role in foreign language learning than vocabulary. While using incorrect grammatical constructions can certainly interfere with communication, selecting the wrong vocabulary words prevents the intended message from getting across; therefore, the focus for instructional materials, even at the very early levels of proficiency, should include appropriate and meaningful vocabulary and opportunities for the development of vocabulary and strategies for vocabulary learning.

2. A second myth is that word lists are not useful. The use of word lists can be an effective strategy, especially for beginning level proficiency students, who can benefit from working with a short list of words and simple definitions or synonyms (Nation, 1994). Text that includes glossed words and their meanings are the most useful for L2 learners when working with new concepts and words (Prince, 1995). Word lists do not promote a deeper knowledge of vocabulary, but they do aid in the memory retrieval process, making it possible to access new words more readily. This fact is especially evident when the vocabulary in lists is used in both written and oral communication strategies. Teachers and curriculum designers must remember that while word lists can be useful, they cannot be the only source of vocabulary learning.

3. The next myth concerns the use of *semantic sets* for introducing vocabulary. Semantic sets are groups of words that all fit into the same semantic category. The most common way of introducing vocabulary at the beginning proficiency levels is through semantic sets, such as days of the week, clothes, sports, transportation, colors, rooms in a house, food, to name a few. L2 learners have difficulty remembering words taught through semantic sets (Tinkham, 1993, 1997; Waring, 1997).

4. Translation can sometimes be useful for L2 learners as a personal choice (de Groot, Dannenburg, & Van Hell, 1994). L2 learners who were exposed to the words and their corresponding translations had better task scores than L2 informants that were exposed to words and their corresponding pictures. This is not to suggest that translation be included in the design of a course or curriculum, but if it is a learner's request or choice, it should not provoke negative feedback from teachers. A quick translation from a peer leads can lead to comprehension, a form of scaffolding (see Chapter 10).

5. While guessing the meaning of vocabulary in context can be a useful reading strategy, it is not an effective vocabulary learning strategy, particularly for

lower-level proficiency learners. While contextual clues may be prevalent in authentic materials, they are often missing from text used for language learners. Even if contextual clues may be present in text, L2 learners must know the contextual vocabulary. Teachers and curriculum designers should remember that L2 vocabulary should be taught and practiced.

6. Another myth is that good L2 learners need to employ only a few strategies to help them learn new L2 words. In fact, L2 learners need a variety of vocabulary learning strategies (VLSs), and they should be taught and practiced and included in the design of a course or a curriculum. VLSs include auditory rehearsal, keyword imagery, and word study.

7. The seventh myth is that only monolingual dictionaries should be used in language classes. Folse (2004) argues that the use of bilingual dictionaries should be encouraged in the design of courses and curricula.

8. The last myth concerns the purposeful teaching of vocabulary. Folse (2004) states that it is a myth to believe that L2 vocabulary does not need to be taught and that L2 learners will pick it up simply by exposure to written text. Teachers and course and curriculum designers must incorporate the purposeful teaching of vocabulary and the use of VLSs in the design process for all proficiency levels in all contexts.

Planning for Vocabulary Instruction

Nation (2001) asserts that teachers and curriculum designers should plan for vocabulary learning just as they plan for other aspects of curriculum design. He makes the following fundamental recommendations.

1. Determine the number and type of words that should be targeted for student learning. In order to make this determination, it is important to consider the four different classes of vocabulary words—high frequency words, academic words, technical words (words related to a specific topic), and low frequency words—and select words from each of the categories. High frequency words, which include function and some content words, should be given priority in beginning proficiency level classes. Targeting fewer words and working with these words in depth is better for retention than targeting more words and providing fewer opportunities for practice.

2. Incorporate the psychological processes used in learning as a model for teaching vocabulary. These processes include: (a) helping L2 learners notice targeted vocabulary in the input in either spoken or written form and getting them to attend to targeted vocabulary by giving them multiple exposures to the vocabulary (Schmidt, 1990, 1995); (b) providing multiple opportunities to retrieve targeted vocabulary; and (c) promoting the creative use of targeted vocabulary by providing opportunities to use new vocabulary in new contexts. The more deliberate attention learners give words, the more likely it is that these words will be learned (Hulstijn, 2001).

3. Space out vocabulary learning. L2 vocabulary learning is a cumulative process that entails learning form, meaning, and use. Teaching L2 vocabulary should be spaced out over time to avoid information overload should teachers try to explore the form, meanings, and use in a single teaching encounter.

Vocabulary Development and the Four Skills

L2 learners develop knowledge about vocabulary based on the different ways in which they learn it. Vocabulary is not simply learned when teachers focus specifically on vocabulary and teach it; it can be learned through all of the four skills—listening, speaking, reading, and writing.

Listening and Speaking

Teachers and curriculum designers should plan listening and speaking activities to increase learners' repertoire of words. Listening activities that focus on vocabulary development should include interesting content and provide an opportunity for learners to receive input that requires them to negotiate meaning. In addition, listening to stories is useful if the story is interesting, comprehensible, and involves repetition (Elley, 1989). Speaking activities provide learners with opportunities to work together cooperatively. Examples of such activities are problem solving activities and role-plays that give learners opportunities to use both their receptive and productive vocabulary. Eliciting specific vocabulary from students in guided discussion is also very useful. Activities such as creating semantic maps focus students on specific vocabulary and also give them an opportunity to explain and justify the connections in the semantic map.

Reading and Writing

In addition to listening and speaking, reading and writing can promote learners' vocabulary enrichment. L2 teachers should select reading materials that are appropriate to the level of their students. Nation (2001) states that materials for language learners should include graded readers, especially at beginning levels of language proficiency. Even though graded readers are criticized as not being authentic materials, Nation argues against such an idea. He proposes that authenticity should be measured by the readers' response to the materials. If L2 learners do not know the meaning of a significant number of words in a text, they will not read it.

L2 learners also need to work with unmodified texts. In this case, teachers must facilitate learners' interaction with the text and guide them through the text. Glosses, visuals such as pictures, graphs, and maps, contribute to text comprehensibility for learners.

Reading large quantities of text in another language promotes vocabulary development. In addition to encouraging reading, L2 teachers should explicitly teach high frequency words. A lack of vocabulary is one of the main difficulties L2 learners have when writing in their target language; therefore, teachers should encourage learners to see writing tasks as opportunities to expand their L2 vocabulary.

Vocabulary Learning Strategies

In order to deal with the larger number of vocabulary items in the lexicon, L2 learners need to develop strategies. These strategies need to be taught and developed in the classroom using the high frequency words so that learners can use the strategies independently to deal with the thousands of low frequency words that they will encounter over time. Nation (2005) identifies four important strategies—inferring meanings from context, learning from word cards, using word parts, and using a dictionary. L2 learners need guidance and opportunities to develop skills with these strategies (see Nation, 2001, 2005 for guidelines for teaching each of these recommended strategies). Teachers and curriculum designers need to remember that vocabulary strategy instruction must also be part of the curriculum design process.

Conclusion

In this chapter, we have outlined some basic considerations for vocabulary instruction in curriculum design. We have considered how to define vocabulary by expanding notions to include formulaic expressions and collocations. In addition, we have looked at some issues in vocabulary learning and English vocabulary more specifically. We also provide some basic guidelines and recommendations for planning vocabulary instruction and including vocabulary instruction in teaching the four skills. We stress the importance of including vocabulary strategies in the design process given the number of low frequency words that L2 learners will encounter.

Task: Expand

Folse, K. S. (2004) *Vocabulary myths: Applying second language research to classroom teaching.*

This book breaks down the teaching of second language vocabulary into eight commonly held myths. The goal is to foster a paradigm shift that views vocabulary development as fundamental in the L2 learning process.

Nation, I. S. P. (2001). *Learning vocabulary in another language.* Cambridge: Cambridge University Press.

This is a book about teaching and learning vocabulary and the role that vocabulary plays in a language development program. The goal of the book is to promote vocabulary development within a balanced language course that consists of four main strands—learning vocabulary from meaning-focused input, form-focused instruction, meaning-focused output, and a balanced course in fluency development. The goal of the book is to help teachers and curriculum designers determine how vocabulary fits into all strands.

Questions for Discussion

1. What does it mean to know a word? What are the different levels of knowing described in this chapter?
2. What are the main concepts that teachers and curriculum designers should know about English vocabulary?

3. Explain your position on each of the following: the use of dictionaries, word lists, and inferring or guessing from context in learning L2 vocabulary.
4. Name one vocabulary learning strategy that you see as important in the curriculum design process and explain why teaching vocabulary strategies to L2 learners is important.

References

Biber, D., Conrad, S., & Reppen, R. (1998). *Cognitive linguistics: Investigating language structure and use*. Cambridge: Cambridge University Press.

De Groot, A. M. B., Dannenburg, L., & Van Hell, J. G. (1994). Forward and backward translation by bilinguals. *Journal of Memory and Language, 33*(5), 600–629.

Elley, W. B. (1989). Vocabulary acquisition from listening to stories. *Reading Research Quarterly, 24*, 174–187.

Folse, K. S. (2004). *Vocabulary myths: Applying second language research to classroom teaching*. Ann Arbor, MI: University of Michigan Press.

Hulstijn, J. H. (2001). Intentional and incidental vocabulary learning: A reappraisal of elaboration, rehearsal, and automaticity. In P. Robinson (Ed.), *Cognition and second language instruction* (pp. 258–286). Cambridge: Cambridge University Press.

McCarthy, M., & Carter, R. (2006). *Explorations in corpus linguistics*. Cambridge: Cambridge University Press.

Nation, I. S. P. (1994). *New ways in teaching vocabulary*. Alexandria, VA: TESOL.

Nation, I. S. P. (2001). *Learning vocabulary in another language*. Cambridge: Cambridge University Press.

Nation, I. S. P. (2005). Teaching and learning vocabulary. In E. Hinkel (Ed.) *Handbook of research in second language teaching and learning* (pp. 581–595). Mahwah, NJ: Lawrence Erlbaum Associates.

Nation, I. S. P. (2009). *4000 essential English words. Books 1–6*. Tokyo, Japan: Compass.

O'Keeffe, A., & McCarthy, M. (2010). *The Routledge handbook of corpus linguistics*. New York: Routledge/Taylor & Francis.

Prince, P. (1995). Second language vocabulary learning: The role of context versus translations as a function of proficiency. *The Modern Language Journal, 80*(4), 478–493.

Schmidt, R. (1990). The role of consciousness in second language learning. *Applied Linguistics, 11*, 129–158.

Schmidt, R. (1995). Consciousness and foreign language learning: A tutorial on the role of attention and awareness in learning. In R. Schmidt (Ed.), *Attention and awareness in foreign language learning* (pp. 1–63). Manoa, HI: University of Hawaii Press.

Tinkham, T. (1993). The effects of semantic clustering on the learning of second language vocabulary. *System, 21*(3), 371–380.

Tinkham, T. (1997). The effects of semantic and thematic clustering on the learning of second language vocabulary. *Second Language Research, 13*(2), 138–163.

Waring, R. (1997). The negative effects of learning words in semantic sets. *System, 25*(2), 261–274.

West, M. (1953). *A general service list of English words*. London: Longman.

Chapter 13

A Skills-based Approach

VIGNETTE

I am working as a private consultant for an English language-teaching center in Brazil. I have been hired to provide an evaluation of the center's curriculum and make recommendations for changes or improvements. I am working closely with the center's administrators, but I report to the Board of Trustees. I have been told that the purpose of the evaluation is part of the board's desire to be proactive in implementing quality control measures at the center. Prior to my arrival, I studied and familiarized myself with a number of written documents, including most of the center's textbooks, a number of sample lesson plans, and the curriculum guides. I believe that I have a good idea about the center's intended curriculum based on what they have sent me. As part of the process, I have been visiting classes and will do so again tomorrow. So far today, I have observed six courses, and I have three more to observe before the day ends. After that, I will spend several days interviewing stakeholders—administrators, staff, instructors, students, and even some parents—before I write my report. On paper the center presents itself as having a very traditional curriculum that is based primarily on the four skills. The center offers eight levels with four courses at each level—listening, speaking, reading, and writing. There are other optional courses available for different levels. For example, at Levels 1 and 2, there is a pronunciation course; for Levels 4–8, there is a conversation club; at Levels 6 and 8, the course is US culture. Today, I have observed two listening classes, two speaking classes, one reading class, and one writing class. The classes were at Levels 3–6. In the Level 4 listening class this morning, the students first read a text, talked about it, and then participated in a cloze listening activity that targeted specific words and phrases from the reading. After that, they participated in a pair dictation with some words from a previous lesson. In this activity one partner listens while the other partner dictates, and then they switch roles. In the Level 6 listening class, the students principally listened to, took notes on, and then discussed a portion of a documentary film about rain forests. Then, they worked in small groups to answer questions with one paper being submitted from each group. In the Level 5 reading class the students talked about the content of a reading they had been assigned from their textbook on the topic of US culture. They had a very interesting and lively discussion about dating and US movies—a discussion that was based more on the students' personal ideas about US culture than on information given in the reading itself. In the Level 2 writing class, students copied lists of words into their notebooks. Then, they wrote in their journals for ten minutes and exchanged letters they had previously written to one another. [Christison, research notes]

Task: Reflect

1. Which of the language skills—listening, speaking, reading, and writing—do L2 learners use in each of the four classes described above?
2. Based on the skills being taught, do you think the courses are appropriately titled?
3. For the purposes of curriculum design, do you think it's possible to separate the four language skills? Why or why not?

Introduction

In this chapter we will focus on the language skills approach to curriculum design. In this tradition, there are basically two models that have had a major impact on the design of instructional materials and English language teaching (ELT) programs and centers. In the first model each language skill—listening, speaking, reading, and writing—is considered separately in different courses. In the second model the skills are integrated in some fashion. One course may include all skills or a combination of skills. Each model will be considered separately in terms of both its history and practice. Then, we will look at each of the skills separately and at some of the basic concepts for skill development that have influenced language teaching and the design of curriculum.

Language Skills as Separated

For the purposes of language teaching, language has traditionally been divided into four separate skills areas—listening, speaking, reading, and writing. The four skills can be separated in other ways. Listening and reading are known as the *receptive* skills, and speaking and writing are known as the *productive* skills. We can also think of the four skills in terms of oral language and literacy. Listening and speaking are the skills needed for oral communication, while reading and writing are skills needed specifically for literacy development. The idea of separating the teaching of language into language skills is considered the norm for most English language teachers, and the view is easily recognized in the research, materials development, language-testing traditions, and the practices of teacher education programs over the past four decades. Considerable research has been conducted on each of the four skills (see Hinkel, 2006 for an overview), textbooks have been created that focus on each of the four skills, language tests focus on different language skills, and teacher education programs frequently include such classes as teaching L2 writing or reading. The skills-based approach to curriculum design has also been widely used by curriculum designers. The English language-teaching center in the vignette conceived of its curriculum in relationship to the four skills with courses in listening, speaking, reading, and writing taught at each of the eight levels. In 1978 when one of us (Christison) took a job as an English language program administrator for an Intensive English Program (IEP) in the U.S., the curriculum she initially designed was skills-based (see Table 13.1) with listening, reading, and writing at each of three levels; pronunciation at two levels; and a conversation program that focused on speaking and interaction with the conversation partners. The advanced group could take one course (with approval of the advisor) in the mainstream curriculum.[1] This type of curriculum was typical of most IEPs in the late 1970s and early 1980s.

Table 13.1 Skills-based Curriculum for a Small IEP

Courses → Levels ↓	Reading	Writing	Listening	Pronunciation	Conversation
Beginning	9:00–9:50 AM–M-F	10:00–10:50 AM–M-F	11:00–11:50 AM–M-F	2:00–2:50 PM–M-F	3:00–4:30 PM–MWF
Intermediate	8:00–8:50 AM–M-F	12:00–12:50 PM–M-F	10:00–10:50 AM–M-F	1:00–1:50 PM–MWF	3:00–4:30 PM–MWF
Advanced	9:00–9:50 AM–M-F	11:00–11:50 AM–M-F	1:00–2:30 PM–T/Th		3:00–4:30 PM–MWF

The four skills approach to curriculum design in North America has its roots in *structural linguistics*. Structural linguistics is based on the early work of Ferdinand de Saussure (Harris, 1987; Joseph, 2012). The purpose of structural linguistics is to classify language in different ways, such as the classification of phonemes, morphemes, lexical categories, phrases and sentence types, or, in this case, language skills. In North America, this approach to curriculum design is easily recognized in the early work of Charles Fries and Robert Lado (Lado & Fries, 1958) at the University of Michigan, who designed a program for ELT that was based on the principles of structural linguistics. The program was separated into language skills but preserved the primacy of spoken language in the methodology, which focused almost exclusively on speaking and listening and using drills for the practice of grammatical structures that were identified for each level. This method ultimately became known as the audio-lingual method.

In the U.K. and Europe, the separation of language into the four skills was a utilitarian decision and motivated by the need to teach academic and technical language; consequently, it was socially rather than structurally driven (Howatt & Widdowson, 2004). Nevertheless, it was similar to the four skills approach in the U.S. in that all four skills were taught and the development of spoken English was given top priority (see Chapter 15 on the topic and situational approach to curriculum design). A four skills approach has also been typical for languages other than English. There were single skills taught such as reading scientific German in the days when most science journals were in German. The same holds true for English today.

Language Skills as Integrated

The rationale for an integration of language skills is that in real-world contexts it is difficult to separate and isolate skills. For example, when you listen to someone, it is likely that you will also need to respond and, therefore, speak. In listening to an academic lecture, it is likely you will need to take notes and, therefore, use the skill of writing. An example can be found in many public schools in North America that embrace the notion of an integrated curriculum (see the examples in the *Expand* activity in this chapter). A rationale for the integration of language skills into content curricula is captured in the following quote from the UNESCO (United Nations Educational Scientific and Cultural Organization) Statement for the United Nations Literacy Decade, 2003–2013.

> Literacy is about more than reading or writing—it is about how we communicate in society. It is about social practices and relationships, about knowledge, language and culture. Those who use literacy take it for granted—but those who cannot use it are excluded from much communication in today's world. Indeed, it is the excluded who can best appreciate the notion of literacy as freedom.

Because literacy development lies at the heart of the educational goals for most public schools, embedding literacy skills across the curriculum and also creating an integrated language curriculum that is dedicated to the acquisition of knowledge and the development of language skills—listening, speaking, reading, and writing—is critical. Language forms the basis for thinking, communicating with others, and learning. It is also a fundamental element of identity and culture (see Volume I, Chapter 5 on identity and language).

With the introduction of the notion of communicative competence (Hymes, 1972), the way in which language-teaching professionals primarily thought about language began to change as his view included form and function in integral relation to each other, as opposed to Chomsky's abstract view of competence in relation to form. Canale and Swain (1980) extended the theoretical bases of communicative competence to include three competencies: grammatical (words and rules that govern them), sociolinguistic (use of appropriate of speech), and strategic (the use of strategies). Bachman and Palmer (1996) added pragmatic competence (using language to accomplish tasks in context). The structural view of language with its separation of language into parts was in contrast to a view of language as communication. In a communicative view of language, language skills are integrated to accomplish certain tasks rather than separated to practice language skills. An integrated skills approach is consistent with communicative language teaching (CLT) as it places an emphasis on helping learners communicate effectively both inside and outside of the classroom.

Widdowson (1978, 1993) led the way in language teaching by requesting that teaching and curriculum design place a strong emphasis on integrating the four skills and providing opportunities in the classroom for meaningful communicative exchanges, such as problem solving activities, discussion, and a wide range of tasks. Nunan (1989) followed suit by providing a set of principles that should guide the design of teaching materials and the integration of skills. These principles include using authentic language (i.e., examples of language actually used by proficient speakers in context), creating opportunities for continuity in the development of language skills from comprehension to production, and creating explicit connections from the classroom to real-world contexts. Carter and Nunan (2001) also state that learner goals in relationship to the context are key components in an integrated skills curriculum.

All four skills are important in the development of communicative competence. Language curricula are designed in such a way that teaching writing is often linked to reading and teaching speaking is often linked to pronunciation, grammar, and such pragmatically-based activities as giving presentations in class and using library resources for research. Most teachers try to incorporate all four skill areas into their planning, though some classes may focus more on one set of skills more than on another due to the role the course plays in the overall curriculum and the objectives of learners (Oxford, 2001).

Defining Language Skills

Each language skill is complex and can be looked at in different ways. How language skills are conceptualized is dependent on context and on the goals of the learners involved. For example, in a curriculum for non-academic adults who are mostly interested in obtaining jobs as soon as possible, the skill of writing will be conceptualized quite differently than it would be in a curriculum for young academic bound adults at the university who are planning to work as researchers or professionals in business. Adults involved in non-academic language-teaching programs may need to write in order to complete a job application, make lists, or write informal letters, while students involved in academic language-teaching programs may need to write a paper presenting the results of their research or to take notes in class.

In addition to differences in how skills are conceptualized in terms of context and learner goals, each skill is made up of different processes that involve "bottom-up" processing in which learners attend to specific data and "top-down" processing in which learners use their knowledge about the word in the process of understanding. In this section of the chapter we focus on some of the key processes that teachers and curriculum designers need to consider as they make decisions about creating materials and curriculum for teaching each of the four language skills.

Listening

Listening is a primary means of acquiring a second language. It involves a set of complex cognitive processes that allow humans to make sense of spoken language. Processing takes place at different levels of cognitive organization, such as phonological, grammatical, propositional, lexical, and discoursal (Rost, 2005). There are two processing phases around which most instruction in L2 listening revolves—*decoding* and *comprehension*—providing opportunities for L2 learners to develop skills in each phase is an important feature of a well-conceived curriculum for teaching listening skills.

When one first begins to listen to input in a language one has not heard before, the language sounds simply like noise. To help learners in the decoding phase, listening activity should be directed towards guiding learners' attention to features of the input, providing opportunities to perceive sounds, recognizing words, and listening for syntactic or grammatical parsing. Ultimately, learners need to listen for phrases and larger chunks of language rather than sounds or individual words. To achieve this goal, some researchers argue for enriched input for L2 learners (Ellis, 2003) in which learners have access to pre-recorded (i.e., scripted) texts that have numerous exemplars of the targeted structures.

Listening comprehension is the process of making meaning from the language input we hear and relating it to real-world experiences, including connecting it to the representations in one's personal memory file. Comprehension involves four processes that are overlapping in nature: (1) identifying salient information in the input; (2) activating appropriate schemata; (3) making inferences; and (4) updating representations (Rost, 2005). An L2 listening curriculum should help learners identify salient information by teaching them to recognize the strategies that proficient speakers use to signal saliency, such as intonation and pausing. Rumelhart (1980) offered the term *schema* (*schemata* as the plural and adjectival forms) to represent the organizing mechanism we have for developing long-term memories. The central component of comprehension is the activation of these schemata or concepts. Comprehending what a speaker says depends to some degree on an activation of the concepts we share with the speaker. L2 learners who may not have shared concepts with mother tongue speakers of the language need opportunities to activate their own background knowledge and to consider it in relationship to new knowledge. Helping learners make inferences and providing opportunities for discussion based on new knowledge are all important components in developing comprehension skills.

Speaking

Speaking in a second language involves knowing the linguistic forms of the language, knowing how the forms are used to fulfill various functions, and using a set of communication strategies to perform the different functions. The focus for teaching the linguistic forms in an L2—the sounds, segments, syllables, and prosodic features—has traditionally been associated with pronunciation courses (see Volume I, Chapter 6). While most English language programs include courses in pronunciation, how to structure the course in terms of learners and their goals has become complicated as English is a world language. Unlike other inter-national languages, the profile for English speakers worldwide is such that non-native speakers outnumber native speakers four to one (Graddol, 2006). This information means that non-native speakers use English more often with other non-native speakers than they do with native speakers, therefore con-founding issues of intelligibility and accent reduction, which are the hallmarks of traditional courses in English pronunciation. Jenkins (2000) offers some inter-esting views on teaching pronunciation from the perspective of English as a world language.

In addition to learning the linguistic forms of spoken English, L2 learners must know how the forms are used to fulfill a variety of functions. These functions are traditionally associated with speaking courses with a focus on interacting with partners or in small groups, and they are for the most part *interactional* (i.e., for the purpose of maintaining social relationships) and *transactional* (i.e., for the purposes of communicating information) (Tarone, 2005). When learners work in small groups and are taught strategies for clarifying, questioning, and including others in a conversation, they are working with interactional functions. When L2 learners are given instruction on how to give presentations in class, they are working with transactional functions of language. English language teachers and curriculum designers need to be certain that both functions are included in the instruction that focuses on the development of speaking skills.

Reading

Reading makes use of numerous processing skills that involve bottom-up and top-down processing. The skills that are included in L2 reading instruction should be driven by the needs of the learners and the context in which the learning is taking place. For example, a young L2 learner acquiring literacy for the first time needs a reading program in English that includes a focus on the development of the alphabetic principle and the use of decodable texts. A young adult in an academic English program at the tertiary level has needs that are different from a young non-literate learner. An academic English learner needs to be able to use text comprehension strategies to be able to understand and work with academic texts.

The following factors are likely concerns for many L2 reading programs although not all programs will include all factors, depending on learners and context (see Christison, 2014 for a discussion of each of these factors).

1. Phonological awareness and development of the alphabetic principle.[2]
2. Decoding.
3. Fluency and automatic word recognition.
4. Vocabulary development.
5. Reading comprehension strategies.
6. Access to reading materials.
7. Opportunities for sustained silent reading.

Writing

The field of L2 writing has emerged as its own discipline in the 21st Century (see Hedgcock, 2005); however, it has become quite diversified in terms of its goals (see, for example, Leki, 2000; Matsuda, Canagarajah, Harklau, Hyland, & Warschauer, 2003; Pennycook, 2001), and to date, no "unitary theory or model of L2 writing has emerged" (Hedgcock, 2005, p. 610). This means that the field encompasses different approaches to teaching L2 writing, such as a structural approach, a rhetorical approach, and a text-based approach (see Christison, 2014 and Hyland, 2003 for a review of the major approaches in L2 writing), and that English teaching programs approach L2 writing in different ways.

Some approaches are bottom-up and focus on learning to write smaller components of language first before tackling longer pieces of prose; others are top-down models and are concerned with communicating a message through an extended piece of prose, such as writing a letter or an essay. Moving from guided to free writing tasks, recognizing key features of expository text, using journals to develop fluency, developing an effective writing process, citing sources correctly, and using rhetorical structures are likely concerns for many L2 writing programs although not all programs will include all of these features. Learners and the context in which they will write should determine the choice of an L2 writing approach. Writing can be a key factor in curriculum design, such as programs that have a series of courses specifically on L2 academic writing. Writing can also be considered as just one of the language skills included in a course in an integrated skills approach to curriculum design.

Task: Explore

Think about the context in which you teach or wish to teach in the future and your understanding of the L2 learners in that context. If you were to design a curriculum for that context, what are the most important components of each of the four skills that you would include? Use the information outlined in the "Defining Language Skills" section in this chapter to focus your response. Share your results with a peer.

Conclusion

In this chapter we have considered the language skills approach to curriculum design by looking at two different models—one model in which each skill is considered separately and one in which the skills are integrated. We have also reviewed some of the theoretical foundations for each model. Finally, a significant portion of this chapter has dealt with each of the language skills and the processes involved that affect choices in a curriculum design process.

Task: Expand

Below you will find links to selected curricula for public schools in Ontario, Canada and in New Zealand. See if you can determine what the approach is to teaching the four skills by reviewing and discussing these documents with a peer.

Ministry of Education. Ontario Curriculum for language arts. Grades 1–8.

www.edu.gov.on.ca/eng/**curriculum**/elementary/**language**18currb.pdf

Ministry of Education. Ontario Curriculum for secondary. Grades 9–12.

www.edu.gov.on.ca/eng/**curriculum**/secondary/english910currb.pdf

The New Zealand Curriculum

www.nzcurriculum.tki.org.nz

Questions for Discussion

1. In your own words explain the two models that are possible for use in a language skills approach to curriculum design.
2. Give an example of a bottom-up and a top-down processing activity for each of the four skills.
3. What is enriched input for the development of L2 listening skills? Do you think it can be effective for improving listening? Why or why not?
4. Give an example of an activity you can use in the classroom to promote interactional language? Transactional language?

Notes

1. Each course met five days a week for 50 minutes or T/Th for 90 minutes. Conversation met Mondays, Wednesdays, and Fridays for 90 minutes. There were two full-time instructors who taught four courses each and an administrator who taught three courses. A part-time coordinator and a group of students who served as conversation partners, either as volunteers or on an hourly wage, staffed the conversation program.
2. *Phonological awareness* includes *phonemic awareness*—the understanding that spoken language is made up of individual speech sounds or phonemes; however, it goes beyond sounds and includes the ability to break sentences into words and words into syllables and recognize and produce rhyming words.

References

Bachman, L., & Palmer, A. (1996). *Language testing in practice.* Oxford: Oxford University Press.

Canale, M., & Swain, M. (1980). Theoretical bases of communicative approaches to second language teaching and testing. *Applied Linguistics, 1,* 1–47.

Carter, R., & Nunan, D. (2001). *The Cambridge guide to teaching English to speakers of other languages.* Cambridge: Cambridge University Press.

Christison, M. A. (2014). *Learning to teach languages.* Ann Arbor, MI: University of Michigan Press.

Ellis, R. (2003). *Task-based language learning and teaching.* Oxford: Oxford University Press.

Graddol, D. (2006). *English next.* London: The British Council.

Harris, R. (1987). *Reading Saussure.* London: Duckworth.

Hedgcock, J. S. (2005). Taking stock of research and pedagogy in L2 writing. In E. Hinkel (Ed.) *Handbook of research in second language teaching and learning* (pp. 597–613). Mahwah, NJ: Laurence Erlbaum Associates.

Hinkel, E. (2006). Current perspectives on teaching the four skills. *TESOL Quarterly Special Anniversary Issue, 40*(1), 109–132.

Howatt, A. P. R., & Widdowson, H. G. (2004). *A history of English language teaching* (2nd ed.). Oxford: Oxford University Press.

Hyland, K. (2003). *Second language writing.* Cambridge: Cambridge University Press.

Hymes, D. H. (1972). On communicative competence. In J. B. Pride and J. Holmes (Eds.), *Sociolinguistics: Selected readings* (pp. 269–293). Harmondsworth: Penguin.

Jenkins, J. (2000). *The phonology of English as an international language.* Oxford: Oxford University Press.

Joseph, J. E. (2012). *Saussure.* Oxford: Oxford University Press.

Lado, R., & Fries, C. C. (1958). *English pattern practice: Establishing the patterns of habits.* Ann Arbor, MI: University of Michigan Press.

Leki, I. (2000). Writing, literacy, and applied linguistics. *Annual Review of Applied Linguistics, 20*, 90–115.

Matsuda, P. K., Canagarajah, A. S., Harklau, L., Hyland, K., & Warschauer, M. (2003). Changing currents in second language writing research: A colloquium. *Journal of Second Language Writing, 12*, 151–179.

Oxford, R. (2001). *Integrated Skills in the ESL/EFL Classroom*. ERIC Digest ED456670. Washington, DC: ERIC Clearinghouse for ESL Literacy Education. Retrieved from http://www.ericdigests.org/2002-2/esl.htm

Nunan, D. (1989). *Designing tasks for the communicative classroom*. Cambridge: Cambridge University Press.

Pennycook, A. (2001). *Critical applied linguistics: A critical introduction*. Mahwah, NJ: Lawrence Erlbaum Associates.

Rost, M. (2005). L2 listening. In E. Hinkel (Ed.), *Handbook of research in second language teaching and learning* (pp. 503–527). Mahwah, NJ: Lawrence Erlbaum Associates.

Rumelhart, D. (1980). Schemata: The building blocks of cognition. In R. Spiro, B. Bruce, & W. Brewer (Eds.), *Theoretical issues in reading comprehension* (pp. 33–58). Hillsdale, NJ: Lawrence Erlbaum Associates.

Tarone, E. (2005). Speaking in a second language. In E. Hinkel (Ed.), *Handbook of research on second language teaching and learning* (pp. 485–502). Mahwah, NJ: Lawrence Erlbaum Associates.

Widdowson, H. G. (1978). *Teaching language as communication* (4th ed.). Oxford: Oxford University Press.

Widdowson, H. G. (1993). Perspectives on communicative language teaching: Syllabus design and methodology. In J. Alatis (Ed.), *Georgetown University Roundtable on Language and Linguistics, 1992—Language communication and social meaning* (pp. 501–507). Washington, DC: Georgetown University Press.

Part IV

Content-based Curricula

Content-based instruction (CBI) refers to any curriculum in which content is the point of departure, rather than language as in Part III. In this approach language is seen "largely as the vehicle through which subject matter content is learned rather than as the immediate object of study" (Brinton, Snow, & Wesche, 1989, p. 5). Advocates of CBI believe that language and content learning support each other. As learners acquire more language, they can access and learn more content; as they learn more content, they improve their language (for example, Stoller, 2004). Various frameworks have been proposed for CBI, the most commonly cited being that of Brinton, Snow, and Wesche (2003), who differentiate among adjunct curricula, topic curricula, and sheltered curricula. Met (1999), on the other hand, places content-based courses on a continuum with content-driven at one end and language-driven at the other.

For this volume, we have divided content-based approaches into two types: those that integrate required content such as academic subject matter in K–12 schools or at tertiary level (i.e., content and language integrated approaches); and those that choose content that is motivating and useful for learners (i.e., topical and situational approaches). Each type has a range of implementations and the differentiation is not distinct. The most defining characteristic of CBI is that language in all its complexity is driven by the linguistic needs of the content.

References

Brinton, D. M., Snow, M. A., & Wesche, M. B. (1989). *Content-based second language instruction.* New York: Newbury House.

Brinton, D. M., Snow, M. A., & Wesche, M. B. (2003). *Content-based second language instruction.* Michigan Classics Edition. Ann Arbor, MI: University of Michigan Press. [Note: The book was reprinted in 2003 by University of Michigan Press as a Classics Edition with a change in copyright and with no change in the body of the text. A preface, glossary of terms, and a short update on CBI since 1989 were added in the front matter.]

Met, M. (1999). *Content-based instruction: Defining terms, making decisions.* NFLC Reports. Washington, DC: The National Foreign Language Center.

Stoller, F. L. (2004). Content-based instruction: Perspectives on curriculum planning. *Annual Review of Applied Linguistics, 24,* 261–28.

Chapter 14

The Integration of Content and Language

VIGNETTE

I am interviewing an IT[1] teacher whose class consists of immigrants and refugees. Attached to the IT class is an English class, taught by an ESL teacher, who observes IT classes and collaborates with the IT instructors to develop a supporting English language curriculum. When asked about the difficulties in trying to arrange such an adjunct class, John explains,[2] "The bureaucracy plain and simple. I have a Certificate 2 in Information Technology. There are minimum entry requirements. I have to prove that they [the immigrants/refugees] met minimum entry requirements. The minimum entry requirements are that they must have studied to Year 10 of high school or done Year 11 IT studies or a particular range of subjects in Year 12, and how can you possibly say that for somebody from the refugee camp who's got no paperwork. How can I enroll them? And I have spent a lot of time trying to convince people that they need to make exceptions to the rules to get this up and under way. As it was, we just got a director's dispensation.

We knew that these students came from a different set of backgrounds, and we knew that teaching styles were going to have to be different. We are going to have to accommodate them. We call it hand holding. We do a lot more hand holding than we probably do with the IT students.

As far as the English side is concerned, I couldn't say whether they're missing out on English. I think it's probably going to be swings and roundabouts. What they lose in a lot of the oral English they'll probably make up with the written because, for example, one of the tasks that we give them is to install Windows. They have to be able to take a computer and install Windows on there and modify it so it suits their requirement or a client's requirements." [Murray, research notes]

Task: Reflect

1. What surprised you about this interview?
2. What do you think John means by "hand holding"?
3. What do you think the English teacher would have to teach to prepare the students for the IT class on installing Windows?
4. How important do you think it is for these particular learners to take an introductory IT course?

Introduction

Pedagogic practices for English language teaching have been evolving in response to the growth of English as a world language. Content and language integration is a practice that has emerged in response to these demographic changes. It provides a means of teaching English through the study of content. In a content and language integrated approach, language learners are not expected to have proficiency in English before working with subject matter content. Language support is provided alongside instruction for content area specializations.

The integration of language and content is a concern for teachers working in many different contexts. For example, in US public schools content and language integrated courses include both native speakers (L1) and ELLs in the same classroom and are most often taught by content area teachers. In the vignette, the IT content and language integrated course for adult learners was taught by a content area teacher who was an IT specialist; however, he also collaborated with a language specialist. Content and language integrated courses can also be taught by English specialists who have developed content area expertise. In Europe and other countries, teaching curriculum subjects, such as math and geography, through the medium of English is often done in secondary schools with learners who have already gained basic skills with English during primary English study. Teachers are also content area specialists who are proficient speakers of English. In each of these different contexts, teachers must be concerned about the development of subject matter expertise alongside English language skills. Many practitioners believe that a general English curriculum (e.g., a skills-based or structured approach) cannot prepare learners for the demanding linguistic, rhetorical, and contextual challenges of the real world (Johns, 1997).

In this chapter we will explore the notion of content and language integration in syllabus design. We will first take a broad overview of the concept by looking at some of the different ways content and language integration is manifested in English language teaching and some of the specific terms that are used. We then turn our attention to options for delivery of instruction and characteristics of content and language integrated courses and programs as we see them. Finally, we look at two specific models for integrating content and language—an adjunct model and a sheltered instruction model known as SIOP (Sheltered Instructional Observation Protocol) (Echevarria, Vogt, & Short, 2008).

Defining Content and Language Integration

There are a number of terms used to describe the integration of language and content. We use the general term content and language integration as an umbrella term to refer to courses and programs that make a dual commitment to the development of subject matter expertise and language skills. We recognize that there are a number of terms that are associated with specific programs or contexts. We review some of the most common ones here, but the list is not meant to be exhaustive.

Content-based Instruction (CBI)

In the U.S., content-based instruction (CBI) is the term most commonly used as an umbrella term to refer to all types of programs that make a dual commitment to content and language development. The term has been widely used to reference programs for both adults and children (Crandall, 1993; Stoller, 2004). Brinton, Snow, and Wesche (2003) were the first to delineate different models that are used for CBI (e.g., theme-based, sheltered, and adjunct models) in a variety of contexts. The term applies to courses taught by both content area specialists who are most often L1 speakers of English, as well as English language teachers. The term has been used to describe content and language integration in programs consistently for over 40 years (see, for example, Cantoni-Harvey, 1987, as well as Bassano & Christison, 1992; Christison & Bassano, 1992, 1997; Grabe & Stoller, 1997). In addition, CBI is not associated with any particular "designer" or researcher.

Content and Language Integrated Learning (CLIL)

Content and language integrated learning (CLIL) is a recent movement for integrating language and content in Europe (see the example of Germany discussed in Volume I, Chapter 3). In general, it involves learning in a curricular subject through the medium of a non-native language, such as studying history or geography in English in countries such as Spain, Germany, or France. The European Commission (www.ec.europa.eu/education/language-teaching/doc236_en.htm) states that CLIL has been found to be effective in all sectors of education from primary through to adult and higher education. This finding is not surprising and mirrors results for content and language integration elsewhere. Teachers working with CLIL in Europe are content specialists in their own disciplines and are proficient speakers of the target language (in this case, English). Implementation varies widely as there is no established orthodoxy for CLIL. Is should be noted that other countries outside of Europe have tried to adopt a content and language integrated model with different results from CLIL in Europe, such as in Malaysia, where they abandoned it. The reasons for the differences in outcomes are complicated (see Chapter 3 for further discussion and Patel, 2012).

Sheltered Instruction

In North America the term *sheltered instruction* has been used to describe an instructional model for content and language integration. The term originally referred to a content and language integrated class for L2 learners that was typically taught by an English specialist with content area expertise. In its current use in the U.S., it refers to a model of providing content and language instruction in classrooms with both first and second language (L2) speakers (Echevarria & Graves, 2007). In the U.S. it is also known as *structured immersion*, SDAIE (specially designed academic instruction in English), CELT (content-based English language teaching), and *mainstreaming*.[3] The primary goal of sheltered instruction is to make grade-level academic subject matter comprehensible for all learners through the use of various types of scaffolding techniques. One of the most widely used models for sheltered instruction in North America is SIOP (Sheltered Instructional Observation Protocol). SIOP will be covered in detail later in this chapter. Another SI model that has been widely used is CALLA (Cognitive Academic Language Learning Approach) (Chamot & O'Malley, 1994). This model focuses on three components: content, language, and learning strategies.

Workplace Literacy

A number of different acronyms have been used to describe programs that integrate language and content in workplace environments (see Volume II, Chapter 9 for an extensive discussion of workplace literacy). In the U.S. the term VESL (Vocational English as a Second Language) has been used (Wong, 1997), and Australians employ the term English for the workplace (EWP).

English for Specific Purposes (ESP)

English for specific purposes (ESP) is a term that has been widely used in international contexts to describe courses for adults who have immediate and identifiable needs, such as specific writing or reading needs related to a workplace or to academic contexts. ESP specialists work closely with experts in the disciplines to determine what learners will be required to do and how to design activities to assist learners in interacting with content in context-appropriate ways. One of us (Christison) taught a small group of four L2 learners who were all studying automotive mechanics in the vocational school at a college. Their automotive mechanics teachers (i.e., the discipline expert) asked the ESP specialist (Christison) to provide instruction that targeted reading of the automotive blueprints and becoming familiar with the required language. The automotive mechanics teacher commented, "It's not their general English skills I'm worried about. I'm not trying to sit down and have a conversation with these boys. My job is to certify them as mechanics. They all have a good sense about cars, but if they cannot read the printouts and the blueprints, I won't be able to recommend them for a certificate." In ESL settings, EAP (English for Academic Purposes) is the term often used in place of ESP (Benesch, 2001; Johns, 1992).

Options for the Delivery of Instruction

There are three potential options available for the delivery of instruction for content and language integrated courses. Either the English language teacher or the content area specialist can deliver the instruction. In addition, the language teacher and content area specialist can collaborate with each other, thereby taking advantage of shared expertise, as in the vignette.

English Language Teacher or Specialist

In this option, the English language teacher or specialist delivers the instruction for the content and language integrated course. The advantage of this option is that the English language teacher already has expertise in how to teach language and is already sensitive to the language needs of the learners. The disadvantage is that the English language teacher may not have sufficient background in the content area. Developing expertise at the level needed for secondary and university content areas may not be a realistic expectation for English language teachers unless they were also content area specialists and had developed expertise in a content area.

Content Area Specialist

In this option, the content area specialist delivers the instruction. The obvious advantage of this option is the content area expertise of the teacher. The disadvantage is that the content area specialist may not know enough about language, thereby making it difficult to provide the necessary modifications in instruction to make content comprehensible for English learners (see Volume I, Part II on language awareness). CLIL teachers are most often content teachers who are proficient non-native speakers of English. In the U.S., content teachers are most often native speakers who may or may not have experience in learning another language. For either of these groups of content area specialists, teacher language awareness is critical.

Collaborative Effort

The third option for the delivery of instruction is a collaborative effort between English language and content area specialists (see the adjunct model in this chapter for further discussion and exemplars). Some programs have had success using this option (Gee, 1997; Johns & Dudley Evans, 1991). This type of collaboration seems to be both desirable and necessary, yet despite the instructional desirability of this option there are often reasons why it is not implemented. For example, programs often lack the financial resources or flexibility in personnel to assign more than one instructor to cover a course.

Characteristics of Content and Language Integration

Although many English language-teaching programs in many different contexts promote the integration of language and content, there is no single methodology supported by the field, but the focus for all of the programs is making content and language comprehensible for language learners. It is beyond the scope of this short chapter to list all of the techniques that teachers might use to make this happen. Instead, we have identified six characteristics that are common to content and language integration in most contexts.

Identifying Content Concepts

In each content area (whether it is in physics or adult life skills), teachers must first be concerned about determining the content knowledge that learners must master. Planning for content does not begin at the level of a lesson, but rather at the level of a unit or a course, so that all content is connected, such as in theme-based teaching. We see the connected feature of content as one of the chief differences between a content and language integrated approach and a topical and situational approach (see Chapter 15 in this volume for more information on a topics and situational approach to curriculum design). In a content and language integrated approach, the most important questions that teachers and course designers can ask themselves are the following: What information should students know at the end of a course or unit? What important questions should they be able to answer? How are the content concepts connected? In terms of planning, this is where teachers who integrate language and content begin. Figure 14.1 provides a conceptual framework or flow chart for the identification of content concepts, beginning at the top level. The bi-directional arrows indicate connections that must be established between concepts, sub-topics, and lessons.

When content concepts have been determined in a hierarchical manner as in Figure 14.1, the essential details associated with individual lessons can be created.

Writing Content and Language Objectives

Once content concepts have been identified (in the hierarchical manner suggested in Figure 14.1) and important questions have been framed, teachers

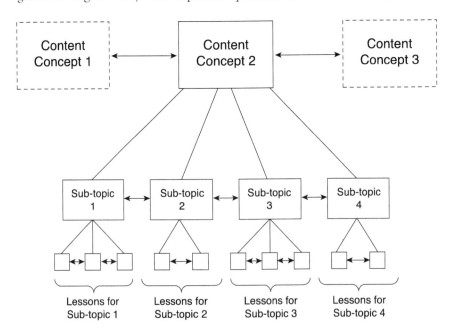

Figure 14.1 A Conceptual Framework for Identifying Content Concepts

Reprinted from Murray, D. E., & Christison, M. A. (2011) *What English Language Teachers Need to Know Volume II: Facilitating Learning* (p.156). New York: Routledge/Taylor & Francis.

determine what learners will do in order to demonstrate their understanding of the content concepts. These understandings are written as performance objectives for content concepts because the focus is on student performance—what they will actually do to demonstrate their knowledge of the content concepts. In Chapter 3 in this volume, we discussed performance objectives and outlined the four main components that are necessary for writing effective performance objectives. We review these components in an abbreviated form here. Criteria for performance objectives include identifying (1) what students will be able to do (e.g., the thinking skills: identify, list, categorize, tell, etc.); (2) what they are expected to learn (i.e., the content concept); (3) how they will demonstrate what they have learned (i.e., what strategies they will use); and (4) what the conditions for practice will be (e.g., grouping strategies, time allocated, type of input, or type of response).

Deriving Language from Content

Most content specialists have difficulty in identifying and creating language objectives. In the planning process, language objectives cannot be determined in advance of content because the content one chooses determines the language that learners will need. Language objectives must be derived from content objectives. In our experience in working with content specialists, those who have experienced the most success in writing language objectives wrote them once content objectives had been established and appropriate texts (construed broadly here to include all types of text, including media, and not simply textbooks) had been chosen.

Many teachers have found it useful to think about the language related to concepts in two different categories—*content-obligatory language* and *content-compatible language* (Snow, Met, & Genesee, 1989). Content-obligatory language is the language that must be learned in order to understand the content concepts. Content-compatible language is language that supports the students in learning the content but is not critical to understanding the content concepts.

Managing Demands on Cognition

Another characteristic of content and language integration is the purposeful attention given to managing demands on cognition. Skutnabb-Kangas and Toukomaa (1976) first made the distinction between "surface fluency" and "conceptual-linguistic knowledge" in a second language. Cummins (1979, 1980, 1992, 2001) later formalized these terms as basic interpersonal skills (BICS) and cognitive academic language proficiency (CALP) (see Chapter 10 in this volume for further discussion on these concepts). Inventories of thinking skills, such as Bloom's Taxonomy (see Chapter 10 in this volume), are useful to both language and content specialists in managing demands on cognition as they help teachers and curriculum designers categorize and select tasks in terms of how cognitively demanding they are. When content concepts are more demanding, teachers should select familiar or less complicated language and process the concepts using familiar learning strategies. When concepts are less cognitively challenging, teachers can select more complicated language and introduce new strategies for learning. When the language is difficult, teachers should think about initially selecting thinking skills that are cognitively less demanding.

It has been our experience in working with both content and language specialists that identifying content concepts, writing clear objectives, deriving language from content, managing demands on cognition, teaching strategies for learning, and checking for understanding are the defining features of second and foreign language programs for integrating language and content that promote positive outcomes for their students.

Task: Explore

Use Figure 14.1 above to help you design a conceptual framework for a content and language integrated unit for a course you teach or might wish to teach in the future.

Content and Language Integrated Models

Content-based programs have been heavily criticized on both pragmatic and theoretical grounds because "instructors can only have a limited understanding of the writing that students compose for their content courses and so [ESP scholars] have thus advocated different forms of collaboration between EAP instructors and instructors in the disciplines" (Molle & Prior, 2008, p. 553). We now discuss one such collaboration between English language teachers and discipline instructors, in an adjunct model, as in the vignette. This section also discusses a model for sheltered instruction referred to as SIOP that has been widely used by content area specialists.

The Adjunct Model

Although *adjunct* programs have been used for some time, Brinton, Snow, and Wesche (1989) were the first to describe a framework for CBI in relationship to the model. They defined an adjunct model as follows:

> In this model, students are enrolled concurrently in two linked courses—a language course and a content course—with the idea being that the two courses share the content base and complement each other in terms of mutually coordinated assignments (p. 16).

While this is the definition for the prototypical adjunct program, many variations exist in actual implementation, so, for our purposes in this chapter, we will use adjunct to refer to any curriculum in which content and language teachers collaborate with the goal of helping learners achieve content goals. We will discuss the variations further in the section on implementation.

Major Characteristics of the Adjunct Model

Although there may be a variety of implementation options, adjunct programs have a number of features in common:

- collaboration and coordination between a content/discipline teacher and a language teacher

- administrative resources to support such coordination
- a need for the language teacher to have some mastery of the content area
- a language component oriented around the discipline content, including:
  - o vocabulary
  - o grammar
  - o materials, often authentic discipline materials
  - o assignments, and
  - o assessments oriented around the discipline.

Adjunct programs are more common in ESL situations, although some do occur in EFL contexts. How then are these principles and characteristics realized in actual curricula?

Implementation

Adjunct approaches have been primarily used in higher education. Higher education itself, however, is diverse. For example, the two programs described by Brinton, Snow, and Wesche (2003) were for freshmen at UCLA and for Francophone and Anglophone students at the University of Ottawa. Benesch's (1988) edited volume details a variety of different college-level programs that have linked courses. In contrast, the program referred to in the vignette was for immigrants and refugees at a Technical and Further Education (TAFE) institute in Australia.

As indicated in the vignette, this TAFE program links an introductory credit-bearing course on IT to a language course. The language instructor observed all the IT classes and based her language instruction on the content of those classes. The two instructors met frequently to coordinate instruction. Students were graded in each class separately. The goal was for the learners to achieve credit for the content class, as well as meet the language requirements for the Adult Migrant English Program (see Chapters 11 and 20 for more information on the curriculum for the AMEP). As well as the language support provided by the adjunct language class, students were supported in the IT class by an instructor who understood their language needs and adjusted instruction accordingly.

Thus, the curriculum for the language course required considerable juggling on the part of the language instructor. She had to include:

- IT language (vocabulary, sentence structures, genres, and pragmatics)
- genres specified by the AMEP curriculum, and
- competencies from the AMEP curriculum.

The link could be achieved because the AMEP curriculum is genre-based and many of the genres are sufficiently broad that genres in the IT class could fit as models and could be used for assessment. One of us (Murray) observed a class in which the language teacher was playing a listening tape for a help desk. She was asking students questions such as: What's the problem? What's the relationship like? What are the suggestions? Do they fix the problem? Then, she elicited from the students some of the language the help desk worker used in the tape, such as: *How can I help you? Can I just ask you a few questions? Is there paper in the printer?* The help desk dialog meets the AMEP language requirement of "Can participate in a spoken transactional exchange." At the same time, it meets IT content curriculum objectives.

Issues in an Adjunct Curriculum

As indicated in the introduction, an issue in both ESP (including EAP) and CBI is whether English language teachers should or can have the knowledge of disciplines in order to teach academic content (Bruce, 2002). Adjunct programs are considered a possible solution to this dilemma. However, as we demonstrated in the examples of implementation, language teachers still need to be able to navigate the discipline content.

A further issue is that such programs place language in the service of other disciplines. There is a tension between content and language, and often language loses out. Students themselves may be more interested in following up on content in their language class than in any general language development the language teacher may choose (Guyer & Peterson, 1988). They may even see the language course as a tutoring program for the discipline (Iancu, 1993). Benesch (1996) adds that the "pragmatic stance" (p. 736) means that teachers have accepted the status quo of institutionalized power differentials, rather than taking a critical pedagogic approach to them. She discusses her own efforts in a linked psychology/ESL class, in which she helped students challenge the anonymous, large-scale lecture mode that alienated them from the psychology lecturer, by inviting him to the smaller ESL class. He willingly engaged in dialogue with the students, humanizing himself and the subject matter for the students. The language teachers themselves may also feel disempowered, being the "flight attendants" to the discipline faculty "in the cockpit" (Goldstein, Campbell, & Cummings, 1997). The collaboration and coordination required for a successful linkage means that the institution has to support the linkage with funding to allow faculty time to talk with each other about their courses (Guyer & Peterson, 1988). Often these collaborations begin through grants but are then not sustainable.

The Sheltered Instruction Model

In this section we discuss SIOP, a sheltered instructional model for CBI. It is a research-based and validated model of sheltered instruction that has been widely and successfully used across the U.S. for over 15 years. The SIOP Model is intended to support K–12 content area teachers who have both L1 and L2 students in their classes. The model helps teachers plan and deliver lessons that support English learners in acquiring academic knowledge as they also develop English language proficiency. The Center for Applied Linguistics (CAL) participated in the development of the SIOP Model and continues to conduct SIOP research (www.cal.org).

Major Characteristics

The SIOP Model consists of eight interrelated components: lesson preparation, building background, comprehensible input, strategies, interaction, practice/application, lesson delivery, and review/assessment. There are 30 teacher indicators (i.e., teachers' actions) associated with the eight components, such as content objectives being defined, displayed, and reviewed with students or use of a variety of question types, including those that promote higher level thinking skills. These indicators are associated with positive outcomes for learners (Echevarria, Short, & Powers, 2006; Echevarria, Vogt, & Short, 2008). Although originally designed as a protocol for classroom observation (Guarino et al., 2001), it has since been updated and revised. Teachers now use SIOP in planning for instruction and in lesson delivery. The original researchers and authors have extended SIOP materials beyond the list of teacher indicators to provide ideas for classroom activities that support the model (Vogt & Echevaria, 2007). Although the teacher indicators have remained consistent, the original researchers and authors have developed versions of SIOP for elementary and secondary foci (Echevaria, Vogt, & Short, 2013a, 2013b).

Implementation

CAL collaborates with schools, states, and districts to design and conduct SIOP Model professional development programs. There are a number of different workshops and support services available (see www.siopinstitute.net or www.cal.org). The SIOP team provides a range of services, including workshops, coaching, site visits, and technical assistance. The team works closely with teachers, professional development specialists, school and district coaches, administrators, and paraprofessionals as they learn to plan, implement, and support instruction using the SIOP Model. They also support the development of district and school level coaches who can assist teachers in implementing the model.

Teachers can work independently with SIOP as the teacher indicators are clearly and succinctly described. Because schools and districts want to make a positive impact on student learning and go beyond what is possible with an individual teacher, they try to implement peer coaching models that support a team of teachers in implementing the SIOP model (see implementation options for SIOP: www.cal.org).

Issues with the SIOP Model

The issues with sheltered instruction and, consequently, with the SIOP Model are not so much issues with sheltered instruction or SIOP but are related to the expectations of teachers, schools, districts, and states for the academic achievement of English learners. This is particularly the case in contexts where English learners are educated in classrooms alongside native speakers. The SIOP Model was never meant to serve as a quick fix. In order for the SIOP or any other model of sheltered instruction to be successful, these indicators need to be implemented consistently over time and built into the teaching culture of schools or districts.

The SIOP Model looks deceptively simple because the indicators are well organized and clearly stated; however, in reality, the model is complex and many layered. It requires commitment and hard work over the long term to unpack the specific features of instruction that underlie the broadly stated indicators. It is difficult for some teachers to remain committed to changing instruction even with the considerable support available for SIOP practitioners. The SIOP Model is often embraced with great enthusiasm initially; however, if expectations are not met, enthusiasm for the model often wanes. Unfortunately, some teachers continue to give lip service to the model when, in fact, they are not diligent in attending to the indicators. This is not a fault of the model.

Conclusion

In this chapter we present the content and language integrated approach to curriculum design. We introduce several terms used to describe programs in this approach, such as CBI, CLIL, workplace literacy, and ESP. The options for the delivery of instruction are also discussed, as well as the defining characteristics of content and language integrated programs. Two models of content and language instruction—the adjunct model and SIOP—are presented and discussed.

Task: Expand

Explore at least one of the following websites and find an activity of a suggestion not covered in this chapter to share with a partner or a small group.

www.ec.europa.eu/education/languages
www.teachingenglish.org.uk
www.clilcompendium.com
www.onestopenglish.com/section.asp?docid=144587
www.tesol.org
www.everythingesl.net/inservices/internet_resources.php
www.siopinstitute.net
www.cal.org/siop/

Questions for Discussion

1. In your own words, explain the advantages and disadvantages of each option for the delivery of instruction in a content and language integrated approach.
2. What are the main characteristics of the content and language integrated approach?
3. What is sheltered instruction? How is it different from an adjunct model?
4. In your own words, explain the adjunct model. In what contexts do you think an adjunct model might be preferable for English learners?
5. What is SIOP? In your own words, explain how it works.

Notes

1. Information Technology.
2. The transcript has only been altered for clarification.
3. We use the term *mainstreaming* here to refer to the placement of L2 students in classrooms originally designed for L1 speakers of English. In other contexts mainstreaming is a term

used only in connection with special education students. Mainstreaming for English language learners (ELLs) has a negative connotation because content area teachers may not have developed skills as language specialists and, therefore, do not know how to integrate language and content effectively. The intent of mainstreaming was predicated on shared responsibility for the education of all children. Content area specialists were to develop skills as language specialists sufficient to be able to integrate language and content for the ELLs in their courses. Developing a cadre of content area teachers who also have skills as language specialists and socializing content area teachers in schools to embrace these dual responsibilities has been immensely challenging.

References

Bassano, S. K., & Christison, M. A. (1992). *Life sciences: Content and learning strategies.* White Plains, NY: Longman.

Benesch, S. (Ed.). (1988). *Ending remediation: Linking ESL and content in higher education.* Washington, DC: Teachers of English to Speakers of Other Languages.

Benesch, S. (1996). Needs analysis and curriculum development in EAP: An example of a critical approach. *TESOL Quarterly, 30*(4), 723–738.

Benesch, S. (2001). *Critical English for academic purposes: Theory, politics and practice.* Mahwah, NJ: Lawrence Erlbaum Associates.

Brinton, D. M., Snow, M. A., & Wesche, M. B. (1989). *Content-based second language instruction.* New York: Newbury House.

Brinton, D. M., Snow, M. A., & Wesche, M. B. (2003). *Content-based second language instruction.* Michigan Classics Edition. Ann Arbor, MI: University of Michigan Press.

Bruce, N. (2002). Dovetailing language and content: Teaching balanced argument in legal problem answer writing. *English for Specific Purposes, 21*(4), 321–345.

Cantoni-Harvey, G. (1987) (Ed.). *Content area instruction: Approaches and strategies.* Reading, MA: Addison-Wesley.

Chamot, A. U., & O'Malley, J. M. (1994). *The CALLA Handbook: Implementing the Cognitive Academic Language Learning Approach.* Reading, MA: Addison-Wesley.

Christison, M. A., & Bassano, S. K. (1992). *Earth and physical sciences: Content and learning strategies.* White Plains, NY: Longman.

Christison, M. A., & Bassano, S. K. (1997). *Social studies: Content and learning strategies.* White Plains, NY: Longman.

Crandall, J. (1993). Content-centered learning in the United States. *Annual Review of Applied Linguistics, 13,* 111–126.

Cummins, J. (1979). Cognitive academic language proficiency, linguistic interdependence, the optimum age question and some other matters. *Working Papers on Bilingualism, 19,* 121–129.

Cummins, J. (1980). The exit and entry fallacy of bilingual education. *NABE Journal, 4,* 25–29.

Cummins, J. (1992). Language proficiency, bilingualism, and academic achievement. In P. Richard-Amato & M. A. Snow (Eds.) *The multicultural classroom: Readings for content-area teachers* (pp. 16–26). New York: Longman.

Cummins, J. (2001). *Negotiating identities: Education for empowerment in a diverse society* (2nd ed.). Sacramento, CA: California Association of Bilingual Education.

Echevarria, J., & Graves, A. (2007). *Sheltered content instruction.* New York: Pearson Education.

Echevarria, J., Short, D., & Powers, K. (2006). School reform and standards-based education: An instructional model for English-language learners. *Journal of Educational Research, 99,* 195–210.

Echevarria, J., Vogt, M. E., & Short, D. (2008). *Making content comprehensible for English language learners: The SIOP® Model* (3rd ed.). New York: Pearson Education.

Echevarria, J., Vogt, M. E., & Short, D. (2013a). *Making content comprehensible for English elementary learners: The SIOP® model*. New York: Pearson Education.

Echevarria, J., Vogt, M. E., & Short, D. (2013b). *Making content comprehensible for English secondary learners: The SIOP® model*. New York: Pearson Education.

Gee, Y. (1997). ESL and Content Teachers: Working Effectively in Adjunct Courses. In M. A. Snow & D. M. Brinton (Eds.), *The content-based classroom: Perspectives on integrating language and content* (pp. 324–330). White Plains, NY: Addison-Wesley Longman.

Goldstein, L. M., Campbell, C., & Cummings, M. C. (1997). Smiling through the turbulence: The flight attendant syndrome and other issues of writing instructor status in the adjunct model. In M. A. Snow & D. M. Brinton (Eds.), *The content-based classroom: Perspectives on integrating language and content* (pp. 331–339). New York: Longman.

Grabe, W., & Stoller, F. L. (1997). Content-based instruction: Research foundations. In M. A. Snow & D. M. Brinton (Eds.), *The content-based classroom* (pp. 5–21). White Plains, NY: Addison-Wesley Longman.

Guarino, A. J., Echevarria, J., Short, D., Schick, J. E., Forbes, S., & Rueda, R. (2001). The sheltered instruction observation protocol: Reliability and validity assessment. *Journal of Research in Education, 11*, 138–140.

Guyer, E., & Peterson, P. W. (1988). Language and/or content? Principles and procedures for materials development in an adjunct course. In S. Benesch (Ed.), *Ending remediation: Linking ESL and content in higher education* (pp. 91–111). Washington, DC: Teachers of English to Speakers of Other Languages.

Iancu, M. (1993). Adapting the adjunct model: A case study. *TESOL Journal, 2*(4), 20–24.

Johns, A. (1992). What is the relationship between content-based instruction and English for specific purposes? *The CATESOL Journal, 5*(1), 71–75.

Johns, A. M. (1997). English for specific purposes and content-based instruction: What is the relationship? In M. A. Snow & D. M. Brinton (Eds.), *The content-based classroom: Perspectives on integrating language and content* (pp. 363–366). White Plains, NY: Addison-Wesley Longman.

Johns, A. M., & Dudley-Evans, T. (1991). English for specific purposes: International scope, specific in purpose. *TESOL Quarterly, 25*, 297–314.

Molle, D., & Prior, P. (2008). Multimodal genre systems in EAP writing pedagogy: Reflecting on a needs analysis. *TESOL Quarterly, 42*(4), 541–566.

Patel, M. (2012). The ETeMS project in Malaysia: English for the teaching of mathematics and science. In C. Tribble (Ed.), *Managing change in English language teaching: Lessons from experience* (pp. 109–113). London: British Council.

Skutnabb-Kangas, T., & Toukomaa, P. (1976). *Teaching migrant children's mother tongue and learning the language of the host country in the context of the socio-cultural situation of migrant family*. Helsinki: The Finnish National Commission for UNESCO.

Snow, M. A., Met, M., & Genesee, F. (1989). A conceptual framework for the integration of language and content in second/foreign language instruction. *TESOL Quarterly, 23*, 201–217.

Stoller, F. L. (2004). Content-based instruction: Perspectives on curriculum planning. *Annual Review of Applied Linguistics, 24*, 261–283.

Vogt, M. E., & Echevaria, J. (2007). *99 ideas and activities for teaching English learners with The SIOP® model*. New York: Pearson.

Wong, K. (1997). VESL and content-based instruction: What do they have in common? In M. A. Snow & D. M. Brinton (Eds.), *The content-based classroom: Perspectives on integrating language and content* (pp. 359–362). White Plains, NY: Addison-Wesley Longman.

Chapter 15

Topical and Situational Approaches

VIGNETTE

One of my former graduate students has taken a job as a materials developer/ curriculum designer for a private language school in Japan. He has been asked to develop ten units of study and has been given four months to develop the materials. In four months' time, he will be departing for Japan and working there for a year creating and adapting teaching materials, doing some program administration, and teaching the course that he is designing, among others. The school has decided to add a course for its students that will focus on higher education study in the U.S., and it is this course for which the ten units are targeted. The school has given him the situations for the ten units already, explaining that these are the situations that they want students to study, and they want communicative language teaching (CLT) as the methodology. Each unit is to have five lessons that can be completed during a 90-minute class. The units they have specified are as follows: at the airport, at the dorm, at the supermarket, at the post office, at school, in the computer lab, in the classroom, at a restaurant, at a party, and on a date. These are not the situations that I would have chosen given the intent of the course, and I suspect they are not the ones that my former graduate student would have chosen either; nevertheless, he believes that they are not really negotiable and that he should try to do his best to accommodate their wishes. He also said that the situations were very general, giving him a great deal of flexibility. Although he is excited about this project, he has come to me for help. He says that he feels a little bit lost in this process and is wondering if I can advise him on how to get started by suggesting a plan or a taxonomy for the first unit. [Christison, research notes]

Task: Reflect

Do you find each of the situations presented to the curriculum designer in the vignette equally useful considering the goals of the project? Are these the situations you would have chosen? If you were asked to develop units for teaching English that were to be based on situations similar to the ones in the vignette, how would you begin? What organizational framework or taxonomy might you use? Do you think that having the situations for the units and the number of lessons in each unit specified in advance will prove helpful in designing the curriculum? Why or why not?

Introduction

Topical and situational approaches to curriculum design are often considered separately, so you may be wondering why we have put both topical and situational approaches together in one chapter. We have linked topical and situational approaches in curriculum design because both approaches are focused on the practice of teaching grammatical structures and vocabulary as dictated by a specific topic and/or situation. In addition, as the field of English language teaching developed and matured and as views of language as communication took prominence among language-teaching professionals, the importance of considering topics within specific situations has grown in popularity.

The relationship between topics and situations can be seen on a continuum. At one end is the general English view, in which topics are seen in relationship to basic language proficiency. In this view topics are included in the curriculum with no specific situation in mind because the topics are basic to all situations (e.g., food, clothing, color, shapes). When approaching curriculum design from this point of view, designers begin with the topics, rather than beginning with the situations in which the topics occur. At the other end of the continuum are topics that are only used for specific situations, such as situations that require a great deal of technical language. When approaching curriculum design from this point of view, designers begin with the specific situation and consider only those topics that are relevant and useful for L2 learners in that situation.

In between the two ends of the continuum are points that represent other types of relationships between topics and situations. For example, one type of relationship begins with situations that are quite general, and then topics are selected. In the vignette, the situations that were given to the curriculum designer were general in the sense that topics within these situations apply to a large number of students who would be seeking higher education experiences in the U.S., however they would not include all learners, for example, non-academic adult immigrant learners. Nevertheless, this relationship is different from the relationship between topics and the situation exemplified in the learner driver example in this chapter (see The Learner Driver Curriculum in this chapter). In this case, the topics are selected for a specific purpose, yet no specific situation has been identified. Both of these examples demonstrate different relationships between topics and situations that can be represented through different locations on a topical-situational continuum. By using the term topical-situational approach, we hope to capture a more realistic view of the relationship between topics and situations in the curriculum design process than we could do by considering each of them separately.

The principal organizing feature of a topical-situational approach is identifying what and how language is used with a particular topic and/or in a particular situation, and grammatical structures and vocabulary are identified and learned as they become important for talking about a topic or in a situation. This chapter will focus on a topical-situational approach to curriculum design by reviewing its beginnings in the Oral Approach or Situational Language Teaching, defining the procedures for creating this type of curriculum, and discussing the issues that arise in its use, as well as its influence on textbook design, including the types of classroom activities that support it. We also offer examples of topical-situational curricula in practice.

Situational Language Teaching

The topical-situational approach to curriculum design that we propose in this chapter has its roots in Oral Approach or Situational Language Teaching. The Oral Approach as a methodology originated in the early 20th Century and is associated with the work of British linguists A. S. Hornby (1954) and Harold Palmer (1923) and their focus on developing an approach to language teaching that was more communicative than structural (see Chapter 8 in this volume). The Oral Approach was based on a set of principles for the selection and organization of content. There was an emphasis on vocabulary and grammatical structures, particularly as they related to improvements in reading. The early work on vocabulary led to the creation of a basic list of vocabulary words for teaching English (West, 1953). Coinciding with the interest in vocabulary was the focus on grammatical content. English was analyzed into sentence patterns that could be used to internalize English sentence structure. The work resulted in a standard reference for English sentence patterns for English teachers and textbook writers (Hornby, 1954).

Another emphasis for the Oral Approach was the situation in which the vocabulary and grammatical structures were to be taught. The focus on a specific situation came about as a result of the influence of linguists such as M. A. K. Halliday (1973, 1975), who emphasized that language structure needs to be tied to meaning and to a context or situation. As a result of this emphasis on situations, the approach became known as Situational Language Teaching.

Hornby's 1954 *Guide to Patterns and Usage in English* presented procedures for developing a curriculum based on situations. It included how to: (1) select vocabulary and grammatical structures; (2) sequence these items; and (3) introduce new items in context or in the situation. For Hornby, the context to which the syllabus was linked was the classroom. Current approaches to situational curriculum design have gone beyond topics that are useful in the context of a classroom. They include a broad array of real-life topics (see examples included in this chapter) depending on the needs and interests of L2 learners (see Richards & Rodgers, 2001, pp. 36–49 for additional background and further discussion on Situational Language Teaching).

Traditionally, situational language teaching began with spoken language. Language forms and vocabulary were taught orally before they were presented in written form. Common techniques for introducing spoken language in situational language teaching were dialogs or short listening passages, and these classroom activities manifested themselves in teaching materials. Language structures were also taught inductively. Explanations of grammar were discouraged as learners were expected to deduce the meaning of vocabulary and structures based on the situation. Teachers tried to make certain that learners had ample opportunities to deduce target language meanings through the practice activities and the specific examples. The language practice techniques that were most commonly used to help learners deduce meaning with this approach were choral repetition (particularly of dialogs), dictation (including partner dictations), drills (including mechanical and communicative), controlled oral-based reading, and guided writing tasks. These language practice techniques found their way into many of the materials associated with situational language teaching. As the field matured and developed and as communicative language teaching grew in popularity, the practices associated with situational language teaching changed. Modern English language teaching methodologies use situations to anchor language-teaching materials but do not necessarily subscribe to the principles or use the traditional practice activities that underpinned early views of Situational Language Teaching.

Topics in Language Teaching

A topic is a concept or an idea that is, hopefully, interesting to the learners but at least necessary. In a general English curriculum, there has been a traditional set of topics covered in most beginning level textbooks, such as colors, food, clothing, shopping, jobs, animals, furniture, or tools. These topics are covered in most general English textbooks because the related vocabulary associated with these topics was thought to be necessary for the development of basic language skills. The vocabulary words that are associated with these topics are called *semantic sets* (see Chapter 12 in this volume). The focus of a topical approach to language teaching is not on learning new concepts but is primarily on learning words in the target language that are necessary for talking about known concepts. Of course, it is also possible that teachers and curriculum designers may select topics that teach L2 learners unknown concepts, such as the use of color and shape in art, the history of jazz, and important inventions, or topics that are life skills and workplace related, such as in the examples that follow in this chapter, but it is not the most common practice.

In a topical approach to curriculum design, topics are not inherently connected through their content as they are in a content and language integrated approach. Some curriculum designers have tried to connect topics in creative ways through creating story lines that link topics or by including the same characters throughout a series of units. In terms of the content, the fact that topics need not be connected is one of the chief differences between a topical-situational approach to curriculum design and the content and language integrated approach (see Chapter 14), and that they are not required topics, such as they often are in academic courses.

A Process of Curriculum Design in a Topical-Situational Approach

We propose a topical-situational approach to curriculum design. In this approach, curriculum is organized around specific topics and/or situations and the purposes that people have for using the topics and/or participating in the situations. There are three basic assumptions that underpin a topical-situational approach to curriculum design. First, language is used to accomplish specific purposes. Second, language use is motivated by topics and situations. In other words, when the topics and situations change, the language and how it is used may also change. Third, different types of performances are necessary to meet the purposes that individuals have for using topics and participating in situations.

Because we see the relationship between topics and situations on a continuum depending on the strength of the relationship, it is not likely that all teachers or curriculum designers will begin the process with a situation. Some may begin by selecting topics without having a specific situation in mind (e.g., see The Learner Driver Curriculum and The First Aid Certificate in this chapter pp. 175–176). Figure 15.1 describes a process for curriculum design that ties topics to a specific situation (i.e., there is a strong connection between topics and a situation). In this process the situation is the basis for selecting and presenting language vocabulary, structures, and genres. In the vignette, the curriculum designer was given a list of situations from which to work. The next step would be to identify and sequence the topics and the grammatical forms. Curriculum designers who begin the process by identifying topics enter the process at Stage 2. Figure 15.1 shows the hierarchical relationships in the procedures for a topical-situational approach to curriculum design. For a curriculum that includes multiple situations, such as in the vignette, this procedure should be carried out for each situation.

Task: Explore

Work with a partner or peer. Describe a group of learners in terms of age and goals for learning. These should be learners that you can see yourself working with in the future. Think of a situation in which these learners are likely to participate. Use the procedures outlined in Figure 15.1 and develop a skeletal outline for one unit using a topical-situational approach to curriculum design.

Issues in a Topical-Situational Approach

There are a number of issues or concerns that need to be addressed in a topical-situational curriculum. One concern that is specifically addressed by a

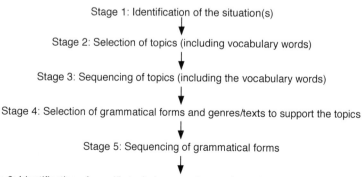

Stage 1: Identification of the situation(s)

Stage 2: Selection of topics (including vocabulary words)

Stage 3: Sequencing of topics (including the vocabulary words)

Stage 4: Selection of grammatical forms and genres/texts to support the topics

Stage 5: Sequencing of grammatical forms

Stage 6: Identification of specific techniques and procedures for teaching vocabulary and grammatical structures and genres

Figure 15.1 Procedures for a Topical-Situational Approach to Curriculum Design

topical-situational approach is the development of skills for communicative purposes. With this approach students learn how to use the target language in communicative situations. The communicative focus motivates learners to see that the "foreign" language they are learning can be used to meet day-to-day communication needs. In addition, the focus is first on topics and situations with grammatical structures surfacing as they interact with topics or with topics in specific situations. In a topical-situational approach, grammatical structures are derived from topics.

The approach poses some challenges for teachers and curriculum designers who are thinking to use this approach for general English teaching. It is much more difficult than it would seem at first glance to predict the vocabulary and structures needed in general situations. The more specific a designer can make the situations the better. In the vignette, the designer was given ten very general situations for the design of a course curriculum. Creating specific situations that are based on his experience and knowledge of higher education in the U.S. would make his task as a curriculum designer much more efficient and would also make the course useful and worthwhile for the learners.

A topical-situation approach to curriculum design is better suited for short-term courses that are geared towards the development of specific skills for specific purposes (see examples in this chapter for The Learner Driver Curriculum and The First Aid Certificate pp. 175–176), than for general English courses that take longer and are geared towards general proficiency. This does not mean that learners cannot develop overall proficiency by participating in short-term courses geared to specific topics or situations or that improved proficiency cannot be a goal for a course.

Another challenge with a situational approach for curriculum designers is that it is also difficult to motivate recurring grammatical patterns in a dialog that does not sound artificial. Often the actual language practiced in the classroom is not the language used in real life. Although the careful sequencing of instructional materials is a historical component of both topical and situational approaches, there have never been any criteria for the sequencing of materials, so it is left up to the curriculum designer to determine the order of presentation of topics and grammatical structures.

Influences on Textbooks and Materials

Topic and situational curricula have had a huge impact on the design of textbooks for both English as a second language (ESL) and English as a foreign language (EFL). Some of the most successful textbook series, beginning in the 1960s, were influenced by Situational Language Teaching. These books include *Streamline English* (Hartley & Viney, 1979), *English for Today* (Slager, 1972), and *Kernel Lessons* (O'Neill, 1973). In fact, all textbooks that have included dialogs as part of the learning materials were an attempt to create language for learner use that was based on situations. Curricula for adult life skills programs were based on specific situations and scenarios that adult immigrant learners would encounter in their new environments or in their jobs. ESP and workplace literacy courses also springboard from a curriculum tied to a specific situation that has relevance for learners' lives.

The Topical-Situational Approach in Practice

In content and language integrated approaches, the content is often selected because it is necessary for the completion of a degree or a certificate. Topical-situational curricula are not necessarily tied to certificates or degrees, although they can be. As well as choosing topics and situations of interest and need for learners, some instructors also select topics that lead to a certification that is useful to the learners. As these examples suggest, it is possible to have a purely topical syllabus without considering the specific situations in which the topics may be used.

We provide three such examples of topical curricula for adult immigrants and refugees in Australia, one leading to learners achieving competency on the written portion of the driver's license test and the other leading to a First Aid Certificate from St. John Ambulance. In each case, the instructors believed that there was a need for the particular certificate. The students who took the learner license course included female refugees from Africa with multiple children, who needed to be able to drive to take their children to school and to medical appointments, and other learners who wanted a driver's license for their work. The First Aid Certificate is required for many occupations in Australia. Additionally, it provides learners with useful personal skills such as CPR. In both cases, learners were high beginners.

The Learner Driver Curriculum

Anyone living in Australia who wants to drive a car must first obtain a learner driver permit. In the state in which this curriculum was used, new drivers must first take a "Learner's License Test." The test has two parts:

- In the **Give Way test** the learner analyzes 12 Give Way diagrams and circles the vehicle that must give way. The learner must get every question correct in order to sit for the Theory test.
- In the **Theory test** the learner completes 40 multiple-choice questions and must get no more than 12 wrong to pass the test. The learner can have an interpreter for this part of the test.

In addition, learners must complete a two-page form, which includes ID details and questions relating to health and organ donation. To get a provisional license, learners must eventually sit for the practical driving test.

The curriculum goals were for learners to:

- develop and use learning strategies to understand the Driving Rules content,
- use effective problem solving skills to correctly interpret the situation inherent in the multiple-choice questions, as well as in the range of answers,
- use L1 and L2 verbal and non-verbal strategies in order to interpret the Give Way diagrams,
- write a formatted text,
- read road and warning signs,
- collate and present ID documents as required by the transport authority,
- follow spoken test instructions in English, and

- budget for the $21 test payment (Hemming, Sydorenko, Lloyd, & Murray, 2004).

These goals motivated the grammar, texts, and vocabulary for the curriculum. In addition, the teachers aligned these linguistic elements with the AMEP curriculum framework (see Chapter 11). The methodology teachers used was modeling and demonstrating the texts, having learners work together to construct the texts, and then to construct them independently. Such texts included directions for cars at different intersections so they follow the Give Way rules.

The First Aid Certificate

The learners in this class had a range of career goals: nursing, engineering, child care, and aged care. They all felt that having a First Aid Certificate would help them enter the job market in such areas, as well as improve their English. The class that one of us (Murray) observed was practical, as the learners practiced CPR on a mannequin lent by St. John Ambulance. They followed the directions of the teacher and then repeated those directions back. The curriculum was developed around the language needed for students to be able to take the practical First Aid test. This language used in the test was integrated with the AMEP competencies (see Chapter 11 for more details on the AMEP curriculum framework), such as "can participate in a transactional telephone conversation." In this case the students phone an ambulance service to request assistance for an elderly woman who has fallen in a suburban street and grazed her hand, which is bleeding; she is in pain and shock. Another curriculum objective from the AMEP curriculum framework is "can provide a spoken explanation." In the first aid lesson, the students explain how to deal with a victim of snakebite.

Air Traffic Controller Training and Aviation English

English is the language of aviation. This flight academy (http://www.panam academy.com/air-traffic-control-training) provides training to air traffic personnel around the world. The academy offers basic courses in aviation English from ICAO (International Civil Aviation Organization) Levels 2–5 and assessment of aviation English proficiency. However, they also offer courses that are directed to specific situations that air traffic controllers encounter. These courses focus on the development of skills and language for the specific situations. These situation-based courses use aerodome simulations that depict the actual aerodome environment with buildings, taxiways, ramps, runways, and variations in aerodome lighting to depict differences in night, day, and dusk conditions, as well as differences resulting from varied weather circumstances. The instruction is tied to specific emergency situations and the skills and language needed in those situations, such as bird strikes, the incursion of ground vehicles and other aircraft, emergency evacuation, landing gear failure, aborted takeoff, missed approach, and emergency landings with fire and rescue. The language is tied to the emergency situation being targeted. The courses are designed to develop the necessary skills, including language skills, in learners to conduct ICAO ATC (Air Traffic Controller) operations.

Conclusion

In this chapter we have considered topics and situations in the curriculum design process. We link the topical and situational approaches by considering the relationship between topics and situations on a continuum that represents the strength of the relationship. It is possible to have a purely topical curriculum; however, most topics can easily be linked to situations. The chapter considers the theoretical basis for a situational approach to curriculum design by reviewing the basic tenets of the Oral Approach and Situational Language Teaching. We also offer procedures for developing curriculum using a situational approach. Finally, we provide examples of topic and situational approaches in practice.

Task: Expand

Conduct an online search. Locate two additional examples of programs or courses for a topical or situational curriculum. Share your results with a peer or with your class.

Questions for Discussion

1. In your own words, describe the differences between a topical and a situational approach.

2. Of the three examples given for topical and situational approaches in practice in this chapter, where would you place the examples on a continuum depicting the strength of the connection between topics and situations?

3. What are the strengths and weaknesses of a situational approach to curriculum design?

4. What are the basic assumptions that underpin a situational approach?

References

Halliday, M. A. K. (1973). *Explorations in the functions of language*. London: Edward Arnold.

Halliday, M. A. K. (1975). *Learning how to mean*. London: Edward Arnold.

Hartley, B., & Viney, P. (1979). *Streamline English*. Oxford: Oxford University Press.

Hemming, P., Sydorenko, T., Lloyd, R., & Murray, D. E. (2004). Fact sheet: Integrating content and language: Meeting the needs of learner drivers [Electronic Version]. *Fact Sheet*. Retrieved from http://www.ameprc.mq.edu.au/docs/fact_sheets/02MiscLearnerDriver.pdf.

Hornby, A. S. (1954). *Guide to patterns and usage in English*. London: Oxford University Press.

O'Neill, R. (1973). *Kernel lessons plus*. London: Longman.

Palmer, H. E. (1923). *The oral method of teaching language*. Reprinted 1968. London: Oxford University Press.

Richards, J. C., & Rodgers, T. S. (2001). *Approaches and methods in language teaching* (2nd ed.). Cambridge: Cambridge University Press.

Slager, W. (1972). *English for today*. National Council for Teachers of English (NCTE). McGraw-Hill College.

West, M. (1953). *A general service list of English words*. London: Longman.

Part V

Learner Centered Curricula

In one sense, all curricula should be learner centered. However, in Part V, by learner centered we refer to curricula where the priority is *process* rather than content, that is, on how the learning environment is arranged. The curriculum is designed around *how* learners learn, rather than around goals of *what* they are to learn. This part consists of three chapters.

For convenience, we have two separate chapters—one on negotiated curricula, and the other on humanistic curricula. This division is not that distinct. However, they have followed two rather different trajectories. Negotiated curricula are largely associated with British and Australian programs, while humanistic curricula have their origins in the U.S. Both have been used in different countries, but negotiated curricula in ELT are especially associated with Candlin and Breen and Nunan; humanistic curricula, with Stevick. Further, in a negotiated curriculum, not only do designers and teachers decide what and how to learn with reference to the learners, but learners themselves are involved in deciding what and how to learn (Nunan & Lamb, 2001).

The remaining chapter is on approaches that grew out of a focus on learner centered curricula. Chapter 18, A Task-based Curriculum, focuses on having learners engage in tasks that they will likely encounter in the world outside the classroom. In this chapter we include project-based curricula because, essentially, projects are extensions of tasks. Projects are an activity that takes place over a long period of instruction, perhaps even an entire term. The project itself may be broken into various tasks. In both cases, curriculum is organized around the tasks or projects.

What is common to all these approaches is:

A strongly-felt pedagogic intuition that the development of competence in a second language requires not systematization of language inputs or maximization of planned practice, but rather the creation of conditions in which learners engage in an effort to cope with communication.

(Prabhu, 1987, p. 1)

References

Nunan, D., & Lamb, C. (2001). Managing the learning process. In D. R. Hall & A. Hewings (Eds.), *Innovation in English language teaching: A reader* (pp. 27–45). London: Routledge.
Prabhu, N. S. (1987). *Second language pedagogy*. Oxford: Oxford University Press.

Chapter 16

A Negotiated Curriculum

VIGNETTE

Sally is a highly experienced teacher in the Australian Adult Migrant English Program[1] (AMEP) in a case study described by David Nunan. In her interview, she describes her experiences trying to implement a learner centered, negotiated curriculum. The AMEP had previously used a centralized curriculum. Sally's previous experiences included advanced learners, but mostly she had worked with low-level, on-arrival learners. Her current group was intermediate students who had already taken several English classes. Although all labeled intermediate, they varied in age, proficiency, literacy skills, confidence, and motivation. In the initial days of the course she tried to conduct a needs analysis, but found that the students could not articulate what they wanted, so she wondered whether she should start by revising what they'd done in previous classes. She believed in a negotiated curriculum and had successfully worked with previous learners to develop their own curricula. She also felt she couldn't develop a list of objectives for such a disparate group of learners. So, she structured the course herself for the first several weeks, asking students at the end of each week what had worked well, what had not, and what they wanted to do differently. Included were all aspects of the curriculum, not just methodology. They all said they did not like pair work. So Sally, committed to it as a chance for more language practice, explained her reasons for using pair work. Students were pleased to have been consulted and agreed to continue with the pair work and in fact they became more engaged in such work and began to both enjoy and learn from it. [Summarized from Nunan, 1988]

Task: Reflect

1. Why do you think these students disliked pair work? How do you feel about learning using pair work—for yourself?—for your students?
2. Why do you think this experienced teacher found it so hard to negotiate with this group of students?
3. How might this teacher have approached the class differently?

4.   Do you think it is useful to ask students how they feel about class activities, content, and structure? Why? When is the best time to do this? Share your ideas with a colleague.

Introduction

> It has been claimed that one important outcome of involving learners in ongoing curriculum development is that not only does it increase the likelihood that the course will be perceived as relevant, but learners will be sensitised to their own preferences, strengths and weaknesses. They will become more aware of what it is to be a learner, will develop skills in "learning how to learn" and will be in a better position to negotiate the curriculum in the future.
>
> (Nunan, 1988, p. 53)

A negotiated approach to curriculum design places the learner in the driver's seat by requiring teachers to respond to learner needs, desires, and reflections on language learning. Such an approach empowers learners to become autonomous. This, therefore, places the responsibility for curriculum development on the individual teacher because each class will differ in its collective needs and desires. While the humanistic approaches discussed in Chapter 17 also rely on learner-centeredness and helping learners become empowered and autonomous, the balance is rather different. In humanistic approaches, teachers become facilitators in the learning process. In negotiated approaches, teachers design the learning process based on ongoing learner feedback. Further, the humanistic approaches were more prevalent in the U.S., while the negotiated approaches were a focus in the U.K. and Australia, and initially associated with Lancaster University.

Defining Negotiation

A negotiated approach grew out of a number of themes prevalent in the 1980s. One theme was the desire to have learners move away from dependence on the teacher to becoming more autonomous learners. Another was learner needs-based design. A third impetus came from the desire to have teachers themselves become more self-directed and independent from textbooks or prescribed curricula. A final direction came from the recognition that curriculum design is an ongoing process during and after instruction, not just in planning instruction. Breen and Littlejohn (2000b) also note that negotiation in the classroom has been shown to facilitate language acquisition. In negotiating the curriculum with learners, the teacher provides more opportunities for rich classroom discourse.

Who then is involved in the negotiation? In the pure version of a negotiated curriculum, only the teacher and the learners are involved. In this approach, the learner is considered to be a fully functional language user (of their first and other languages), who has "a highly relevant initial competence of communicative knowledge and abilities" (Breen & Candlin, 2001, p. 12). Further, the learner, from previous experience, has views about language and language learning, whether previously articulated or not. Learners also have their own interests both in terms of content and the learning process. These then provide learner input in the negotiation. Teachers in turn have their own beliefs about language and language learning, and even specific content interests. However, because learners' needs and wants are critical to engagement, they supersede teachers' predispositions. However, as a professional, the teacher can use learners' expectations, needs, desires, and interests to fashion the learning experiences.

Further, "[t]he extent to which it is possible or desirable for learners to be involved in their own learning will obviously vary from context to context (and, indeed, from learner to learner)" (Nunan & Lamb, 2001, p. 28). As in the vignette, Sally was committed to pair work, but students expressed dislike for it. However, through her explanations of its usefulness, students were willing to try it again. With their more positive attitudes, they began to enjoy and learn from pair work. Öztürk (2012), for example, contends that English preparatory programs at universities in Turkey provide a context in which a negotiated curriculum is almost unavoidable: There is no national curriculum, learners come from different sociocultural, ethnic, and socioeconomic backgrounds, have different levels of English, and different needs and wants. Additionally, teachers have different backgrounds from the learners. In this context, Öztürk claims that a pre-course needs analysis is not possible. However, some learners in some contexts might still resist.

In this chapter, we will define a negotiated curriculum as one where "the discussion between all members of the classroom to decide how learning and teaching are to be organized" (Breen & Littlejohn, 2000a, p. 1) determines the curriculum. They provide a pyramid of the various curricular components that can be negotiated: the wider educational curriculum, a specific language/subject curriculum, a course, a series of lessons, a sequence of tasks, and a task (Breen & Littlejohn, 2000b, p. 35). In other words, what is to be negotiated is *all* aspects of the curriculum that we discussed in Chapter 5.

Task: Reflect

Think about your own language learning. Were any aspects of the curriculum negotiated between teacher and learners? Why/why not? How would you have felt had the teacher asked for your input on content, activities, or materials?

Major Characteristics of a Negotiated Curriculum

Nunan (1985) sets out how teachers can work with learners in each aspect of the curriculum: needs analysis, goal setting, deciding input, deciding content, ordering input, staging language, choosing materials, choosing activities, and evaluating instruction. We will discuss only a few of these aspects, looking at how teachers and learners can work together to plan instruction. We have chosen aspects and examples that teachers in almost any educational context could make use of, acknowledging that most teachers will not be in a position to implement a negotiated curriculum approach in its purest form.

Needs Analysis

Needs analysis is one of the areas in which most curriculum design experts agree that learners need to have some involvement. There are problems, however, because often teachers have no idea who will be in their class (their English level, their reason for learning English, etc.) until the first day of class. "Establishing the learning needs of the individual student can only come about through the often lengthy process of getting to know each individual student" (Nunan, 1985, p. 4).

Because curriculum design is ongoing throughout instruction, needs analysis can be conducted at different times and for different purposes. For example, before a particular lesson or unit a teacher might conduct a needs analysis to determine what types of learning activities students prefer. The needs analysis might have the types of questions in Table 16.1.

Choosing Activities

The choice of activities and class arrangements is the aspect of curriculum for which teachers most often seek learner input. Some teachers survey students at the beginning of the course, others assign activities and then ask students to evaluate the activity, as Sally did in the vignette. This feedback can be in response to a survey or can just be a quick like/don't like response using check marks. Some teachers have students hold up different colored cards for whether they liked it or did not like it. While a quick response is useful, it often does not get at why students like or do not like a particular activity and so how it might be adjusted to meet learner needs and desires. As well as asking whether students like/dislike a particular activity, it is also useful to find out whether they have learned from it. For example, a survey such as that used in Table 16.1 could be expanded as in Table 16.2.

Table 16.1 Language Learning Needs Analysis

Learning Situation	How important is this for you? Circle a number. 1 = not important 2 = a little important 3 = important 4 = very important			
Grammar rules	1	2	3	4
Pronunciation	1	2	3	4
New words	1	2	3	4
Speaking	1	2	3	4
Listening	1	2	3	4
Reading	1	2	3	4
Writing	1	2	3	4

Table 16.2 Learning Activity Needs Analysis

Learning Activity	How much did you like this activity? Circle a number. 1 = did not like it 2 = liked it a little 3 = liked it 4 = liked it very much				How much English did you learn from this activity? Circle a number. 1 = nothing 2 = a little 3 = quite a lot 4 = a lot			
Using a textbook	1	2	3	4	1	2	3	4
Practicing with the whole class	1	2	3	4	1	2	3	4
Practicing with a partner	1	2	3	4	1	2	3	4
Practicing in a group	1	2	3	4	1	2	3	4

Choosing Content

Subject matter content (as opposed to language content) provides a unique opportunity for learner-centeredness. The content can be chosen for a number of learner related reasons:

- the content is of intrinsic interest to the particular learners
- the content is what learners will need for either their social life or their work life, or
- the content is learner generated.

Many textbooks choose subjects dear to the hearts of their teachers, but of little interest to learners. However, finding out what learners actually need in order to conduct their lives in English can be a useful starting point for choosing content. Table 16.3 provides a set of sample questions that can be asked of

Table 16.3 Learner Content Needs in English

Content Area	How important is this for you? Circle a number. 1 = not important 2 = a little important 3 = important 4 = very important				How confident are you in this area? Circle a number. 1 = not confident 2 = a little confident 3 = confident 4 = very confident			
Reading a newspaper	1	2	3	4	1	2	3	4
Understanding TV	1	2	3	4	1	2	3	4
Reading signs and notices	1	2	3	4	1	2	3	4
Listening to lectures	1	2	3	4	1	2	3	4
Talking to my co-workers	1	2	3	4	1	2	3	4
Talking to the doctor	1	2	3	4	1	2	3	4
Reading websites	1	2	3	4	1	2	3	4
Writing emails for work	1	2	3	4	1	2	3	4

students, depending on their context. Some could be used for any context; others, such as listening to lectures, would be used for students preparing to study in English.

Learner generated content can include student writing that is used as texts in the classroom (see, for example, Dixon & Nessel, 1983). It can also mean that all texts used in the course are found and brought to class by the students (Hall, 2001). This is particularly effective in advanced English for Specific Purposes (ESP) courses, where learners are all interested in the same subject matter, as was the case in the example Hall provides. Learner generated content can also include having students collect samples of language use in their contexts and bring them to class. These samples can be printed texts or they can be a dialog they overheard or were engaged in (see, for example, Murray, 2005). Chapter 5 in Volume I of this series also has a detailed discussion of using learners' lives as resources in the language classroom (Murray & Christison, 2011).

Designing Assessment

Assessment is probably one of the areas that teachers are most reluctant to negotiate with learners, and in some contexts only negotiated formative[2] assessment is possible. One type of formative assessment that can be used with learners of all ages and proficiency levels is a learner diary. Advanced learners can keep a narrative diary. For beginners, the teacher can provide headings (negotiated with the learners) or sentence frames for learners to complete, such as the following:

- This week I studied . . .
- This week I learned . . .
- This week I used English with . . .

Learners can be prompted in their writings with starters such as "Things I find hard in English are . . ." or "Things I'd like to be able to do in English are . . ." Or, after an instructional unit on paraphrasing, the teacher can have students respond with yes/no or rate themselves on a five-point scale to various statements, such as:

- I can think of synonyms for words.
- I can re-write verbal phrases.
- I know that I must not take phrases from the original.

For a writing course where the task was an autobiographical essay, Litz (2007) negotiated the scoring rubrics with his learners using the following steps:

- students examined and discussed teacher provided samples that represented each level for the task
- in groups students commented on each sample
- students decided the attributes of the task, such as organization and vocabulary, and

- students discussed and decided on the criteria for each attribute for each level, such as "Poor organization of ideas. No paragraphs and sentence marker errors" for organization at Level 1.

How then are these principles and characteristics realized in actual curricula?

Implementation

The most system-wide reform based on a negotiated approach to curriculum was attempted in Australia in the Adult Migrant English Program (AMEP), referred to in the vignette. Prior to 1980, the program used a centralized curriculum. From 1980, it devolved the curriculum in the hope that teachers better understood their own local context and were therefore better able to make curriculum choices for their learners. Teachers were expected to negotiate content, materials, and methodology with their learners.

Nunan's (1988) study of the program showed that teachers felt the need for a number of supports if they were to achieve an effective negotiated curriculum. These needs included:

- non-mandatory curriculum guidelines
- in-service for the development of program-planning skills
- procedures for deriving more homogeneous class groups
- more resources such as counseling, and bilingual and curriculum support
- more appropriate teaching/learning materials, and
- smaller classes (adapted from p. 163).

This list is probably not dissimilar from what teachers using other curricular types might request if asked. The third point regarding more homogeneous groupings is clearly one of the issues that Sally in the vignette had to deal with. She was used to a more homogeneous group of learners who were beginners and had very recently arrived in Australia. Therefore, many of their needs would be in common, unlike those of the disparate intermediate group she was faced with in the vignette. It is intriguing that the characteristic that Sally found most impeded a negotiated curriculum was the one that Öztürk (2012) considered to be a reason for choosing a negotiated curriculum. We would concur with Sally, however, that negotiating with a homogeneous group is much easier than with a disparate group.

Task: Explore

Select a language program with which you are familiar. Interview several teachers. Ask them which aspects of the curriculum they negotiate with learners or not. Ask them why they do or do not negotiate these aspects. Also ask them whether they have a disparate learner group or not. Does this affect their decisions? Share your results with a colleague.

Issues in Negotiated Curriculum

The major criticisms leveled against negotiated curricula have been: (a) they expect each teacher to be a curriculum designer; (b) learners may not be the best judges of what and how to learn or learners may consider teachers are "lazy," and (c) it makes progression through a range of courses quite difficult. We will deal with each of these issues in turn.

Teacher as Curriculum Designer

Although we have set out a process for teachers to be able to engage in curriculum design, experience with negotiated design in the AMEP in Australia has shown that for all aspects of curriculum to be negotiated between teacher and learner is an overwhelming task that most teachers do not have the training or experience to be able to implement. In a review of the AMEP, Bartlett and Butler concluded that "the learner-centred curriculum created a great deal of stress, that teachers were required to have a range of new skills if the ideals of the learner-centred curriculum were to become reality, and that teachers required assistance and support in a number of areas" (cited in Nunan, 1988, p. 37). These support areas included needs analysis, course planning skills, educational counseling, conflict resolution, and assessment skills.

The Learner as Curriculum Co-designer

In Chapter 7 (Quality Assurance and Curriculum), we noted that Bogue (1998) expressed grave reservations about whether learner satisfaction was a viable measure of quality. He claimed that students can state they are highly satisfied in a survey and yet remain uneducated. Many educators have experienced the popular teacher who actually does not help learners achieve their learning objectives and outcomes. Öztürk (2012) notes that in his Turkish context, although a negotiated curriculum might seem "unavoidable," students expect the teacher to be "the source of knowledge" (p. 38) and students are likely to feel uncomfortable discussing instruction with "highly respected" teachers. In some cultural contexts, for the teacher to ask instructional opinions from the class implies the teacher is lazy or has abandoned them (Grognet, 1996).

Establishing Continuity Across Programs

Lack of continuity across programs so that learners could progress easily from one course to the next was cited as a major reason for the abandonment of the learner centered curriculum model in the AMEP. In the early 1990s the program underwent major curriculum and policy changes. A national curriculum framework was adopted in 1992, in response to a 1985 review of the AMEP (Campbell, 1986), a review that recommended a curriculum that had clearly defined learner pathways. The national curriculum framework is text-based and the certification of learner progress is achieved through the assessment of competencies. Providers of the AMEP are evaluated based on three criteria—reach, retention, and results.[3] These changes, while allowing for local syllabi and methodologies, resulted in less negotiation, although teachers still valued learner input into their instructional decisions. They did, however, allow students to progress more smoothly from one class to another, as well as provide data for program evaluation.

Conclusion

While in some sense, all curricula should focus on learners' needs, the negotiated curriculum is the most all-embracing manifestation of a learner centered curriculum. In its purest form, all aspects of the curriculum are negotiated between teacher and learner at the class level. This, however, places considerable responsibility and burden on both teacher and learner. It expects the teacher to have curriculum design skills, as well as negotiating skills. It expects learners to be self-aware about their own learning needs and desires. It also makes articulation between courses within a program quite difficult and time consuming because there are no pre-established standards for exit from any given course. Despite these drawbacks, teachers might want to consider including some aspects of negotiation in any curriculum.

Task: Expand

Nunan, D. (1988). *The learner-centred curriculum: A study in second-language teaching.* Cambridge: Cambridge University Press.

This volume provides details of the components of a learner centered curriculum, as well as an evaluation of the AMEP's negotiated curriculum.

Breen, M. P. & Littlejohn, A. L. (Eds.), *Classroom decision making.* Cambridge: Cambridge University Press.

This volume has an excellent introductory chapter by the editors, in which they trace the origins of the negotiated curriculum and provide a detailed description of such a curriculum. The various chapters provide examples of negotiation in K–12 and tertiary education around the world and cover all aspects of the curriculum.

Questions for Discussion

1. Explain the relationship between a learner centered and a negotiated curriculum.
2. How can learners' lives be used as input into the curriculum?
3. For what types of learners do you think a negotiated curriculum works best?
4. How could a teacher build learner self-assessment into any type of curriculum?
5. Why do you think some people are critical of negotiated curricula?

Notes

1. The AMEP is a national program for teaching English to immigrants and refugees who do not have functional English. In the Australian context, "migrant" refers to immigrants.
2. Formative assessment is any assessment conducted during instruction to provide learners and teachers with information about what has/has not been learned. Teachers and learners

can then use this information to plan the next stages of instruction. Formative assessment contrasts with summative assessment, which provides a final summation of student learning.
3. Reach refers to how many potential eligible immigrants/refugees the program teaches. Retention refers to whether students stay in the program, that is, do not drop out.

References

Bogue, G. E. (1998). Quality assurance in higher education: The evolution of systems and design models. *New Directions for Institutional Research, 99*, 7–18.

Breen, M. P., & Candlin, C. N. (2001). A communicative curriculum. In D. R. Hall & A. Hewings (Eds.), *Innovation in English language teaching: A reader* (pp. 9–26). London: Routledge.

Breen, M. P., & Littlejohn, A. L. (2000a). Introduction and overview. In M. P. Breen & A. L. Littlejohn (Eds.), *Classroom decision making* (pp. 1–4). Cambridge: Cambridge University Press.

Breen, M. P., & Littlejohn, A. L. (2000b). The significance of negotiation. In M. P. Breen & A. L. Littlejohn (Eds.), *Classroom decision making* (pp. 5–38). Cambridge: Cambridge University Press.

Campbell, W. J. (1986). *Towards active voice: Report of the Committee of Review of the Adult Migrant Education Program*. Canberra: Australian Government Publishing Service.

Dixon, C. N., & Nessel, D. (1983). *Language experience approach to reading (and writing)*. Hayward, CA: Alemany Press.

Grognet, A. G. (1996). *Planning, implementing and evaluating workplace ESL programs*. Washington, DC: Center for Applied Linguistics, Project in Adult Immigrant Education.

Hall, D. R. (2001). Materials production: Theory and practice. In D. R. Hall & A. Hewings (Eds.), *Innovation in English language teaching: A reader* (pp. 229–239). London: Routledge.

Litz, D. (2007). Student-directed assessment in ESL/EFL: Designing scoring rubrics with students [Electronic Version], *13*. Retrieved from http://iteslj.org/Lessons/Litz-StudentDirectedAssessment.html

Murray, D. E. (2005). Use of L1 in adult ESL settings. In D. E. Murray & G. Wigglesworth (Eds.), *First language support in adult ESL in Australia*. (pp. 12–23). Sydney: NCELTR.

Murray, D. E., & Christison, M. A. (2011). *What English language teachers need to know Volume I: Understanding learning*. New York: Routledge.

Nunan, D. (1985). *Language teaching course design: Trends and issues*. Adelaide, Australia: National Curriculum Resource Centre.

Nunan, D. (1988). *The learner-centred curriculum: A study in second-language teaching*. Cambridge: Cambridge University Press.

Nunan, D., & Lamb, C. (2001). Managing the learning process. In D. R. Hall & A. Hewings (Eds.), *Innovation in English language teaching: A reader* (pp. 27–45). London: Routledge.

Öztürk, G. (2012). A negotiated syllabus: Potential advantages and drawbacks in English preparatory programs at universities. *International Journal on New Trends in Education and their Implications, 4*(1), 35–40.

Chapter 17

A Humanistic Curriculum

VIGNETTE

I am in Rabat, Morocco working at the Summer Institute of English (SIE) for four weeks. We came a week early to plan and work together; SIE will be three weeks long with one week for inspectors and two additional weeks for teachers. SIE is designed for secondary school English teachers and is an initiative sponsored by the Ministry of Education (MOE) in cooperation with the British Council and the English Language Teaching Division of the US Embassy. The teaching staff at SIE consists of two university professors from Morocco, six senior inspectors, two English language specialists sponsored by the British Council and four from the U.S., and one Fulbright awardee. One English language specialist from the U.S. serves in a part-time administrative capacity. Each member of the teaching staff is responsible for four eight-hour workshops over the course of the three-week program so that teachers and inspectors will have choices. The Moroccan professors and the English language specialists from the U.K. and the U.S. also give at least one plenary. One of the workshops that I have prepared focuses on how teachers can facilitate classroom interaction among their students. In this workshop, I have focused on six different activity types that promote interaction and can be used with different content, topics, or grammatical structures. In an attempt to get teachers thinking out of the box, I have also chosen some content and topics that are humanistic in nature; these are topics I thought would be interesting to them but may not be typical for their classrooms based on what I have seen in their textbooks. I prepared a "Find Someone Who" activity that included questions about the teachers' wants and desires for the future, past experiences, and opinions about things happening in the world. I told them about the origins of the activity[1] and a bit about a humanistic approach to language teaching. The Moroccan teachers participated fully in the interactive activities that I had planned. On day four of the workshop, they used the activity blueprints that I had given them to plan their own activities and then present them to one another. At the conclusion of the workshop, the teachers told me they were eager to try some of the activities with their own students. After the last class a couple of students approached me and asked if we could talk about humanistic teaching during the tea break. Because I consider myself a humanist at heart, I was eager to discuss this topic with them. In discussion they told me that while they truly

enjoyed the interactive activities and could see that the interaction would be useful for language acquisition, they were worried about implementing the activities in their classrooms. The two young men were deeply religious and were worried because they had read a definition of humanism somewhere that attached prime importance to human rather than divine matters. I explained that my own definition of humanistic education was simply as a philosophy that affirmed an individual's ability and responsibility to lead an ethical and personally fulfilled life that would, hopefully, contribute to the greater good of humanity. I told them that in order to do this, I thought that one must reflect on one's beliefs and values and that the classroom could give learners opportunities to do this. They considered my definition, and we agreed that there were likely many different definitions of humanism and humanistic education and that the workshop had given them much to consider and think about in terms of their future teaching.
[Christison, research notes]

Task: Reflect

1. What is your definition of humanistic education?
2. What are the two different definitions of humanistic education given in the vignette?
3. Do you think it is possible to merge these two definitions? If yes, how? If no, why not?
4. How do you think small group/interactive activities support a humanistic language-teaching curriculum?

Introduction

The humanistic approach to curriculum design presented in this chapter differs from the negotiated curriculum that was discussed in Chapter 16 in some important ways. Even though a humanistic approach also promotes a learner centered curriculum that emphasizes helping learners become empowered and autonomous, the balance is different from a negotiated curriculum. In humanistic approaches, teachers become facilitators in the learning process. Furthermore, and as mentioned in Chapter 16, humanistic approaches have been more prevalent in the U.S., while the negotiated approaches have been a focus in the U.K. and in Australia.

In the late 1970s, one of us (Christison) attended a workshop given by Gertrude Moskowitz at an English language-teaching conference. We participated in many unusual language-learning activities that she had created, including the now famous "Find Someone Who" activity (Moskowitz, 1978). We also participated in small group activities in which we gave our opinions, talked about our preferences, shared information about ourselves, and acknowledged others in our group. As a group of workshop attendees, we were very enthusiastic about the experiences we had, and most of us were eager to take what we had learned in the workshop back into our classrooms. When we were asked if we enjoyed our experiences in the workshop, felt positive about learning, and could see our students responding in a similar way, the overwhelming majority answered with a resounding "yes." Ms. Moskowitz then told us that what we had experienced were language-learning activities that supported ideas associated with humanistic education.

Humanistic education is an approach to education that is based on the early work of humanistic psychologists, most importantly the works of Abraham Maslow (1998) and Carl Rogers (1969). Carl Rogers has been called the Father of Humanistic Psychology, and he devoted a great deal of his professional effort towards applying the results of his research in psychology to person centered teaching. In person centered teaching, the teacher serves as a learning facilitator who demonstrates empathy, caring about students, and genuine interest in their thoughts, feelings, opinions, and ideas. In terms of humanistic education, these qualities are thought to be key traits of effective teachers. Humanistic education also applies to the work of other humanistic pedagogues, such as Maria Montessori (2006), who proposed an educational philosophy that builds on the way that children naturally learn and considers the whole child in the learning process—their social and emotional learning, as well as their cognitive development—and John Dewey, US philosopher and educational reformer, who championed a humanistic approach to education in the U.S. in the late 19th and early 20th Centuries (Dewey, 1897, 1910, 1916).

In second language (L2) and foreign language (FL) teaching, humanistic approaches emerged in the 1970s and 1980s, and are most often associated with the works of Charles Curran (1976), Caleb Gettegno (1976), and Georgi Lozanov (1979). The approaches that these educators promote seek to engage the whole person: the intellectual, emotional, social, artistic, and the practical lives—as they are all important for growth and development. The objectives of humanistic education include developing an individual's self-esteem, the abilities to set and achieve appropriate goals, and the skills that contribute towards full autonomy as a learner.

Humanistic education in L2 learning is also associated with the work of Earl Stevick (1976, 1989, 1990). Unlike Curran, Gattegno, and Lozanov, Stevick did not propose a specific methodology for humanistic language teaching. Stevick stated that his intention was "neither to promote 'humanism' in language teaching nor to discourage it—neither to attack nor to defend any form of it. Instead, [he] tried to sort out a few terms and the ideas that have sometimes been attached to them and to provide certain new information" (1990, p. 144). His work has made it possible for other language teaching professionals to consider the ideas associated with humanistic language teaching in greater depth.

Humanistic approaches to curriculum design emphasize the "natural desire" of everyone to learn; consequently, they focus on the need for learners to feel empowered and to have control over their learning process. The teacher must relinquish some control and take on the role of a facilitator of learning, working to create positive learning experiences for the students and positive affect in the classroom. Helping learners build a positive self-concept and understand themselves as learners are also important components of humanistic approaches. This chapter explains this approach and provides humanistic principles that teachers and designers can follow in the curriculum design process to show the wide range of possibilities for addressing the humanistic element in curriculum design.

Defining Humanism

At its very basic level humanism is concerned with any activity that involves humans—our needs, wants, desires, or experiences. Humanism can also be described as a particular attitude or perspective on life or on humanity. Humanists share certain attitudes, beliefs, and perspectives about the human experience. In the vignette, the author's students asked her about a definition of humanism that "attached prime importance to the human experience" leaving them to wonder about the role of "divine matters" in humanistic education. The author of the vignette proposed a definition of humanism as "a philosophy that affirms an individual's ability and responsibility to lead an ethical and personally fulfilled life that, hopefully, contributes to the greater good of humanity"; as such, it was a definition that neither embraced nor excluded the possibility of "divine matters." In fact, for many humans, "divine matters" are an essential part of the human experience. How one embraces and interprets humanism is to some degree very personal. The general definition of humanism provided in the vignette does not seem controversial. There are few, if any, educators who would argue with the basic tenets put forth in the definition. Educators want their learners to be personally fulfilled, and teachers should be their strongest supporters and the ones they can count on. We want our learners to be concerned about others' welfare and to contribute to making the world a better place. The practice of bringing these values into a second or foreign language classroom is what we refer to as humanistic language teaching.

Stevick (1990) outlines five overlapping components associated with a definition of humanism. These overlapping components and their orientation appear in Table 17.1.

Teachers and curriculum designers must determine how each of these components can be realized in the curriculum design process. The following questions are associated with each of the components and can help focus the curriculum design process:

- Feelings: What parts of the curriculum promote positive affect?
- Social relations: How are friendship and cooperation encouraged and developed?

Table 17.1 Components of Humanism

Components of Humanism	Orientation
Feelings	Embraces what makes people feel good about themselves and about learning
Social relations	Encourages friendship and cooperation
Responsibility	Accepts the need for scrutiny of one's own work and a process for considering others' points of view
Intellect	Supports making personal choices and having the freedom to control one's own mind and how one thinks
Self-actualization	Pursues the realization of one's deepest true qualities

- Responsibility: What processes contribute to learners giving and receiving opinions from others and evaluating their own learning?
- Intellect: What control do students have over their own learning and freedoms do they enjoy?
- Self-actualization: How can students learn about themselves?

Principles of Humanistic Education

The components of humanism can be addressed in the classroom through the use of six principles that are related to the basic components of humanism and apply to the curriculum design process. Table 17.2 can serve as a tool for evaluating a curriculum based on the six principles for humanistic language teaching.

Principle 1: Learner Choice and Control

In humanistic language teaching students are always given opportunities to exercise control over their own learning. Learners are encouraged to make choices that range from deciding what book to read, which classmates to work with, or what roles to assume during group work, to larger choices such as periodically setting future life goals. Exercising some control and choice in their own learning allows students to focus on the content of interest to them and for the amount of time they choose (within reason). It supports the component of humanism referred to as "intellect," which is defined as making personal choices and having the freedom to control one's own mind and how one thinks. Humanistic language teachers believe it is important for students to be motivated and engaged in the material they are

Table 17.2 Principles for Humanistic Language Teaching

Humanistic Principles	Curriculum Design Question(s)	Checklist and Indicators
Principle 1: Learner Choice and Control	Are the students given opportunities to exercise choice or control in their own learning?	
Principle 2: Learner Concerns and Interests	In what ways does the curriculum reflect students' interests, needs, and concerns? How are learners given input into the content of the curriculum?	
Principle 3: The Whole Person	Are both the cognitive and affective domains an integral part of the learning process?	
Principle 4: Self-evaluation	Are students given an opportunity to evaluate their own learning? If yes, then how? Do they learn about themselves in the process?	
Principle 5: Collaboration	Are cooperation and collaboration encouraged? If so how?	
Principle 6: Teacher as a Facilitator	Is the teacher functioning as a facilitator of learning? What are the indicators?	

learning, and giving learning choices and control over their learning contributes to these factors.

Principle 2: Learner Concerns and Interests

Humanistic education focuses on learners' concerns and interests because it is believed that the overall mood and feeling of the students can either hinder or foster the process of learning. Learners respond best to learning when the content is interesting, meaningful, and relevant to their lives and experiences. In humanistic language teaching it is important to embrace what makes people feel good about themselves and about learning.

Principle 3: The Whole Person

Humanistic educators believe that both feelings and knowledge are important to the learning process. Humanistic language learning activities are those that "explore the students' values, ideas, opinions, goals, and feelings, as well as their experiences" (Terrell, 1982, p. 281). Unlike traditional educators, humanistic teachers do not separate the cognitive and affective domains. This aspect also relates to the curriculum in the sense that lessons and activities provide focus on various aspects of the student and not just rote memorization through note-taking and lecturing.

Principle 4: Self-evaluation

Humanistic educators believe that the process of grading done by the teacher is mostly irrelevant because the traditional grading process encourages students to work for the grade and not for satisfaction associated with personal achievement. Humanistic educators often disagree with routine testing because success in testing frequently involves the need for rote memorization as opposed to meaningful learning. They also believe testing does not always provide appropriate educational feedback to the teacher. Self-evaluation supports the component of humanism called "responsibility," which is defined as accepting the need for scrutiny of one's own work and a process for considering others' points of view.

Principle 5: Collaboration

The ability to work together successfully with others is an important component of success in working among friends, in families, at the workplace, or in modern societies. The concept of social relations is a component of humanism, and humanistic language teaching encourages friendships and cooperation in the classroom through collaborative work on class projects, problem solving in small groups, and revision and modification of assignments. The approach that language teachers have used to foster interaction among learners is called Cooperative Learning, which is defined by the presence of two overarching principles—positive interdependence and individual accountability. The presence of these principles in the design of activities and tasks for learners makes cooperative learning different from collaborative learning. For a comparison of the two concepts—collaboration and cooperation—see Christison (2014). For recent accounts of cooperative learning in different contexts in language teaching see McCafferty, Jacobs, and DaSilva-Iddings (2006).

Principle 6: Teacher as a Facilitator

The teacher's role in humanistic language teaching is to guide and assist learners as they take on more responsibility for their learning. Envisioning the teacher as a facilitator requires a change in standard teaching approaches. The purpose of the facilitation is to move the responsibility for learning from the instructor to the student (see Volume II, Chapter 3 for information on gradual release models of teaching) so that ultimately students take responsibility for learning with teachers providing assistance, encouragement, and monitoring in the learning process. A teacher who sees her role in the classroom as a facilitator of learning tends to be more supportive than critical and more understanding than judgmental. In order to be successful as a facilitator, a teacher must also come across as genuine rather than as simply playing a role. This is best accomplished if the teacher is, in fact, genuinely concerned for her students. A facilitator's job is to foster an engaging environment for the students and ask inquiry-based questions that promote meaningful learning and thereby promote learner freedom that is essential in a humanistic approach to language teaching.

The Affective Domain

In almost all formal classroom environments, teachers spend considerable time addressing the cognitive aspects of learning, however the affective aspects are also important and comprise an important part of humanistic language teaching, as reflected in the component of humanism defined as "feelings." The Affective Domain includes learners' emotions, values, motivations, and attitudes, and all of these can affect learning. For several decades, L2 researchers and teachers have talked about the importance of creating a low affective filter in the classroom (i.e., creating a low-stress and low-anxiety environment) (e.g., Krashen & Terrell, 1983). The ability of teachers to recognize that learners have varied orientations to learning (both positive and negative) and differing commitments to the process of learning are important in creating positive affect.

    Benjamin Bloom (see Krathwohl, Bloom, & Masia, 1964) conceived of five categories or levels in the affective domain. These levels are useful for teachers and curriculum designers in trying to identify learners' orientations and commitments to learning, and, consequently, are important in the curriculum design process. Each of the levels represents the degree of commitment required on the part of the learners. There are five levels—*receiving, responding, valuing, organizing,* and *characterizing,* with the level of receiving (i.e., awareness) representing the lowest degree of commitment and characterizing (i.e., learners are firmly committed to the experience) representing the highest. The basic premise is that when learners are committed to the process of learning they have a positive orientation towards it. Just above the level of awareness is the responding level. Learners at the responding level react to classroom information in some way but nothing more. At the valuing level, learners begin to attach value to classroom information, and at the organizing

Table 17.3 Levels of Learner Commitment

Level of Commitment	Description
Receiving	Learners are aware of classroom information, but they do not react
Responding	Learners react to classroom information in some modest way, but there is nothing more
Valuing	Learners begin to attach value to classroom information and see its relevance
Organizing	Learners begin to put together information according to their own schemata, which will ultimately lead to the development of a commitment to learning
Characterizing	Learners are firmly committed to the experience of learning in the classroom and have a positive orientation towards it

level they begin to put together information according to their own schemata, which leads to the development of a commitment to learning. Table 17.3 provides a summary of these levels of commitment.

The difficulty for teachers and curriculum designers in identifying learners' overall commitment to learning is that each learner in a class may have a different orientation, and all groups of learners are different. For teachers who have multiple groups of students in a teaching day, the latter is an important consideration. Teachers and curriculum designers can balance these two concerns by making a plan for the affective domain that best represents the particular group of learners with whom they are working even through the plan may not be a perfect fit for all learners. In the process of developing a plan, teachers recognize that learners are likely to have different commitments to learning. In a humanistic approach, teachers work with learners to help them recognize their level of commitment; consequently, a humanistic curriculum should help learners recognize their level of commitment to learning and give them skills to move to a higher level if that is a goal.

Task: Explore

Select two lessons that you have prepared or two that you use in the program in which you are teaching. Use Table 17.1 to help you determine how the principles of humanistic language teaching are being realized in the materials that you use or intend to use in your teaching. Create a rubric to show how the humanistic principles were applied in the materials you selected. Share your results with a colleague. Talk about whether you were pleased with the results or whether you intend to make changes to the lessons. If you intend to make changes, explain why.

Humanistic Language Teaching in Practice

In this section of the chapter, we take a closer look at humanistic language teaching in practice as we briefly review Stevick's work (1980, 1990) as a model for evaluating methods and approaches in relation to their humanistic components. The purpose in reviewing Stevick's work is to determine if his methods can be helpful to curriculum designers as a way of determining the degree of humanism present in a given language teaching model or curriculum.

Second and foreign language teaching methods most notably associated with humanistic language teaching, such as Curran's Counseling Learning, Gettegno's Silent Way, and Lozanov's Suggestopedia have been reviewed and evaluated in relation to humanistic principles (see, for example, Stevick, 1980, 1990). By looking at Counseling Learning and the Silent Way in relation to the five components of humanism—feelings, social relations, responsibility, intellect, and self-actualization— (see Table 17.1) he not only gave us a way to understand humanism, but he indirectly gave teachers and curriculum designers a model for evaluating the components of humanism that may be present in any model, approach, or curriculum.

Conclusion

In this chapter we have taken a closer look at the role of humanism in language teaching. We defined humanism in terms of its basic components—feelings, social relations, responsibility, intellect, and self-actualization—and translated them into a set of principles for use in the curriculum design process. We also discussed the affective domain and its importance in L2 teaching. Finally we looked at humanistic language teaching in practice by reviewing Stevick's work with the purpose of determining its usefulness in evaluating different models, approaches, and curriculum in language teaching.

Task: Expand

Earl Stevick's book *Humanism in Language Teaching: A critical perspective* (1990) is available online as a free download. In this book he introduces key elements of humanism in language teaching and provides an in-depth discussion of both Curran and Counseling Learning and Gettegno and the Silent Way.

www.sil.org/lingualinks/languagelearning/booksbackinprint/onhumanismin
   languageteaching/humanism.pdf

Questions for Discussion

1. In your own words, explain humanistic language teaching to a colleague or peer.
2. Choose one of the principles for curriculum design that supports humanistic language teaching and explain how is it connected to at least one of the components of humanism.
3. What is the teacher's role in a humanistic curriculum? How is it different from the role of the teacher in a negotiated curriculum?
4. In terms of second language acquisition, why is the affective domain important?

5. Select four learners that you are teaching or have taught and one that you know well. Explain to a partner the level of commitment to learning for each of them and provide a short comment to explain why you placed these learners where you did.

Note

1. The "Find Someone Who" activity originated with Gertrude Moscowitz in a book entitled *Caring and sharing in the foreign language classroom* (1978).

References

Christison, M. A. (2014). *Learning to teach languages: A basic methods book for TESOL*. Ann Arbor, MI: University of Michigan Press.

Curran, C. (1976). *Counseling-learning: A whole person model of education*. New York: Grune & Stratton.

Dewey, J. (1897). *My pedagogic creed*. Public domain. Retrieved from http://en.wikisource. org/wiki/My_Pedagogic_Creed

Dewey, J. (1910). *How we think*. New York: D. C. Heath & Co. Public domain. Retrieved from http://archive.org/details/howwethink000838mbp

Dewey, J. (1916). *Democracy and education*. Public domain. Retrieved from http://www. gutenberg.org/files/852/852-h/852-h.htm

Gattegno, C. (1976). *The common sense of teaching foreign language*. New York: Educational Solutions.

Krashen, S. D., & Terrell, T. D. (1983). *The Natural Approach: Language acquisition in the classsroom*. Oxford: Pergamon Press.

Krathwohl, D. R., Bloom, B. S., & Masia, B. B. (1964). *Taxonomy of educational objectives: The classification of educational goals. Handbook II: The affective domain*. New York: Longman/ Green.

Lozanov, G. (1979). *Suggestology and outlines of Suggestopedy*. New York: Gordon and Breach.

Maslow, A. (1998). *Toward a psychology of being* (3rd ed.). Hoboken, NJ: Wiley Blackwell.

McCafferty, S. G., Jacobs, G. M., and Iddings DaSilva, A. C. (2006). *Cooperative learning in second language teaching*. Cambridge: Cambridge University Press.

Montessori, M. (2006). *The Montessori Method*. New York: Cosimo. (originally published in 1909; translated and published in English in 1912).

Moskowitz, G. (1978). *Caring and sharing in the foreign language classroom: A sourcebook on humanistic techniques*. Rowley, MA: Newbury House.

Rogers, C. (1969). *Freedom to learn*. Columbus, Ohio: Charles E. Merrill.

Stevick, E. W. (1976). *Memory, meaning, and method*. Rowley, MA: Newbury House.

Stevick, E. W. (1980). *Teaching language: A way and ways*. Rowley, MA: Newbury House.

Stevick, E. W. (1989). *Success with foreign languages: Seven who achieved it and what worked for them*. London: Prentice Hall.

Stevick, E. W. (1990). *Humanism in language teaching: A critical perspective*. Oxford: Oxford University Press.

Terrell, T. (1982). The Natural Approach to language teaching: An update. *Modern Language Journal, 66*(2), 121–132.

Chapter 18

A Task-based Curriculum

VIGNETTE

I am teaching a class called "American Culture," but the course in practice is really a course in US history with some cultural components integrated into the curriculum as motivated with historical topics. It is an ESL class in the Intensive English Program (IEP) at the college where I work, and it is intended for intermediate-high to advanced level proficiency students. There are 24 students in my class from six different language backgrounds—Arabic, Korean, Japanese, Portuguese, Spanish, and Thai. The students are from ten different countries. We are about halfway through a 15-week semester, so there is a college expectation (but not a requirement) that teachers will give midterm exams. Midterms are to occur either this week or next week. As students have several short assessment opportunities throughout the term and as I am required to give a final exam, I have decided not to give a midterm. Instead I have decided to give my students the option of pursuing projects. This is a huge experiment for me, and I must admit that I am a bit nervous. I have prepared a set of guidelines for the students and provided a shortlist of possible projects they might pursue, including creating their own midterm exam based on the content of the course to date, asking peers to take the exam and provide feedback, compiling a summary of the feedback, and making a short class presentation about what they learned. I also included ideas for projects such as resource papers that would go beyond the information we covered in class and creative projects that involved incorporating art and music into their subject matter. The list is not meant to be exhaustive, and I will encourage the students to propose original projects. They are also required to create a rubric for the evaluation of their project and grade themselves against the rubric. As we have used rubrics in class, students are familiar with the concept. I am requiring that they review the rubric with me in advance so that I can work with them on their indicators of effectiveness. They can work alone or in groups of two, three, or four persons. I'm thinking that I should also give students who want to take the midterm exam the option of doing that; however I don't think that anyone will take me up on that. [Christison, research notes]

Task: Reflect

Why do you think the teacher in the vignette decided to use a task-based or project-based assessment for her students instead of a midterm exam? Why do you think she would allow some students to take the midterm instead of doing a project? Why do you think the teacher required a rubric for the project? If you were the teacher in the vignette, what kind of project options might you give your students? Do you agree with the teacher that projects would be a good option for students in lieu of a midterm exam?

Introduction

One of the major developments in language teaching and learning that came about in the 1980s, in conjunction with the popularization of communicative language teaching (CLT) methodology, was the emergence of task-based language learning (TBLL). TBLL is also referred to as task-based language teaching (TBLT) or task-based instruction (TBI). TBLL is an important movement because it highlights the fact that learners need both knowledge about language and the ability to use language to achieve communicative or other goals. A task-based approach to curriculum design focuses on tasks, and language is the instrument that learners use to participate in and complete the task. Tasks can be small or can be as large as projects that cover a full semester. By focusing on tasks, learners are afforded opportunities for meaningful interaction with the target language and can process and recycle language more naturally. A task-based curriculum creates the need to learn language by using it, so it is consistent with communicative language teaching.

Definition of Task-based Language Learning

TBLL is a subcategory of communicative language teaching (CLT) (Nunan, 1991, 2004). The concept of organizing language instruction around tasks came into the field of second language (L2) teaching from mainstream education (Shavelson & Stern, 1981). However, the concept of pedagogic tasks has been a topic of discussion among practicing teachers in all content areas for decades. It is not a recent invention.

Central to a discussion of TBLL is a definition of a task—what it is and how to define it. Long (1985, p. 89) states:

> tasks include painting a fence, dressing a child, filling out a form, buying a pair of shoes, making an airline reservation, borrowing a library book, taking a driving test, typing a letter, weighing a patient, sorting letters, taking a hotel reservation, writing a cheque, finding a street destination, and helping someone across the road. In other words, by "task" is meant the hundred and one things people *do* in everyday life, at work, at play, and in between. "Tasks" are the things people will tell you they do if you ask them and they are not applied linguists.

In order to make the concept of task viable within TBLL, it must involve language; however, within the scope of tasks that involve language, how should tasks be defined?

Prabhu's provocative research (1987) showed that his students were able to learn language by participating in non-linguistic motivated tasks as well as when they were concentrating on linguistic questions. In non-linguistic motivated tasks, language is likely involved, however the motivation for participation in a task is not simply to complete a language exercise or drill but to communicate meaning—to achieve one's purpose or accomplish one's goal. Prabhu's work encouraged researchers and teachers to focus on meaning-focused language tasks instead of on language drills or exercises, which may have focused on form with little concern for meaning. Widdowson (1998) cautions, however, that the distinction that some researchers have made between drills and exercises and meaning-focused tasks is far too simplistic and that learners must ultimately pay attention to both form and meaning. Within the framework of TBLL, teachers and curriculum designers are interested in tasks whose successful completion involves "meaning-focused language use" (Ellis, 2003, p. 3); consequently, in this chapter, we will adopt this view of tasks as they relate to TBLL.

Categorizing Tasks

There has been an extensive debate on what constitutes a "task" for the purposes of language teaching and learning; and teachers, curriculum designers, and researchers have categorized them in different ways.[1] The most common distinction is the one made between *exercises* (focused on accuracy and the form of language) and *tasks* or *activities* (focused on developing fluency through meaning and use of language). Researchers have also tried to distinguish between *pedagogic* tasks (tasks accomplished for the purposes of classroom learning) and *real-life* tasks (tasks involving the real-world use of language), although there are arguments among researchers that real-life tasks are not possible in the language classroom. The fact that pedagogic tasks differ from real-life tasks is not a bad thing. By their very nature, pedagogic tasks make language accessible for language learners, particularly at the early proficiency levels when the language associated with real-life tasks (e.g., complicated syntax, speed of delivery, unfamiliar vocabulary) affect comprehensibility. Tasks are differentiated in other ways. There is an emphasis in mainstream education on critical thinking and differentiating between *higher-order thinking* tasks and *lower-order thinking* tasks (see Chapter 10 on academic functions in this volume). Tasks may be categorized and grouped based on almost any prominent feature of tasks. These groupings are called *task-types*. The most common and most frequently used way of categorizing tasks is according to the four language skills—listening, speaking, reading, and writing. Teachers and curriculum designers must always keep the development of the four skills in mind when they plan for and select tasks. Prabhu (1987) divides tasks into three main categories—*information gap*, *reasoning gap*, and *opinion gap*. Each of these categories is discussed below.

Information-gap tasks involve a transfer of information from one person to another, from one form to another, or from one place to another. In order for this to happen, language learners are generally required to decode or encode information. An example of an information-gap activity is pair or small group work in which each member has a part of the total information and attempts to convey it verbally to the other(s) in order to solve a problem or answer a set of questions.

Reasoning-gap tasks require learners to derive new information from information that has been given to them either orally or in writing through inference, deduction, or perceiving patterns or relationships. Problem solving processes that ask learners to decide on a solution and support their decision or explain their decision-making process work well with language learners. One example that we have used is asking learners to decide on a travel itinerary for an upcoming trip and determine how arrival and departure times, layovers, airline choice, cost, travel dates, etc., will affect their decisions, or to compare and contrast a fairy story such as Cinderella as described in different cultures.

Opinion-gap tasks involve identifying and articulating a personal preference, feeling, or attitude in response to information or a situation. One example is story completion; another is taking part in the discussion of a social issue. Learners may use factual information to support their opinions. They may also formulate arguments to justify their opinions. In opinion-gap tasks, there is no objective procedure for demonstrating whether outcomes are right or wrong, and there is no reason to expect the same outcome from different learners.

Another way of categorizing tasks was created for the *Australian language level guidelines* (Scarino et al., 1988). Curriculum designers looked at the purposes of tasks to offer these categories:

* interacting and discussing
* interacting and deciding or completing a transaction
* obtaining information and using it
* giving information
* making a personal response, or
* providing a personal expression.

Another system of task-types used in the level guidelines focuses on higher-order thinking skills. These task types include the following:

* enquiring
* interpreting
* presenting information
* problem solving
* creating
* composing, and
* judging/evaluating (see Clark, Scarino & Brownell, 1994).

The purpose of categorizing tasks is to ensure that in the curriculum design process there is a means for students to engage with a range of learning experiences and participate in a range of language learning tasks in different contexts so that they are prepared to manage the variability of context in the real world. In the process of categorizing tasks, teachers and curriculum designers need to consider how tasks fit together and how each task builds on or extends previous learning. Learning, after all, is continuous and cumulative.

TBLL in the Classroom

L2 classrooms have expanded their role in the teaching and learning process. While they remain formal settings for instruction and guided practice, we must also recognize that L2 classrooms have also become "center[s] for purposeful communication and meaningful exchanges" (Pica, 2005, p. 439). In many classrooms this change has resulted in learners taking a more active role in their learning by participating in collaborative tasks and projects. While the classroom activities have become popular with teachers and learners alike, the nature of instruction has changed, making some researchers wonder about the long-term effects of a lack of emphasis on language (Pica, 2002). How teachers select tasks and how they decide to implement them in the classroom are of primary concern in TBLL. Task characteristics need to be identified so that tasks can be selected to support learners' needs. In addition, there must be a system for task implementation that allows for a focus on language and meets communicative needs.

Task Characteristics

In terms of designing tasks for instructional use, it is helpful to think about the characteristics of the task, particularly if tasks are to be purposeful and contextualized. Task characteristics include the following:

- Purpose – the reason for undertaking the task (i.e., the learners' goals and objectives).
- Context – a context may be real, simulated, or imaginary. In considering context teachers and curriculum designers should consider who, how (interactional circumstances), where, when, and what (in terms of experiences and relationships).
- Process – the procedures for completing the task, including the roles of the learners and teacher. It is important for teachers to determine how the procedures or processes get communicated to the learners.
- Result – the specifications for the expected response(s), including the product that is to be produced.
- Input – the characteristics of the input that learners receive (see also Nunan, 2004 and Bachman and Palmer, 2010). Teachers need to determine whether the input needs to be modified and, if so, how.
- Difficulty factor – linguistic, cognitive, and performance time. These can be manipulated to make tasks easier or more difficult.
- Language factor – the characteristics of the task that are related to language. How does the task support learners in developing their language skills?

Task Implementation

In TBLL, the core of the lesson and the main organizing principle is the task itself (see Nunan, 2004; Willis, 1996; and Willis & Willis, 2007 for example frameworks for creating tasks and task-based learning lessons). Using Doyle's (1983) definition of "academic task," Simpson & Nist (1997, p. 378) enumerate three components that are necessary for teachers and curriculum designers to consider in task implementation:

1.   the products that learners formulate,
2.   the operations or procedures they use to formulate the products, and
3.   the resources that learners have available to them while they are generating a product.

The operations or procedures for task sequencing or a task implementation cycle include pre-task, task completion, and task review.

Pre-task

In the pre-task phase, the teacher focuses students' attention on what will be expected of them during the task cycle. A teacher could also prime the students with key vocabulary words or grammatical concepts, although this priming activity for the task makes the task cycle very similar to the traditional present-practice-produce (PPP) paradigm. Some teachers prefer that learners themselves be responsible for selecting the appropriate language for a given context. In the pre-task phase, the instructor models the task either by doing it or by presenting a picture, audio, or video demonstrating the task.

Task Completion

During the task phase, the students normally work in small groups to complete the task. This is typically done in small groups, although how a task is processed is dependent on the task itself. The teacher's role is typically limited to an observer or facilitator.

Task Review

If completion of the task has resulted in tangible linguistic products, e.g., a text (narrative or expository), collage, a PowerPoint presentation, an audio or video recording, or an exhibition, learners can critique one another's work and offer constructive feedback. Rubrics are helpful for this phase of the task so that learners are clear about whether they have achieved the objectives or not. The teacher can also, with input from learners, summarize what language students have learned during the task. Such a summary can alleviate anxiety of learners who are used to more traditional approaches and worry that they are just doing a task, not learning language.

If a performance or presentation factor is built into procedures for task implementation, there are additional phases that must be considered—planning for the presentation, practicing with peers, making the presentation, and analysis (i.e., students reflect on what they learned).

Task: Explore

Choose a task you have done in the classroom that your students seemed to enjoy or locate a task in a text. Identify the task characteristics and create a plan for task implementation as per the specifications given in the chapter.

Issues in TBLL

As with all types of instructional activity, there are issues related to TBLL. Table 18.1 offers teachers and curriculum designers a list of issues to consider based on perceived advantages and disadvantages. There is no perfect approach to curriculum design. Teachers and curriculum designers must consider the issues and make choices based on what they believe to be in the best interests of their learners.

Table 18.1 Advantages and Disadvantages of TBLL

Advantages	Disadvantages
Task-based activity is student centered	It is not for beginners
Learners have more freedom in learning	Tasks make it difficult to predict
Learners are exposed to more and varied	learning
input	It is difficult to focus on specific
A natural context of language use can develop	language
among learners	Some students speak too much while
Language arises from learner needs	others may not speak enough
Learners develop strong communication skills	Some learners may feel they are not
	learning language

Project-based Curricula

Projects are an extension of tasks. They come from the same theoretical understandings of language learning, that is, that language learning takes place when learners are engaged in purposeful communicative activities (Ellis, 2003). They also require learners to work collaboratively to achieve a certain goal or outcome and they change the role of the teacher. "In project-based teaching, the rigorous application of curriculum gives way to the skill or art of managing the learning process" (Debski, 2006, p. 41). As one learner stated, "There's a real task for us to drain our brains. It offers us a good chance to learn what we want to learn. So we feel responsible and interested in the project" (Gu, 2002, p. 24), thus allowing for learner agency.

Projects have been used in general education long before the task-based approach to ELT developed out of CLT. For example, the Dalton Plan originated from the work of progressive scholars such as Dewey and Montessori, in which students engaged in monthly assignments, using the classroom as a laboratory. Direct instruction was minimal, with learners discovering solutions through their own explorations. One such implementation is at Ascham School in Australia, where one of us taught. They explain their project-based system as:

> Dalton at Ascham comprises three main components: the lesson, the study and the assignment. Girls attend lessons in class groups where teachers deliver the curriculum. In studies, girls learn to work in different ways; in groups, independently and in partnership with their teacher. The assignment sets out the work for each topic so that girls are able to plan their work for the week, in conjunction with their teachers.

(Ascham School, 2013)

Within ELT, projects can vary as the following examples demonstrate:

- high school students researching higher education institutions to practice an admissions interview (TESOL, 1997),
- students interviewing community members to write a report about attitudes towards building a playground in the local park,
- students creating a resource website for an intensive English program (IEP) to provide useful information for future students (Debski, 2006), and
- Chinese and American students collaborating via the web to create a PowerPoint presentation on strategies for marketing Suzhou freshwater pearls in Georgia, U.S. (Gu, 2002).

Projects can be semester-long or for a period each week. The strong version bases the entire curriculum on projects. In weak versions, projects are included, along with a variety of other activities. For example, one of us (Murray) taught in an IEP that used a topic/situational approach (see Chapter 16 in this volume), with a different topic each week. Each Wednesday afternoon was devoted to learners in groups undertaking a research project off campus. The lessons prior to the project afternoon were spent providing language input and practice to help them prepare for their project. So, for example, if the project involved interviewing local people at the beach about beach safety, the previous lessons would include how to interview, as well as the language of safety and beach culture. The days after the project excursion were spent with students writing up their project, requesting help for what they found difficult in the project, and so on.

Assessment of project-based curricula is more complex than in some other approaches. Aspects other than acquisition of language may need to be assessed, such as student investment in the project, the quality of collaboration, and the amount of English used in the project. Because one of the goals of project-based learning is learner empowerment and the application of the project to real-world issues, assessment can be self-, peer-, and/or teacher-based. Portfolios are also a useful assessment tool for projects.

Conclusion

In this chapter we have focused on key components of TBLL by defining tasks; introducing models for organizing tasks; providing suggestions for identifying characteristics of tasks; and creating a system for task implementation, thereby making it feasible to incorporate tasks within lessons, courses, and programs. We also discuss the advantages and disadvantages of the approach and take a detailed look at one task-type—project-based tasks.

Task: Expand

Additional resources on task-based language learning (TBLL) and task-based language teaching (TBLT) include

http://tesolexpert.com/home/CommunicativeTasksAndTheLanguage Curriculum.pdf

http://www.asian-efl-journal.com/pta_February_2007_tr.pdf
http://www.gwinnett.k12.ga.us/HopkinsES/Alfonso_Web/ESOL%20
Modification%20Research/Pica_classroom_learning_teaching_research.pdf
http://www.etlc.ntust.edu.tw/data/090425/TBL_presentation.pdf
http://www.kansai-u.ac.jp/fl/publication/pdf_education/04/5rodellis.pdf

Questions for Discussion

1. In your language teaching, do you make a distinction between exercises and tasks or pedagogic tasks and real-life tasks? Why? Why not?
2. How do you ensure that your students experience a range of tasks through your teaching and through interactions with you?
3. How might you modify one of the tasks you currently use to make it more complex and worthwhile for your students (see task characteristics and task implementation in this chapter)?
4. What are the issues involved in project-based curricula?

Note

1. Ellis (2003, pp. 4–5) offers an excellent summary of different definitions of *task* that have been proposed by researchers. For the purposes of this chapter, we will consider meaning-focused language tasks.

References

Ascham School. (2013). A Dalton education. Retrieved from http://www.ascham.nsw.edu.au/About-Ascham/Why-Ascham/A-Dalton-Education/A-Dalton-Education

Bachman, L., & Palmer, A. (2010). *Language assessment in practice.* Oxford: Oxford University Press.

Clark, J., Scarino, A., & Brownell, J. (1994). *Improving the quality of learning: A framework for target-oriented curriculum renewal.* Hong Kong: Institute of Language Education.

Debski, R. (2006). *Project-based language teaching with technology.* Sydney: NCELTR.

Doyle, W. (1983). Academic work. *Review of Educational Research, 53*(2), 159–199.

Ellis, R. (2003). *Task-based language teaching and learning.* Oxford: Oxford University Press.

Gu, P. (2002). Web-based project learning and EFL learners: A Chinese example [Electronic Version]. *Teaching English with Technology, 2,* 4–41, Retrieved from http://www.tewtjournal.org/VOL%202/ISSUE%204/ARTICLE.pdf

Long, M. (1985). A role for instruction in second language acquisition: Task-based teaching. In K. Hyltenstam and M. Pienemann (Eds.), *Modelling and assessing second language acquisition* (p. 89). Clevedon, UK: Multilingual Matters.

Nunan, D. (1991). Communicative tasks and the language curriculum. *TESOL Quarterly, 25*(2), 279–295.

Nunan, D. (2004). *Task-based language teaching.* Oxford: Oxford University Press.

Pica, T. (2002). Subject matter content: How does it assist the interactional and linguistic needs of classroom language learners? *Modern Language Journal, 86*(1), 1–19.

Pica, T. (2005). Classroom learning, teaching, and research: A task-based perspective. *Modern Language Journal, 89*(3), 339–352.

Prabhu, N. S. (1987). *Second language pedagogy.* Oxford: Oxford University Press.

Scarino, A., Vale, D., McKay, P., & Clark, J. (1988). *Australian Language Level Guidelines.* Canberra: Curriculum Development Centre.

Shavelson, R., & Stern, P. (1981). Research on teachers' pedagogical thoughts, judgments, decisions, and behavior. *Review of Educational Research, 51*(4), 455–498.

Simpson, M. L., & Nist, S. L. (1997). Perspectives on learning history: A case study. *Journal of Literacy Research, 29,* 363–395.

TESOL. (1997). *ESL standards for pre-K-12 students.* Alexandria, VA: TESOL.

Widdowson, H. G. (1998). Skills, abilities, and contexts of reality. *Annual Review of Applied Linguistics, 18,* 323–333.

Willis, D., & Willis, J. (2007). *Doing task-based teaching.* Oxford: Oxford University Press.

Willis, J. (1996). *A framework for task-based learning.* New York: Longman.

Part VI

Learning Centered Curricula

We have chosen to use the term "learning centered" for the three approaches in Part VI. Others have used this term differently. For example, Nunan and Lamb (2001) said that learner centered curricula were focused on learning, by which they meant on the *process* and *content* of learning. We have preferred to call these approaches learner centered (Part V). For us, "learning centered" refers to the commonality of the three approaches in this part—that they are all focused on *what* is learned. Others have referred to this approach as a focus on *product* (Nunan, 1988*)*, rather than process, with which we agree.

The three approaches focus on what learners know and are able to do, that is, on the learner and the learning, rather than on the teacher and the teaching. Chapter 19 explains outcome-based curricula, a design advanced by Spady (1994). Chapter 20 examines competency-based curricula, where learning outcomes are expressed in terms of competencies. Chapter 21 explores standards-based curricula, where outcomes are expressed in global goals that can then be broken down into smaller "can do" statements. All these approaches are interested in *outcomes* and what learners can do. While many documents use competency, outcomes, and standard interchangeably, each has a rather different history and trajectory. Therefore, rather than trying to deal with them all together, we have chosen to provide individual chapters so that readers can see more clearly how they differ and are similar in implementation.

References

Nunan, D. (1988). *The learner-centred curriculum: A study in second-language teaching*. Cambridge: Cambridge University Press.

Nunan, D., & Lamb, C. (2001). Managing the learning process. In D. R. Hall & A. Hewings (Eds.), *Innovation in English language teaching: A reader* (pp. 27–45). London: Routledge.

Spady, W. (1994). *Outcome-based education: Critical issues and answers*. Arlington, VA: American Association of School Administrators.

Chapter 19

Outcome-based Education

VIGNETTE

I am working with a group of English language teachers from a university in Thailand who are required by university management to revise all their courses to be outcome-based. The university itself has overarching outcomes for all graduates. All courses that students take need to align with these outcomes. The general descriptors of these overarching outcomes are "being knowledgeable, being ethical, proficient thinking, capability, a thirst for knowledge and a capacity to learn, leadership, public mindedness, and retention of Thai identity amidst globalization." The English language teachers are exploring how they can align and revise their content-based courses. These are courses they teach for other departments such as business, law, architecture, and medicine. After I provide brief presentations about the nature of outcome-based curricula, I meet with groups of teachers who teach courses in the different subject areas. They bring with them their current syllabi as starting points. Each group focuses on one aspect of the capability outcomes, that is, communication skills, because this seems to fit their programs best. In fact, many complain that they are at a disadvantage because they are teaching language skills, so only this overarching outcome applies to their courses. I challenge them to think also about the other outcomes and how their courses address those attributes. One group, teaching business English, recognizes that in teaching business oral presentations, they need to address aspects of proficient thinking, such as critical thinking and problem solving, as their students choose a topic for their presentation, select specific content to argue their point, and organize their presentation with main ideas and supporting details. They decide that their course also teaches skills in information technology, one of the attributes of capability identified by the university. Students achieve this by researching content online and using PowerPoint for their presentations. [Murray, research notes]

Task: Reflect

1. How might this group of teachers also include *leadership* in their courses?
2. How might this group of teachers include *being ethical* in their courses?
3. Do you agree with the list of outcomes developed by this university? What would you do differently? Why? Share your ideas with a colleague

Introduction

> Outcome-based education [OBE] means clearly focusing and organizing everything in an educational system around what is essential for all students to be able to do successfully at the end of their learning experiences. This means starting with a clear picture of what is important for students to be able to do, then organizing the curriculum, instruction, and assessment to make sure this learning ultimately happens.
>
> (Spady, 1994, p. 1)

Although many other educators and scholars have contributed to OBE, Spady is often considered the world authority. The definition he provides above requires that in a particular educational context, the stakeholders know exactly "what is essential for all students to be able to do," and know how to embody that in curriculum design and how to design assessment to measure this "essential doing." OBE has been interpreted in two ways. The first focuses on student mastery, usually of subject matter, with some generic skills outcomes, such as the critical thinking referred to in the vignette. The other focuses on outcomes that are related directly to students' future life roles, such as being a productive worker or an active, responsible citizen. The second focus is what Spady calls transformational OBE, as opposed to traditional or transitional OBE. Because competency- and standards-based approaches can be considered traditional or transitional OBE, in this chapter we will discuss only transformational OBE, in which educational outcomes reflect the complexities of life outside the classroom. Transformational OBE is the approach favored by Spady. Competency-based and standards-based approaches are discussed in Chapters 20 and 21. Spady (1994) relates transformational OBE to total quality management (see Chapter 7) used in the corporate world with its shift to "[e]stablishing within the organization the conditions that motivate and empower individuals to use the potential that is within them" (p. 41).

Task: Reflect

Think about your own language learning. Was the approach transformational? Did you have a clear understanding of what you were to do in that language? How did the assessments you took align with what you were required to do? How did both align to your life outside of school?

Defining Outcome

Outcome is used loosely by many educators and businesses for many different types of programs. Here, we will use Spady's conceptualization because this chapter is explicitly about OBE as Spady and his colleagues have elaborated and implemented it. For OBE practitioners, outcome is "a culminating demonstration of learning" (Spady, 2008, p. 4), where demonstration means that learners actually perform the skill or competence, not just demonstrate knowledge about it. These OBE practitioners, therefore, focus on outcomes with action verbs such as describe, construct, or design, rather than non-demonstration verbs such as know, understand, or value. By "culminating" they meant "what [learners] could do as a result of all the learning experiences and practices they had engaged in" (Spady, 2008, p. 5). Therefore, the focus is on *whether* and *what* students learn, not on *how* or *when* they do.

Unlike many of the competency-based models (see Chapter 20), which have focused on behavioral objectives that are discrete skills and tasks, such as "students will be able to read, interpret, and follow directions found on public signs," Spady (1994) has developed a framework of complexity with six different types of demonstrations of learning from the simple to the complex:

- discrete content skills
- structured task performances
- higher-order competencies
- complex unstructured task performances
- complex role performances, and
- life-role functioning.

The higher-level performances are grounded in the contexts in which people operate as workers, parents, sons and daughters, citizens, and players, that is, the transformational aspect of OBE. While the Thai university referred to in the vignette includes outcomes such as "public mindedness" and "being ethical," the framework rubrics are not all described in demonstrable terms; instead, most refer to "having." Higher-level performances require integration, synthesis, and application of knowledge and skills so that learners are able to perform.

Major Characteristics of OBE

Although there may be a variety of implementation options, all successful transformational OBE is supported by four underlying principles:

- having a clear focus on learning results, sharing and modeling that focus, and aligning all instruction and assessment to those results
- designing curriculum (in all its aspects) back from the desired results
- having high expectations of all learners, while recognizing not all learn in the same time or in the same way, and
- employing a range of opportunities for learners to learn and demonstrate successful learning.

These principles need to be applied consistently, systematically, creatively, and simultaneously.

In addition, OBE has a very specific definition of what "based" means. For Spady, "based" in this context means five closely related things: (1) defined by; (2) designed from; (3) built on; (4) focused on; and (5) organized around. This combination of five things implies something much deeper and more impactful than simply being "oriented toward" and/or "related to" something (Spady, 2008, p. 7). In other words, in OBE all aspects of the curriculum are driven by the outcomes.

OBE has been primarily implemented in general education (not English language education) in North America and elsewhere, with very specific approaches to defining and assessing outcomes. Instructional and learning activity is governed by progress towards specific objectives. Outcomes are specified in the form of learner behaviors, skills, attitudes, and abilities. Instruction is then designed so that teachers can coach learners to a mastery level of each outcome. Learners are assessed against these outcomes. Such assessment needs to determine what is to be assessed, how the learner is to carry out the demonstration, and in what setting or circumstance. Each of these criteria has to be considered in designing the assessments. Within the Spady model, the outcomes need to be transformative to help learners become productive citizens, problem solvers, and autonomous learners. Such outcomes, he believes, require a systemic restructuring of education, of curriculum, courses, and programs.

The generic types of role performances used by a number of K–12 school districts in the U.S. and Canada include learners (who are self-directed, continuously developing, lifelong, and collaborative learners) and thinkers (who are capable of perceptive, constructive, and complex thinking). He sets out a framework of these roles that can be used as a basis for developing outcomes:

- listeners and communicators
- teachers and mentors
- supporters and contributors
- team members and partners
- leaders and organizers
- implementers and performers
- problem finders and solvers
- planners and designers, and
- creators and producers.

Many of the roles in Spady's framework are ones that industry and governments have identified as essential skills, generic skills, job-readiness, or soft skills. For example, the Canadian Office of Literacy and Essential Skills identifies reading, document use, numeracy, writing, oral communication, working with others, thinking, computer use, and continuous learning (Office of Literacy and Essential Skills, 2007). The Australian Chamber of Commerce and Industry and Business Council of Australia (ACCI/BCA) identify communication skills, teamwork skills, problem solving skills, initiative and enterprise skills, planning and organizing skills, self-management skills, learning skills, technology skills, and personal attributes (Australian Chamber of Commerce and Industry and Business Council of Australia, 2002). See Chapter 20 on competency-based approaches to curriculum design for a more detailed discussion of workplace skills and their role in English language instruction. The Thai example in the vignette includes role qualities such as leadership, creative thinking, problem solving skills, and communication skills. Thus, we can see the connection between OBE's goal of developing productive citizens and workplace skills defined by industry.

How then are these principles and characteristics realized in actual curricula?

Implementation

The most system-wide reform based on Spady's approach was attempted in South Africa. South Africa is a diverse country in terms of culture, language, religion, and ethnicity. There are 11 official languages, as well as braille and South African Sign Language. Each official language can be learned as a home language, a first additional language, or a second additional language. OBE was first introduced in 1998 and implemented with a Revised National Curriculum in 2002. Inspired by the constitution, the Revised National Curriculum Statement had identified 12 critical and developmental outcomes across all education, outcomes that are to be embedded in every curriculum.

The South African Department of Education states that the critical outcomes envisage learners who will be able to:

- Identify and solve problems and make decisions using critical and creative thinking.
- Work effectively with others as members of a team, group, organisation and community.
- Organise and manage themselves and their activities responsibly and effectively.
- Collect, analyse, organise and critically evaluate information.
- Communicate effectively using visual, symbolic and/or language skills in various modes.
- Use Science and Technology effectively and critically showing responsibility towards the environment and the health of others.
- Demonstrate an understanding of the world as a set of related systems by recognising that problem-solving contexts do not exist in isolation.

The developmental outcomes envisage learners who are also able to:

- Reflect on and explore a variety of strategies to learn more effectively.
- Participate as responsible citizens in the life of local, national, and global communities.
- Be culturally and aesthetically sensitive across a range of social contexts.
- Explore education and career opportunities.
- Develop entrepreneurial opportunities (Department of Education, n.d., p. 11).

For English as an additional language, the South African Department of Education's (2002) curriculum describes five learning outcomes:

- Listening: The learner will be able to listen for information and enjoyment, and respond appropriately and critically in a wide range of situations.
- Speaking: The learner will be able to communicate confidently and effectively in spoken language in a wide range of situations.

- Reading and viewing: The learner will be able to read and view for information and enjoyment, and respond critically to the aesthetic, cultural and emotional values in texts.
- Writing: The learner will be able to write different kinds of factual and imaginative texts for a wide range of purposes.
- Language structure and use: The learner will know and be able to use sounds, words and grammar of the language to create and interpret texts (pp. 10–11).

A closer look at the application of the 12 critical and developmental outcomes in English as an additional language can illustrate how the overarching outcomes become instantiated in curriculum. In addition to defining the learning outcomes, the curriculum also delineates assessment standards and texts. For example, the learning outcome for grade 4 reading and viewing, along with its assessment standards that determine whether the learner has mastered the outcome, is presented in Table 19.1.

While the learning outcome remains constant across grade levels, the assessment standards change at different grade levels, using more and more complex tasks and texts. For example, a sample of the Assessment Standards for grade 9 is:

- reads different kinds of stories (e.g., adventure stories) and factual texts
- reads some short authentic texts (e.g., a valentine card)
- critically views an advertisement, and
- demonstrates a reading vocabulary of about 3,000 words (Department of Education, 2002, p. 39).

In addition to establishing assessment standards for each learning outcome for each grade level, the curriculum details assessment principles, continuous assessment, and managing and recording assessment results. These details provide teachers with guidelines for instruction and assessment, creating standards for instruction across the cultural, religious, and ethnic diversity of the nation.

Table 19.1 Sample South African Learning Outcome Grade 4

Learning Outcome Grade 4	Assessment Standards
READING AND VIEWING The learner will be able to read and view for information and enjoyment, and respond critically to the aesthetic, cultural and emotional values in texts	• Reads short texts with visual support: • matches words and sentences with pictures • an advertisement • picture stories with simple captions • comic strips • signs in the environment (e.g. traffic signs). • Reads, listens to and/or sings a simple, popular song • Uses reference books for language learning: • bilingual/monolingual dictionary • grammar reference book • multimedia courses, where available

Adapted from Department of Education (2002). *Revised National Curriculum statement Grades R-9 Languages—English Second Additional Language* (p. 18).

Spady (2008) expressed disappointment in the development and implementation of OBE in South Africa on the grounds that the critical outcomes were not expressed in outcome language and were inconsistent across the 12 outcomes. He further claimed that they were not being used as the driver of curriculum, instruction, and assessment, nor were they transformational. In fact, Spady's framework for OBE education includes standards for implementation, which include not only instruction and assessment, but also a collectively agreed upon mission statement, ongoing program improvement (see Chapter 7), and the need for the outcomes to be publicly derived.

Task: Explore

Examine the reading and viewing outcome with its attendant assessment standards and determine to what extent this standard reflects (or not) the overarching critical and developmental outcomes. What do you think might account for any differences? To what extent do they reflect Spady's approach to OBE learning?

OBE Curriculum Design

From Spady's own writings and the curriculum developed in South Africa, we can see to what extent OBE incorporates the features of curriculum design described in Chapter 5. Most emphasis is placed on defining outcomes and on assessing them. While Spady does note that the mission needs to be collectively agreed, he does not argue for the need for either stakeholder or learner needs analyses. They are perhaps implied because OBE outcomes should be transformative so that learners become productive citizens, problem solvers, and autonomous learners. This implies that institutions or governments wanting to base their curriculum on OBE design would need to determine the characteristics of productive citizens, problem solvers, and autonomous learners in their particular context. In the case of South Africa, the outcomes are inspired by the constitution, whose preamble states that the aims of the constitution are to:

- heal the divisions of the past and establish a society based on democratic values, social justice and fundamental human rights
- improve the quality of life for all citizens and free the potential of each person
- lay the foundations for a free and open society in which government is based on the will of the people and every citizen is equally protected by the law. and
- build a united and democratic South Africa able to take its rightful place as a sovereign state in the family of nations (Department of Education, 2002, p. 1).

From this document, we can see the genesis for some of the critical and developmental outcomes and how those in turn are realized as specific outcomes for English as an additional language. In the case of the Thai university in the vignette, the overarching outcomes derived from the university's 2008 decision to have all curricula outcome-based in order to produce "valuable global citizens." This in turn was motivated by the Office of the Higher Education Commission's Thailand

Qualifications Framework for Higher Education, which instituted a quality assurance system across higher education institutions.

Curricula need to identify the content and its sequencing, and both language content and contexts for that language. The EAL curriculum includes a language structure and use outcome, but it is very general. However, on examining the range across grade levels, it is easier to see the sequencing. What the curriculum does delineate is recommended text types (see Chapter 11 for text-based curricula). For example, for grade 4, oral, written, and multimedia texts are suggested, such as short, simple instructions; simple songs; signs in the environment; simple forms; and short extracts from television programs.

Although in principle any methodology could be used, OBE supports integrated approaches. So, for example, the South African curriculum states that, although the outcomes are presented separately, they are expected to be integrated when taught and assessed. OBE also supports a constructivist approach, that is, OBE is learner centered and collaborative, with learners actively interpreting, processing, and creating knowledge (Lave & Wenger, 1991; Wenger, 1998).

While the context for the language content is not mandated in OBE, the South African curriculum suggests that teachers might use themes of interest (see Chapter 15) to the specific learners in their setting, whether rural or urban, that unite the country. In the case of the Thai university in the vignette, the language courses were all content-based and so the outcomes needed to include the content area such as business or law.

Issues in OBE Curriculum

Because OBE focuses on *whether* and *what* students learn, its implementation is in conflict with the way schools are organized, especially K–12 schools. Most school systems are regulated, with calendars that determine "[s]chool years, curriculum structures, courses, Carnegie units of credit,[1] promotions processes, funding and teacher contracts" (Spady, 1994, p. 153), all of which mitigate against a curriculum that is focused only on *what* is learned, not *how*, or *when*.

As we indicated in Chapters 1 and 2, how the curriculum is resourced, implemented, and its effect on learning can be quite different from the intended curriculum. These differences result from decisions made by institutions, teachers, and learners. It is for this reason that Spady and other OBE proponents argue for a whole institutional commitment to change.

OBE has been heavily criticized as promoting personal values and beliefs, rather than academic excellence. Spady specifically notes that OBE curricula need to separate personal and religious values from civic values, such as honesty and fairness, that make for stable communities. He further notes that OBE requires that outcomes be demonstrable and measurable, which is not possible with personal values such as positive self-concept. The South African implementation does discuss values, but it considers values in the context of language learners needing to be able to analyze and contest the values in texts produced by others and to know how they express their own values in the texts they produce. Similarly, the Thai university includes public mindedness and retention of Thai identity amid globalization.

Conclusion

OBE focuses on learning and how learners can demonstrate their learning. Further, that learning should contribute to the development of civic life by developing learners who can fulfill the roles of community life, such as being team members or problem solvers. Because it assumes that all learners should achieve to their capacity, learners need to have the time to achieve, as well as be provided with the educational experiences that help them to achieve.

Task: Expand

Spady, W. (1994). *Outcome-based education: Critical issues and answers.* Arlington, VA: American Association of School Administrators.

In this volume Spady sets out a detailed framework for OBE and also addresses the criticisms that have been leveled against OBE.

Schlebusch, G., & Thobedi, M. (2004). Outcomes-based education in the English second language classroom in South Africa. *The Qualitative Report, 9*(1), 35–38.

This article provides an evaluative study of the implementation of OBE learning of English in Black townships.
   It is also available online: http://www.nova.edu/ssss/QR/QR9-1/schlebusch.pdf

Puhl, C. A. (1997). Develop, not judge: Continuous assessment in the ESL classroom [Electronic Version]. *Forum, 35*, from http://dosfan.lib.uic.edu/usia/E-USIA/forum/vols/vol35/no2/p2.htm

This article provides excellent examples of continuous assessment tools used in OBE in South Africa.

Questions for Discussion

1. Explain the relationship between outcomes and assessment.
2. Think of English language learning examples for the six different types of demonstrations of learning. Share with a colleague and compare your examples.
3. How could a teacher build Spady's framework of roles into her own classroom, even if she is not using OBE?
4. Why do you think South Africa chose a "language structure and use" outcome as well as outcomes for speaking, listening, reading, and writing?
5. Why do you think South Africa chose "reading and viewing," not just "reading" as an outcome?
6. Why do you think some people are critical about including personal values in curricula? Is this the case in your context?

Note

1. US schools use the Carnegie unit to measure educational attainment. It is time-based, being 120 hours of contact time with an instructor over a year for secondary students. Universities translate this into Student Hour or Credit Hour, which is 12 hours of contact.

References

Australian Chamber of Commerce and Industry and Business Council of Australia. (2002). *Employability skills*. Canberra: Department of Education, Science and Training.

Department of Education. (2002). *Revised National Curriculum statement Grades R-9 Languages—English Second Additional Language*. Retrieved from http://www.education. gov.za/LinkClick.aspx?fileticket=n9K7kiqSvFs%3D&tabid=266&mid=720

Department of Education. (n.d.). *Revised National Curriculum statement grades R-9 (Schools)*. Retrieved from http://www.education.gov.za/LinkClick.aspx?fileticket=JU1Y7NGqqm k%3D&tabid=390&mid=1125

Lave, J., & Wenger, E. (1991). *Situated learning: Legitimate and peripheral participation*. Cambridge: Cambridge University Press.

Office of Literacy and Essential Skills. (2007). Workplace skills: Essential skills [Electronic Version]. Retrieved from http://www.nald.ca/fulltext/sticht/31jan05/31jan05.pdf

Spady, W. (1994). *Outcome-based education: Critical issues and answers*. Arlington, VA: American Association of School Administrators.

Spady, W. (2008). It's time to end the decade of confusion about OBE in South Africa [Electronic Version]. Retrieved from http://edulibpretoria.files.wordpress.com/2008/08/ spadyobeconfusionpaper.pdf

Wenger, E. (1998). *Communities of practice: Learning, meaning, and identity*. New York: Cambridge University Press.

Competency-based Curriculum

Task: Reflect

1. How does this lesson excerpt help learners achieve the CASAS competencies?
2. What else do you think this teacher might do during the rest of the lesson?
3. What activities might the teacher use to help learners practice the new concepts?

4. Why do you think CASAS includes non-language competencies, such as appropriate behavior and attitudes? Do you think that this is appropriate? Why? Why not? How can those competencies be measured?

Introduction

Competency-based education (CBE) has a long history outside of language education, especially in training programs. One impetus for the development of CBE was to divide skills or qualifications into their component parts such that leaners could achieve credit for learning parts of an overall skill, as opposed to having to meet all requirements for a particular qualification, such as for a trade. Additionally, within training programs was the recognition that some competencies were applicable to many different jobs and, therefore, allowed for joint training. For example, in the Australian Vocational Education and Training (VET) system, a unit on basic communication skills can be used in the following training packages: sport, fitness and recreation industry, racing, public safety, information and communications technology, pulp and paper manufacturing, visual arts, crafts and design, community services, business services, defense, and automotive (Training.gov.au, 2013).

The application of CBE to English language teaching began in the U.S. in the 1970s. These Competency-based Language Teaching (CBLT) programs were developed to teach recent immigrants and refugees who had an immediate need to be able to use English in their daily lives. They were therefore sometimes labeled "survival skills" or "life skills." Since then CBE has been adopted in many countries, but it still remains a major focus in adult English language teaching (ELT) in immigrant receiving countries, and in workplace ELT.

Defining Competency

Competency or competence has different meanings in the field of ELT. It has been contrasted with "proficiency" in Chomsky's (1957) model of language. In this model, competence refers to the underlying knowledge about the language that a native speaker has. Competence, on the other hand, is language in use. Hymes (1971) formulated "communicative competence," placing language in its sociocultural context, in contrast to Chomsky's individual, cognitive model. For Hymes, communicative competence includes not only the rules of speaking but also the sociocultural norms and values that guide interaction and cultural behavior within specific speech communities. Others have expanded on this notion, such as the intercultural work of Liddicoat and Crozet (2000), who described and researched "intercultural competence," the intercultural space that educators need to help their learners develop. Communicative competence as a concept and goal in language teaching was taken up by advocates of communicative language teaching (CLT). In CBLT, however, "competency is an instructional objective described in task-based terms such as "Students will be able to ... that include a verb describing a demonstrable skill such as *answer, interpret*, or *request*" (Peyton & Crandall, 1995).

Like outcome-based approaches (see Chapter 19 in this volume), the focus is on *whether* and *what* students learn, not on *how* or *when* they do it. Critical to this definition is the necessity for objectives/competencies to be demonstrable so that they can be measured.

Task: Explore

Use the table below to examine the list of verbs used in ELT objectives. Categorize them into demonstrable and not demonstrable. How could each be measured?

Objective Students will be able to:	Demonstrable or not?	Measurement tool
Understand word stress		
Write grammatical sentences		
Develop skill in using and evaluating evidence		
Use comparative adjectives and conjunctions correctly		
Be familiar with various styles of writing such as description, narration, and argumentation		
Use learning strategies in academic contexts ranging from science, mathematics, social studies, to literature and composition		
Use a variety of lexical phrases to participate in a discussion		
Become aware of the language of giving thanks		
Take part in an opinion-gap activity		
Analyze essay prompts		

Major Characteristics of CBLT

Although there may be a variety of implementation options, all successful CBLT programs include (Weddel, 2006):

- assessment of learner needs
- selection of competencies based on those needs

- instruction targeted to those competencies, and
- evaluation of learner performance in those competencies.

Auerbach (1986), in a critique of CBLT, expanded on these four steps in CLBT curriculum design as a result of a broad literature review of CBE:

1. A focus on successful functioning in society: The goal is to enable students to become autonomous individuals capable of coping with the demands of the world.
2. A focus on life skills: Rather than teaching language in isolation CBLT in adult ESL teaches language as a function of communication about concrete tasks.
3. Task or performance centered orientation: What counts is what students can do as a result of instruction.
4. Modularized instruction: "Objectives are broken down into manageable and immediately meaningful chunks" (quoted from Center for Applied Linguistics, 1983, p. 2; cited in Auerbach).
5. Outcomes which are made explicit a priori: Outcomes are public knowledge, known and agreed upon by both learner and teacher.
6. Continuous and ongoing assessment: Students are pre-tested to determine what skills they lack and post-tested after instruction in those skills.
7. Demonstrated mastery of performance objectives: Rather than the traditional paper-and-pencil tests, assessment is based on the ability to demonstrate pre-specified behavior.
8. Individualized, student centered instruction: In content, level, and pace, objectives are defined in terms of individual needs (adapted from pp. 414–415).

The teacher in the vignette was implementing CBLT as Weddel and Auerbach have described. She was targeting specific competencies that focus on essential life skills. She made explicit to learners what they were learning and why.

How then are these principles and characteristics realized in actual curricula?

Implementation

CBLT approaches have largely been used in the adult ESL sector, although many countries have used such an approach in other sectors. For example, the Arlington, Virginia public schools developed High Intensity Language Training (HILT) as a competency-based program to teach English and academic content to limited-English-proficiency students. In Cameroon, Nkwetisama (2012) found that, while the curriculum was learner centered, teachers and learners were not making full use of CLT methodologies so that learners could use English in communicative situations. He therefore proposed a competency-based approach because CBLT "seeks to bridge the wall between school or the classroom and everyday real life" (p. 519). To help teachers implement such an approach, he lays out the content and language components for different competencies in the curriculum, such as "describing a job." Riyandari (2004), in contrast, details the difficulties of implementing such CBLT in Indonesian universities. The goal of the introduction of CBLT across sectors in Indonesia was to prepare students for the job market.

Adult ESL Education in the U.S.

As indicated in the vignette, CASAS is a competency-based model. It grew out of California's concern in the 1970s with the variety of instructional models used in adult education that had no overarching rationale. CASAS was developed by the California Department of Education and a consortium of local adult education agencies in order to provide a consistent approach to adult ESL. Since then, it has been adopted in all states, largely because, initially, refugees had to be enrolled in a CBLT program for the institution to receive federal funding. It "is the only adult assessment system of its kind to be approved and validated by the U.S. Department of Education in the area of adult literacy" according to the CASAS website (http:// www.casas.org). As well as being used in all US states, it is used in Singapore and other countries of the Pacific Rim. CASAS focuses on employment and life skills for adults and youth, using specific, measurable competency statements. The competencies cover a range of content areas:

- basic communication
- community resources
- consumer economics
- health
- employment
- government and law
- math
- learning and thinking skills
- independent living (CASAS, 2012).

Each content area has components. For example, health includes "understand basic principles of health maintenance" and "understand forms related to heath care." Competencies related to understanding principles of health maintenance include:

- interpret information about nutrition, including food labels
- identify a healthy diet
- identify practices that promote dental health, and
- identify how to handle, prepare, and store food safely (CASAS, 2008).

Institutions using CASAS choose among the competencies based on their learners' needs and current language proficiency. They may also make use of the ESL Model Standards developed in California (see Chapter 21 for detailed descriptions of these standards). These standards are based on developmental stages in second language acquisition and the nature of communicative competence. Taken together with the CASAS life skills competencies, they provide a framework for developing individual curricula in adult ELT.

   In addition to the CASAS and ESL Model Standards, ESL adult programs in the U.S. are required to teach to the Secretary of Labor's Commission on Achieving Necessary Skills competencies (U.S. Department of Labor, 1991), commonly referred to as SCANS Competencies. This commission identified specific skills needed by the workforce, such as "participate as members of a team," "select and apply appropriate technology," and "organize time."

Adult Migrant English Program in Australia

A competency-based model was also developed in Australia's Adult Migrant English Program (AMEP), in response to a 1985 review of the program. The review found that the then current negotiated curriculum was placing burdens on teachers as curriculum developers, and not providing continuity and progression for learners (see Chapter 16 on negotiated curricula). Additionally, funding bureaucrats wanted more accountability, developing a three-category evaluation of institutions providing the AMEP: reach, retention, and results. The curriculum developers layered a competency model over a text-based model (see Chapter 11 for more details of the AMEP's text-based model). This choice was pragmatic, because the curriculum was accredited within Australia's Vocational Education and Training system, a system that had adopted competency-based training models. Feez and Joyce (1995), in discussing the competency-based model they developed, indicated:

> an acknowledgement by NSW AMES[1] of the reality of competency-based training did not mean a lack of awareness of its limitations. However, in order to influence the training agenda providers had to be part of that agenda and could not merely criticise it from a safe distance as has been the privileged position of some academic commentators (p. 27).

Canadian Language Benchmarks Assessment

Canada also developed a CBLT model for teaching adult immigrants and refugees. Canada's Language Instruction for Newcomers to Canada (LINC) Program provides free basic language instruction in English and French. The curriculum is based on the Canadian Language Benchmarks Assessment (CLBA), which indicates the amount of training required to achieve specific LINC Program outcome competency levels. The CLBA has 12 benchmarks or reference points along a continuum from basic to advanced. Benchmarks are described in "can do" statements such as:

- can write short letters and notes on a familiar topic
- can complete extended application forms, and
- can write down everyday phone messages.

The benchmarks, as well as assessing learners, are used as the basis for curriculum design.

Workplace ELT

Another ELT area in which CBLT has been used extensively is in workplace programs. Grognet (1996), for example, describes the process for planning, implementing, and evaluating workplace programs. While she does not explicitly refer to CBLT, the process she describes is the same as that delineated earlier in this chapter. Grognet includes in the needs analysis, task analysis, and observation of workers on the job, as well as interacting in other work functions such as union meetings. She notes that needs and instruction do not have to be restricted to on-the-job skills, but can include skills for positions that learners may hope to have in the future. She argues that her model is learner centered, that learner centered processes (see Chapter 16, for example) are not inconsistent with workplace ESL.

Task: Explore

Below are competencies taken from a variety of different CBLT curricula. For each competency, decide for which type of program it would be suitable, and describe the methods and materials you would use to help learners achieve the competency.

Competency Learners will be able to	Types of program it would be suitable for	Methods and materials for mastering this competency
Communicate simple personal information on the telephone		
Request time off at work		
Clarify or request clarification		
Read a procedural text		
Take notes during an academic lecture		
Distinguish between fact and opinion in a newspaper article		
Point to letters corresponding to the sounds made by the teacher		
Identify the sequence of a simple narrative passage		
Identify and paraphrase pertinent information		
Identify a problem and its probable causes		
Interpret data in a graph		
Negotiate a spoken transaction for goods/services		
Use and respond to basic courtesy formulas (greetings, welcoming, introductions, etc.)		

Competency-based Curriculum Design

The claim for CBLT is that jobs, tasks, or activities require certain competencies, "each of which is composed of a number of elements of competency" (Docking, 1994, p. 11). Therefore, any task can be divided into its component competencies, such that the accretion of the parts leads to competency as a whole. The curriculum, therefore, consists of these elements, often expressed as competencies themselves. While superficially these elements may seem to be objectively derived and discrete items, Docking (1994) identifies the influences on educators during the process of determining competencies:

1. Philosophical: our beliefs about education and training and about work.
2. Sociological: our concerns about equity and mobility.
3. Economical: concerns about employability and cost/benefit.
4. Political: concerns about award conditions and national productivity.
5. Pragmatic: what we believe can be reasonably taught and learned.
6. Historical: what has always been taught.
7. Occupational: what makes us feel unique and useful.
8. Psychological: what we believe can be meaningfully defined.
9. Institutional: what we are required to include for professional recognition.
10. Assessable: what we believe can be assessed and certified (pp. 11–12).

All these beliefs impact the curriculum design so that any competency-based curriculum is responsive to context and not highly portable. Contexts for the language content in ELT competency-based curricula often seem self-evident because the competencies are related to specific life skills areas, such as in CASAS or the CSWE. However, the principle behind CBE is that specific competencies are transferable. The CSWE, therefore, does not specify the context for achieving a particular competency, often stating "in a relevant context" or "in a range of contexts."

Although in principle any methodology could be used, most competency-based systems have supported CLT because it "is based on a functional and interactional perspective on the nature of language. It seeks to teach language in relation to the social contexts in which it is used" (Richards & Rodgers, 2001, p. 143).

Issues in CBLT Curriculum

As we indicated in Chapters 1 and 2, how the curriculum is resourced, implemented, and its effect on learning can be quite different from the intended curriculum. These differences result from decisions made by institutions, teachers, and learners.

Competency-based curricula have been heavily criticized as "socializing immigrants for specific roles in the existing economic order" (Auerbach, 1986, p. 411) or more broadly as subscribing to economic rationalism. Auerbach claims that this focus may prevent teachers from using learner centeredness in their classrooms. This claim is related not only to survival curricula, but also to vocationally-oriented ones, where "there would be pressure to adopt a narrow focus of competence, focusing on a restricted repertoire of behaviour based on tight specifications of standards" in contrast to methodologies "that develop the capacity to deal with the new, the innovative and the unexpected" (Bottomley, Dalton, & Corbel, 1994, p. 22). CBLT is not the only curriculum model to have been accused of being rationalist, instrumentalist, reductionist, and product-driven. Outcome-based and standards-based approaches, because they are focused on outcomes, have also had to address such charges. Even task-based language teaching has been seen as normative in some contexts (see Gong & Holliday, 2013 for a discussion of TBLT textbooks in China).

While Auerbach, among others, has recognized the possible restrictions of CBLT, others such as Docking (1994) have identified its potential as:

- a means of promoting and rewarding excellence, by writing competencies that demand sophisticated and high level performance
- a means of justifying certification decisions, not on a normative basis but based on *real* standards
- a means of ensuring consistency in standards between lecturers, across time, across campuses and between internal and external modes of delivery
- a means of raising standards to meet competency profile requirements and *not just pass marks*[2]
- a means of ensuring the credibility and continued resourcing of education and training providers
- a means of avoiding cultural bias and facilitating equity
- a means of meeting the need for flexibility and diversity *and* consistent comparable standards
- a means of interfacing and integrating different forms of learning including different education and training sectors, and different levels of education
- a means of communicating curriculum expectations to students and colleagues and providing a shared language of outcomes for education, training and work
- a means of empowering learners to take more responsibility for their learning, to increase their options, and to take advantage of opportunities for learning as they arise (pp. 15–16).

CBE proponents have also been accused of being behaviorist, largely because CBE divides tasks into discrete components and assumes the whole is comprised of its components alone. In fact, as van Ek (1976, p. 5) noted when talking about the Council of Europe's Threshold Level (a precursor to the Common European Framework of Reference for Languages):

[I]t should perhaps be pointed out right at the beginning . . . that a behavioral specification of an objective by no means implies the need for a behavioristic teaching method. The way in which the objective has been defined does not impose any particular methodology—behavioristic or otherwise on the teacher.

This is borne out by implementations discussed above, where we have seen that CBLT has largely adopted more communicative methodologies, rather than ones based on structuralism. Indeed, Auerbach herself noted that CBLT is learner centered.

Because assessment is a crucial part of any curriculum, but is built into CBLT, what is assessed and how is critical. CBLT has been criticized because for learners to achieve the competency requires that they achieve all aspects of it in order to be considered competent. While full completion of the task is necessary in many training situations, language creates a quite different situation. A trainee plumber who cannot correctly replace the washer on your tap cannot be considered to be competent in this skill. However, in language, for example, for the competency "can write a recount" in the CSWE, learners must be able to correctly use the schematic structure, as well as the specific syntactic features. If the learner fails to use temporal connectives, then they have not achieved the competency. There is no partial completion. However, in life, partial completion of texts can still communicate.

Conclusion

CBLT focuses on what is learned and how learners can demonstrate their learning. While it has mostly been adopted in adult education for immigrants and refugees, it has also been adopted in other countries and for different sectors. While there are potential disadvantages to CBLT, these can be overcome with careful planning and by providing learners with opportunities to explore both language and different contexts. Competencies do not have to be restricted to ones that are instrumentalist, but can include competencies of higher complexity as in Spady's (1994) model (see Chapter 19).

Task: Expand

http://www.cal.org/caela/

This is the website for the Center for Adult English Language Acquisition in the U.S. It hosts numerous digests and other documents that outline CBLT approaches for adult ESL.

http://www.casas.org

This is the website for CASAS, used in adult ESL in the U.S. It provides lists of competencies in a variety of areas.

http://www.training.gov.au

This is the website for Australia's competency-based training programs. Although it is not specific to ELT, it provides excellent examples of competencies across a range of communication skills.

Pettis, J. C. (2007). Implementation of the Canadian Language Benchmarks in Manitoba: 1996 to the present. *Prospect, 22*(3), 32–43. Also available at: http://www.ameprc.mq.edu.au/docs/prospect_journal/volume_22_no_3/Implementation_of_the_Canadian.pdf

This article provides an excellent case of using a competency-based assessment system for curriculum development.

Questions for Discussion

1. Explain the relationship between competencies and assessment.
2. Think of English language learning examples for the health competencies in CASAS. Share with a colleague and compare your examples.
3. How could a teacher build Spady's more complex competencies into a CBLT curriculum?
4. Why do you think some people are critical about competencies restricting learners, rather than empowering them?
5. What is your opinion of the influences on determining competencies listed by Docking? How can curriculum designers ensure that no one influence dominates or controls decisions?

Notes

1. NSW AMES (New South Wales Adult Migrant Education Service) was the provider that developed the CSWE curriculum framework for use across the AMEP nationally.
2. In Australia, "marks" refers to points assigned for a performance/assignment.

References

Auerbach, E. R. (1986). Competency-based ESL: One step forward or two steps back? *TESOL Quarterly, 20*(3), 411–415.

Bottomley, Y., Dalton, J., & Corbel, C. (1994). *From proficiency to competencies: A collaborative approach to curriculum innovation.* Sydney: NCELTR.

CASAS. (2008). *CASAS Competencies: Essential life and work skills for youth and adults.* Retrieved from http://www.casas.org/docs/pagecontents/competencies.pdf?Status= Master

CASAS. (2012). CASAS Competencies. Retrieved from https://www.casas.org/product-overviews/curriculum-management-instruction/casas-competencies

Chomsky, N. (1957). *Syntactic structures.* The Hague: Mouton.

Comprehensive Adult Student Assessment System. (1996). *CASAS Life Skills Test.* San Diego, CA: Author.

Docking, R. (1994). Competency-based curricula: The big picture. *Prospect, 9*(2), 8–17.

Feez, S., & Joyce, H. (1995). Systemic functional grammar meets competency-based training in the NSW AMES. *Interchange: Journal of the NSW Adult Migrant English Service, 27,* 11–16.

Gong, Y., & Holliday, A. (2013). Cultures of change: Appropriate cultural content in Chinese school textbooks. In K. Hyland & L. L. C. Wong (Eds.), *Innovation and change in English language educaiton* (pp. 44–57). London: Routledge.

Grognet, A. G. (1996). *Planning, implementing and evaluating workplace ESL programs.* Washington, DC: Center for Applied Linguistics, Project in Adult Immigrant Education.

Hymes, D. (1971). *On communicative competence.* Philadelphia: University of Philadelphia Press.

Liddicoat, A. J., & Crozet, C. (Eds.) (2000). *Teaching languages, teaching cultures.* Melbourne: Applied Linguistics Association of Australia and Language Australia.

Nkwetisama, C. M. (2012). Competency based approach to English language education and the walls between the classroom and the society in Cameroon: Pulling down the walls. *Theory and Practice in Language Studies, 2*(3), 516–523.

Peyton, J. K., & Crandall, J. (1995). Philosophies and approaches in adult ESL literacy instruction [Electronic Version]. *Digests.* Retrieved from http://www.cal.org/caela/esl_resources/digests/PEYTON.html

Richards, J. C., & Rodgers, T. S. (2001). *Approaches and methods in language teaching* (2nd ed.). New York: Cambridge University Press.

Riyandari, A. (2004). Challenges in implementing competency-based English language teaching at university level. *TEFLIN Journal: A publication on the teaching and learning of English, 15*(1).

Spady, W. (1994). *Outcome-based education: Critical issues and answers.* Arlington, VA: American Association of School Administrators.

Training.gov.au. (2013). BBSBCMM101A: Apply basic communication skills. Retrieved from http://training.gov.au/Training/Details/BSBCMM101A

U.S. Department of Labor. (1991). *What work requires of schools: A SCANS report for America 2000* (ERIC No. ED 332 054) Washington, DC: Author.

van Ek, J. A. (1976). *The threshold level for modern language learning in schools.* London: Longman.

Weddel, K. S. (2006). Competency based education and content standards [Electronic Version]. Retrieved from http://www.cde.state.co.us/cdeadult/download/pdf/Competency BasedEducation.pdf

Chapter 21

Standards-based Curriculum

VIGNETTE

TESOL International Association colleagues and I are on a task force to develop Pre-K–12 standards for English language learners in the U.S. Through an iterative process involving members and affiliates, the task force has decided on three overarching goals: Goal 1: To use English to communicate in social settings; Goal 2: To use English to achieve academically in all content areas; and Goal 3: To use English in socially in culturally appropriate ways. Each goal has three standards, each of which has descriptors that elaborate student behaviors that meet the standard, and sample progress indicators that teachers can use to determine whether learners have reached the standard. The progress indicators are assessable and observable. The standards specify what learners should know and be able to do and have been developed in grade level clusters. For each standard for each grade level cluster, we are developing vignettes to help teachers understand the standards by showing classroom-based instructional sequences. We have solicited real-life vignettes from teachers around the country. At this particular meeting, we are working on choosing a vignette for grades 9–12 for Goal 1, Standard 3: Students will use learning strategies to extend their communicative competence. The vignette we are evaluating is for an intermediate class of learners who have completed driver's education, and are about to do the practical driver training. The teacher has invited a police officer to talk to students about road safety, peer pressure, and so on. He plays them a video of teenage car accidents, asking them to look for the causes of the accidents. One student did not understand much of the officer's lecture, including "excess speed." But, in the video, he notices the camera move from a speed limit sign saying 65 to the speedometer reading 80. He asks his friend in their home language whether he thinks excess means "too much." The teacher and the officer ask what "excess speed" means and the student is able to answer correctly. The officer asks how he figured it out. The student explains and the teacher compliments him on his use of strategies. [Murray, research notes]

> **Task: Reflect**
>
> 1. How does this lesson excerpt demonstrate that this learner's performance met Goal 1, Standard 3? Do you think this one sample is sufficient evidence to determine that the student has achieved the standard?
> 2. What else do you think this teacher might do during the rest of the lesson to build on strategy use?
> 3. What activities might the teacher use to help other learners use these strategies?
> 4. Why do you think the TESOL standards include learner strategies?

Introduction

Standards-based education, like outcome-based and competency-based, is focused on what learners *know* and are *able to do*. The standards movement in education began in the U.S., in response to the publication of *A Nation at Risk* (National Commission on Excellence in Education, 1983). Because of concern over the U.S.'s dismal education outcomes, various groups began looking for educational reform. In 1988, the National Council of Teachers of Mathematics began developing standards for mathematics. In 1989, the National Governors' Association education summit agreed on six goals for education to be reached by 2000, leading to federal money to support the development of standards in mathematics and other subject areas. In 1994 Congress passed Goals 2000: Educate America Act. Starting in 1991, TESOL International Association responded to these goals by investigating standards for ESL learners (not funded by the federal government). The writing and field reviewing of the TESOL Pre-K–12 standards was conducted over a three-year period, mostly by volunteers, resulting in the 1997 publication of the standards (TESOL, 1997). This document was supported by documents on assessment (TESOL, 1998, 2001), implementation (Agor, 2000; Irujo, 2000; Samway, 2000; Smallwood, 2000), and teacher education (Snow, 2000).

The movement was not confined to the U.S. In more or less the same time frame, Australia was developing its framework of stages (McKay & Scarino, 1991) and Alberta, Canada was developing its learner outcomes (Alberta Education, 1997). Since then, standards have been developed in many countries for different types of learners: English for Occupations in Thailand (English Language Development Center, 2005) and English as an additional language/dialect in Australia (ACARA, 2012).

Defining Standards

Standard has different meanings in different arenas. For example, most countries have a standards organization responsible for overseeing standards setting professional associations and other entities. Standards Australia defines them as "published documents setting out specifications and procedures designed to ensure products, services and systems are safe, reliable and consistently perform the way they were intended to. They establish a common language which defines quality and safety criteria" (Standards Australia, 2013). TESOL defined standard as a statement that indicates "what students should know and be able to do as a result of instruction" (TESOL, 1997, p. 15). Critical to this definition is the necessity for standards through which learners can demonstrate learning so that they can be assessed. This often involves benchmarks of performance.

Task: Explore

1. Does your country have a standards organization such as Standards Australia?
2. Are there standards documents for ELT in your country?
3. Do they include performance indicators and benchmarks of performance? Why? Why not?

Major Characteristics of Standards-based Curricula

Although there may be a variety of implementation options, all successful standards-based programs include:

*   overarching goals or standards
*   descriptors that provide "can do" statements for what learners can do to achieve that particular standard, and
*   assessment criteria to determine whether learners have achieved the standard and to what extent.

Some standards are described in terms of levels of proficiency. Others describe the standards and then the performance at different levels of proficiency. All standards-based systems aim to ensure transparency and accountability, as well as provide guidance for curriculum developers, textbook writers, and classroom teachers. Many standards specify either language or subject matter content because they are designed for a specific context in which they will be used. However, they usually do not mandate a particular methodology, although the nature of the standards often implies one, such as communicative language teaching.

Sample Standards-based Curricula

Standards have now become common worldwide. In this chapter, we have chosen to focus on only a few of these standards and how they affect curriculum design. We will discuss the standards developed by the professional association—TESOL International Association—and the Common European Framework of Reference for Language (CEFR), which is used in Europe for curriculum design, textbook writing, and assessment. In addition, we will discuss the California Model Standards for Adult ESL that we referred to in Chapter 20, and the Standards of English for Occupations developed in Thailand. These four sets of standards provide contrasting contexts and interpretations of standards for ELT.

TESOL Pre-K–12 Standards

In the vignette, we described part of the process used in the first iteration of TESOL's Pre-K–12 standards. Since then, educational changes at the US national level have led to a revision of the standards so that they interact more easily with more recent legislation and national curricula efforts[1] by connecting them to the core curriculum content areas. TESOL's framework includes five standards, at different grade level clusters, accompanied by performance indicators (Gottlieb, Carnuccio, Ernst-Slavit, & Katz, 2006).

Standard 1: English language learners **communicate** for **social, intercultural, and instructional** purposes within the school setting.

Standard 2: English language learners **communicate** information, ideas, and concepts necessary for academic success in the area of **language arts**.

Standard 3: English language learners **communicate** information, ideas, and concepts necessary for academic success in the area of **mathematics**.

Standard 4: English language learners **communicate** information, ideas, and concepts necessary for academic success in the area of **science**.

Standard 5: English language learners **communicate** information, ideas, and concepts necessary for academic success in the area of **social studies**.

Each of these standards is applied to grade level clusters: Pre-K–K, 1–3, 4–6, 6–8, and 9–12. Each standard is also grouped into the four language skills: listening, speaking, reading, and writing. Student performance on the standards is judged according to five levels: starting, emerging, developing, expanding, and bridging. The latter demonstrates that the learner is ready to work effectively in English in a mainstream classroom with minimum support. Performance is measured according to indicators of success.

The 1977 version of the TESOL standards did not establish detailed proficiency levels; rather, it specified goals and standards for learners at beginning, intermediate, and advanced levels of English proficiency. The 2006 version, therefore, like the CEFR, establishes a proficiency scale.

Common European Framework of Reference for Language

The CEFR developed from the Council of Europe's threshold level (van Ek, 1976), the level at which learners could independently use the second language in its country of use. Because it was used for curriculum development across many countries in Europe, it was a de facto standard for the 36 languages for which curricula were developed. While neither the threshold level nor the CEFR specifically ascribe to the standards movement, the descriptors parallel those of other standards documents. The CEFR documents refer to competencies: general competencies and communicative language competencies. However, we have chosen to include the CEFR in the chapter on standards rather than in Chapter 20 on competency-based curricula because of its broad scope and its implied Europe-wide standards of use. In contrast, the competency-based approaches have been used in limited domains, such as workplace or adult immigrants. The CEFR in fact details such a wide range of domains that Cook (2011, p. 145) has claimed that "the CEFR aims at a whole description of human existence," and the framework itself is context-free.

The CEFR's goal is "to facilitate communication and interaction among Europeans of different mother tongues in order to promote European mobility, mutual understanding and co-operation, and overcome prejudice and discrimination" (CEFR, 2001, p. 2). The focus, therefore, is on communication, on "what language learners have to learn to do in order to use a language for communication and what knowledge and language skills they have to develop so as to be able to act effectively" (p.1). CEFR's full title includes learning, teaching, and assessment. To that end, it identifies six levels of proficiency, described in "can do" statements as in Table 21.1 below. EAQUALS (The European Association for Quality Language Services, n.d.-b) has expanded these six levels into 11 through the addition of "+" to provide finer distinctions between levels, which are necessary in many programs, especially short courses. The CEFR refers to the "can do" orientation as an "action-based approach." B1 is equivalent to the threshold level in van Ek (1976), with C2 being mastery. The descriptors cover all four of the language skills—listening, speaking, reading, and writing. In Table 21.1, we provide all levels, but only one of the specifications at each level. For the full level descriptors, see the Council of Europe's website (http://www.coe.int/t/dg4/linguistic/Source/Framework_en.pdf).

The CEFR also provides a self-assessment grid so that learners can identify their level for listening, reading, spoken interaction, spoken production, and writing. The category of spoken interaction seeks to demonstrate the way listening and speaking interact in actual use. For example, at A1, the lowest level, the self-assessment for spoken interaction is:

> I can interact in a simple way provided the other person is prepared to repeat or rephrase things at a slower rate of speech and help me formulate what I am

Table 21.1 Common European Framework of Reference for Language Levels

Description	Level	Sample Specification
Proficient user	C2	Can understand with ease virtually everything heard or read
	C1	Can understand a wide range of demanding, longer texts, and recognize implicit meaning
Independent user	B2	Can understand the main ideas of complex text on both concrete and abstract topics, including technical discussion in his/her field of specialization
	B1	Can understand the main points of clear standard input on familiar matters regularly encountered in work, school, leisure, etc.
Basic user	A2	Can understand sentences and frequently used expressions related to areas of most immediate relevance (e.g., very basic personal and family information, shopping, local geography, employment)
	A1	Can understand and use familiar everyday expressions and very basic phrases aimed at the satisfaction of needs of a concrete type

trying to say. I can ask and answer simple questions in areas of immediate need or on very familiar topics (p. 26)

This example very clearly shows not only how an individual uses language but how speakers also need to work with their interlocutors to achieve each person's communicative goal.

Task: Explore

Go to the Council of Europe's website (http://www.coe.int/t/dg4/linguistic/Source/Framework_en.pdf). Use the self-assessment to assess some of your students. How useful are these descriptors for describing the achievement of your students? How could they be used to determine the curriculum for their next stage of English learning?

English-as-a-Second Language Model Standards for Adult Education Programs[2]

As mentioned in Chapter 20, these model standards are to be used in conjunction with the competency-based CASAS. These standards go beyond curriculum standards of what learners need to know and be able to do. They include the following:

- program standards
- curricular standards
- instructional standards
- standards for student evaluation
- descriptions of proficiency levels
- descriptions of course content
- sample lessons
- general testing standards, and
- testing materials (California Department of Education, 1992).

This list shows that the document serves as a basis for quality assurance (see Chapter 7) because of its comprehensiveness. The three curricular standards are quality principles:

- Curricular Standard 1: The curriculum is focused on meeting students' needs as determined by assessment of students' language proficiencies, goals, and interests (p. 3).
- Curricular Standard 2: ESL instruction integrates language components—vocabulary, grammatical structures, language functions, pronunciation—in units on topics that are important to the students (p. 4).
- Curricular Standard 3: In the design of curriculum, students' levels of literacy skills—whether in their primary languages or in English—are an essential consideration (p. 4)

The proficiency levels are written as student "can do" statements, as in other standards documents. Each level includes performance indicators in terms of what students can do at work, in listening, in speaking, in reading, in writing, and in comprehensibility. A performance indicator for Beginning Level High for speaking is: Students can communicate survival needs using very simple learned phrases and sentences (p. 15). This performance contrasts with Advanced High Level speaking: Students can engage in extended conversation on a variety of topics but lack fluency in discussing technical subjects. Students generally use appropriate syntax but lack thorough control of grammatical patterns (p. 18).

Standards of English for Occupations

The Ministry of Education in Thailand developed standards for English language needed in 25 occupations in order for "workplace personnel [to] communicate competently in English" (English Language Development Center, 2005, n.p.). The purpose of the standards was to provide guidance for curriculum developers, for individual self-assessment, and for workplace training needs and courses. Each occupation has four standards:

- Standard 1: Understanding and interpreting spoken and written language on a work topic.
- Standard 2: Using spoken and written English to participate in work interaction.
- Standard 3: Using an appropriate language variety and register according to audience, purpose, setting, and culture.
- Standard 4: Understanding and using nonverbal communication appropriate to audience, purpose, setting, and culture.

Standards 3 and 4 are similar in scope to Goal 3 in the vignette. Occupations range from caddies to doctors, to hotel front desk staff, to spa therapists, to IT project managers. The 25 occupations reflect the industries in which Thailand has been developing an international presence.

Each standard has benchmarks at basic, intermediate, and advanced levels, with benchmark indicators. Because of the complex nature of the work doctors and IT project managers do, the performance indicators are more complex than for other occupations. For example, the benchmarks for spa therapists are only at the basic level. The indicators for Standard 3 are:

1. Respond appropriately to basic compliments, complaints, criticism, etc.
2. Use polite language to interact with guests, especially when persuading, and negotiating.
3. Respond to and use humor appropriately (p. 56).

Standards-based Curriculum Design

Like competency-based and outcome-based, standards-based curriculum design is a backward design, starting with the goals or standards. The CEFR, for example, has six levels, but it is possible to design a curriculum for a specific group for whom the objectives are a subset of the standards in the descriptors, even though the framework is context-free. For example, the CEFR defines many settings within the larger domains of personal, public, occupational, educational. For each domain, they list contexts of use for locations, institutions, persons, objects, events, operations, and texts. Therefore, it could be possible to develop a curriculum for adult learners of English who are beginning learners who need immediate language to negotiate government agencies and their English classroom (if they are not yet working or in school other than language school). Or, in a different context, the objectives may be focused on the receptive skill of reading (for example, to read university textbooks in English). The CEFR provides lists of tasks, strategies, and texts that can guide curriculum development. However, the starting point would be the descriptors, that is, the "can do" statements.

A series of case studies of curriculum design based on the CEFR (The European Association for Quality Language Services, n.d.-a) shows that, rather than starting with a needs analysis, many of the language schools examined their current curriculum documents and re-wrote them as "can do" statements. These case studies also showed that the institutions implemented the new approach and evaluated it, often leading to different assessment procedures such as changes in report cards that identified student learning in terms of "can do" statements. This adaptation is common for institutions that already have curricula developed over time, ones that meet their learners' needs. In the face of curriculum renewal efforts, they often adapt rather than re-invent. However, in order to determine whether the new approach meets stakeholder needs, it is essential to evaluate the implementation from the perspective of all stakeholders.

In contrast to the CEFR, TESOL's Pre-K–12 2006 standards are not context-free. Although the general standards might provide some guidance for another context, they are specific to the US current context. The ESL Model Standards for Adult ESL Programs are also context-specific, describing course content and instructional standards in contexts for immigrant/refugee learners, such as shopping and transportation. The sample standard provided earlier referred to "survival needs," clearly indicating that the content is around immediate survival. The Standards for Occupations are also completely context-specific so that language and subject matter content are determined by the occupation.

A vital aspect of standards-based curriculum approaches is assessment, the determination of to what extent learners have achieved the standards. The CEFR framework has extensive descriptors for use in assessment. The self-assessment tool can be used to establish a portfolio (Council of Europe, 2009) to present to prospective employers, for example. While TESOL does not specify particular assessments, the standards are aligned with the Common Core State Standards and its assessment procedures (National Governors Association for Best Practices Council of Chief State School Officers, 2010). However, as Ross points out, at issue is "how curriculum content can be validly assessed to demonstrate that target-level benchmarks have been achieved" (Ross, 2011, p. 794). This is especially vexing for language learners taking subject matter assessment in English because the language of the test affects performance (for example, Wiley & Wright, 2004).

Issues in Standards-based Curriculum

As we indicated in Chapters 1 and 2, how the curriculum is resourced, implemented, and its effect on learning can be quite different from the intended curriculum. These differences result from decisions made by institutions, teachers, and learners. The standards we have described are intended curricula. How they are implemented varies.

Like competency-based language teaching and outcome-based education, standards-based curricula have been accused of being rationalist, instrumentalist, reductionist, and product-driven. In addition, in the U.S. and Australia, a major criticism has been of federal government overreach. In both countries, states have the responsibility for education and the notion of national standards has always been rejected. The counterargument for a national standard has been the need for learners to be able to move seamlessly from one state to another, as well as the need to reduce the inequality of achievement across states. Furthermore, without standards of performance, not only is there variation across language programs, but also, in many cases, the textbook or the national examination (see, for example, Stewart, 2009 on Japan's entrance examination) becomes the de facto standard.

Often, standards-based curricula are a top-down change to the status quo, what Nation and Macalister (2009) call "power-coercive." Top-down change is often resisted or adapted (see Chapters 1 and 2 and the CEFR case studies). However, as we saw with the TESOL standards, standards can be developed using a bottom-up process. The Common Core Standards in the U.S. were instigated by governors from a number of states, along with state school chiefs who believed their state standards were insufficient. They received extensive input from national subject matter associations, teachers' unions, parents, and other stakeholders. Like most standards frameworks, their implementation is left to the local level to determine methodologies and activities and tasks. However, particular orientations to learning are embedded in many standards documents. For example, the TESOL standards advocate for language in use and the acquisition of academic language so that learners can succeed in their content areas.

Conclusion

Standards-based education focuses on what is learned and how learners can demonstrate their learning. Standards have been adopted throughout the world as a means of guiding curriculum, improving levels of student performance, and demonstrating accountability to government and citizenry. While there are potential disadvantages to standards, these can be overcome with careful planning such that the process is both top-down and bottom-up and by maintaining some flexibility in delivery at the local level.

Task: Expand

http://www.coe.int/t/dg4/linguistic/Cadre1_en.asp

This is the website for the Common European Framework of Reference for Languages.

http://www.tesol.org/advance-the-field/standards

This is the website for TESOL's standards projects. As well as the Pre-K–12 standards, TESOL has also developed standards for teachers, adult education, technology, and teacher education programs.

http://www.acara.edu.au/verve/_resources/English_as_an_Additional_Language_or_Dialect_Teacher_Resource_05_06_12.pdf

This is the website for the Australian EALD resource. The resource includes learners' proficiency levels in the different skills at different stages in terms of "can do" statements. The resource is a supplement to the Australian Curriculum: Foundation to Year 10, which is standards-based.

http://www.adultedcontentstandards.ed.gov/Source/GetStandard.cfm

This US government website houses the various standards documents developed for adult ESL in 22 states. Comparing and contrasting them provides useful insights into standards-based curricula.

http://www.excellencegateway.org.uk/node/1516

This website hosts the Adult ESOL Core Curriculum in the U.K., which is a standards-based curriculum.

Questions for Discussion

1. Explain the relationship between standards and assessment.
2. Think of English language teaching tasks and strategies that could be used to teach the spa therapist benchmark indicators. Share with a colleague and compare your examples.
3. How do standards-based curricula differ from competency-based curricula? What do they have in common?
4. Why do many standards include proficiency levels and descriptors?
5. How can curriculum developers using standards ensure buy-in from teachers?

Notes

1. Most recently, the National Governors Association and the Council of Chief State School Officers have led the development of Common Core State Standards to provide US students with high-quality education in subject areas such as mathematics and language arts.
2. The model standards and CASAS are just one of several curricula guidelines used by US states in adult education.

References

ACARA. (2012). *English as an additional language or dialect teacher resource*. Retrieved from http://www.acara.edu.au/verve/_resources/English_as_an_Additional_Language_or_Dialect_Teacher_Resource_05_06_12.pdf

Agor, B. (Ed.). (2000). *Integrating ESL standards into classroom practice: Grades 9–12*. Alexandria, VA: TESOL.

Alberta Education. (1997). *English as a second language*. Edmonton, Canada: Author.

California Department of Education. (1992). *English-as-a-Second Language model standards for Adult Education programs*. Sacramento, CA: Author. Also available from https://www. casas.org/docs/pagecontents/ca_esl_model_standards_1992_-2-.pdf?Status=Master

CEFR. (2001). *Common European framework of reference for languages: Learning, teaching, assessment*. Cambridge: Cambridge University Press.

Cook, V. (2011). Teaching English as a foreign language in Europe. In E. Hinkel (Ed.), *Handbook of research in second language teaching and learning* (Volume II, pp. 140–154). New York: Routledge.

Council of Europe. (2009). European language portfolio. Retrieved from http://www.coe. int/t/dg4/linguistic/Portfolio_EN.asp

English Language Development Center. (2005). *Standards of English for occupations*. Bangkok, Thailand: Ministry on Higher Education, Ministry of Education.

Gottlieb, M., Carnuccio, L., Ernst-Slavit, G., & Katz, A. (2006). *PreK-12 English language proficiency standards: An augmentation of the WIDA language proficiency standards*. Alexandria, VA: TESOL Publications.

Irujo, A. (Ed.). (2000). *Integrating ESL standards into classroom practice: Grades 6–8*. Alexandria, VA: TESOL.

McKay, P., & Scarino, A. (1991). *ESL framework of stages: An approach to ESL learning in schools*. Melbourne: Curriculum Corporation.

Nation, I. S. P., & Macalister, J. (2009). *Language curriculum design*. London: Routledge.

National Commission on Excellence in Education. (1983). *A nation at risk: The imperative for educational reform*. Washington, DC: U.S. Government Printing Office.

National Governors Association for Best Practices Council of Chief State School Officers. (2010). *Common Core State Standards*. Washington, DC: Author.

Ross, S. J. (2011). The social and political tensions in language assessment. In E. Hinkel (Ed.), *Handbook of research in second language teaching and learning* (Volume II, pp. 786–797). New York: Routledge.

Samway, K. D. (Ed.). (2000). *Integrating ESL standards into classroom pracice: Grades 3–5*. Alexandria, VA: TESOL.

Smallwood, B. A. (Ed.). (2000). *Integrating ESL standards into classroom practice: Grades Pre-K–2*. Alexandria, VA: TESOL.

Snow, M. A. (Ed.). (2000). *Implementing ESL standards for Pre-K-12 students through teacher education*. Alexandria, VA: TESOL.

Standards Australia. (2013). What is a standard? Retrieved from http://www.standards.org. au/StandardsDevelopment/What_is_a_Standard/Pages/default.aspx

Stewart, T. (2009). Will the new English curriculum for 2013 work? *The Language Teacher, 33*(11), 9–13.

TESOL. (1997). *ESL standards for Pre-K-12 students*. Alexandria, VA: Author.

TESOL. (1998). *Managing the assessment process: A framework for measuring student attainment of the ESL standards. TESOL Professional Papers #5*. Alexandria, VA: Author.

TESOL. (2001). *Scenarios for ESL standards-based assessment*. Alexandria, VA: Author.

The European Association for Quality Language Services. (n.d.-a). *CEFR curriculum case studies: Examples from different contexts of implementing "Can do" descriptors from the Common European Framework of Reference*. Budapest, Hungary: Author.

The European Association for Quality Language Services. (n.d.-b). Descriptors. Retrieved from http://www.eaquals.org/pages/?p=7399

van Ek, J. A. (1976). *The threshold level for modern language learning in schools*. London: Longman.

Wiley, T., & Wright, W. (2004). Against the undertow: Language minority education policy and politics in the "Age of Accountability". *Educational Policy, 18*(1), 142–168.

Index